£1·25

RUBENS AND HIS TIMES

P. P. Rubens and Isabella Brant by P. P. Rubens. (Pinakothek, Munich)

RUBENS
AND HIS TIMES

BY

ROGER AVERMAETE

TRANSLATED BY
CHRISTINE TROLLOPE

London
GEORGE ALLEN AND UNWIN LTD
RUSKIN HOUSE   MUSEUM STREET

Translated from the French

RUBENS ET SON TEMPS

© Editions Brepols, Brussels 1964

PRINTED IN GREAT BRITAIN
in 11 point Juliana type
BY THE BLACKFRIARS PRESS LTD
LEICESTER

All glory to this Homer of painting, this father of warmth and rapture, whose art cancels out all that has gone before him, not in the perfection he brings to one or another part of it, but in that mysterious power, that inner life which pervades the whole.

DELACROIX

CONTENTS

CONTENTS

ILLUSTRATIONS

INTRODUCTION

After eight years in foreign parts, a painter came back to settle in a country ravaged by years of war. He had left at the very beginning of his career, and when he returned he was thirty-three years old. Immediately he took his place as leader, easily outshining all the other painters, numerous as they were, who worked in the town in which he had come to live. Commissions flowed in, and pupils too. The cleverest craftsmen used their special skills to collaborate with him, and in accepting their assistance he changed their whole conception of their art and drew them effortlessly into his own Dionysian world. Once he had decided to take an active part in politics, he became a diplomat despite the opposition of those who ended by employing him. He became rich and respected; honours were conferred upon him; kings, princes, ministers were his friends. For some thirty years a strict self-imposed discipline kept at bay the lust for power he felt within himself. And although he spent his last years in the peace of the countryside like any great lord to whom the years have brought some measure of disillusionment, it can only have been because he coveted the supreme delight of savouring and rejecting all the vanity of worldly pomp.

Such a man was Rubens. He strove after success, and his career is one of the most amazingly successful ever known. What is rarer still, this success has been maintained over the years. In life, Rubens was so famous that his radiance made the colourless reign of the archduke Albert and his wife Isabella pass for a golden age; but his fame did not stop there. In that magic world of painting, that mysterious road to rapture and escape, whose strangeness remains hidden from the indifferent eyes of men, his position has always been among the highest.

Much has been written about Rubens. His work has been studied with fervour, clarity and enthusiasm; and shrewd scholars have estimated his influence. His biographers have been legion. Following an excellent principle, they have attempted to explain the work by the man. But the work has always befogged them so that they show an irritating tendency towards exaggeration, and legend has taken precedence over history. The tendency

13

began with the earliest. Some made Rubens the descendant of a Styrian prince. Details without proof abound in all of them. Since these details tended towards the deification of the Master, later biographers have often simply repeated the nonsense without further examination. It is scarcely necessary to recall the quarrels which broke out in the nineteenth century when the researches of Bakhuizen van den Brink established beyond a doubt that the painter's birthplace was the little town of Siegen. Up to that time, Antwerp and Cologne had contended for that honour. With touching dishonesty, Belgian historians and art critics—Pierre Gerard, Barthelemy Dumortier, F. J. van den Branden, Max Rooses etc.—upheld the claims of Antwerp with the most subtle of quibblings, while Dr L. Ennen flung himself into battle in support of those of Cologne! For years a plaque attached to the ruins of his house on the Wapper shamelessly declared that the master was born in Antwerp, and it was not until a brand-new 'Rubens house' was built, as a belated contribution of the people of Antwerp to the Rubens legend, that the misleading inscription finally disappeared.

Another example of the determination to exaggerate common to all Rubens' biographers is provided by the death of his first wife. We are constantly told that his grief was immense. Several writers declare that he retired for a while to the abbey of Saint Michael where Isabella Brant had been buried side by side with Maria Pypelincx, the painter's mother. No one knew on what this conjecture is based. But it so happens that the extant correspondence of Rubens includes a whole series of letters dating from this period. At that time he was corresponding with Pierre Dupuy; and he replied to Dupuy's letter of condolence with a fervent eulogy of the dead woman. Speaking of his own grief, he suggests that a voyage might do him good. The letter is rather frigid and stilted, and completely in the spirit of 'humanism'. It is impossible to draw any conclusion from it; a serenity worthy of the Stoics was a favourite pose of the time. The letters which followed, week by week, to this same correspondent, are much more revealing. Rubens was concerned only with politics, and seemed very excited by current events; he speaks about himself only once, to say that he has recovered from a fever. This example is typical. His first eulogists may well have given free rein to their fantasy, but it seems astonishing that later on, when all available documents had been searched, it should never have occurred to his biographers to reduce the best-known episodes to their true proportions.

Truth to tell, Rubens wore a mask all his life. His amiability, his charming manners, his love of outward show, his 'humanist' pretensions are so many defences. We can reach him only through his correspondence and his work. And even so, he was capable, pen in hand, of erecting still more impenetrable barriers. He left some 230 letters, and we can find in them scarcely half a dozen touches which shed sudden and unexpected light on the inner depths of the man. His work speaks more eloquently, for although he may have hoped to hide behind the motley caval-cade of his subjects, it did not occur to him that an artist's sub-jects are no more than pretexts; his nature was bound to betray itself in the painter's own language—a language of lines and colours woven together in the inimitable manner of the great artist. And because we are all sensitive to this language which speaks to us through the intermediary of works of art, we are drawn towards anyone who can bring us this mysterious message. Because men have described Rubens' pictorial language in religious or mythological scenes, in landscapes or portraits, they have longed for better acquaintance of this brother so divinely favoured. What, after all, is the life of a successful man? Very little if the truth were known; but if he is one of the chosen ones, who have the gift of drawing us, too, into the enchantment of their vision—then it is a different matter. Art is a mystery, and who is to lay bare its secrets? Who can tell why men remain for centuries under the enchantment of one particular work, while others on the same subject leave them cold? To speak in this respect of the quality of a painting would be an over-simplification, reducing the mystery to a technical problem—a betrayal, and a pointless one at that, since art goes far beyond mere technique. Art is like a religion, and its com-municants are bound together by mystic ties.

We must not allow the great impetus which draws us towards Rubens to be weakened by falsehoods, even pious ones. A man of his stamp should stand in the full light of day. And if he had human failings, so much the better; there is great solace in the knowledge that a man, living as other men live, can scale the highest peaks by the magic of his art. The present work contains no sensational discovery or newly-found document. It is intended to evoke Rubens as he appears through the messages he has left. It contains no flights of fancy and no arbitrary manipulation of the texts. And this means that Rubens can now step down from the unreal pedestal where most of his biographers left him, and walk on the same level as the rest of mankind, who are his brothers. We shall love him all the more.[1]

[1] The only new thing in the studies devoted to Rubens during the last few decades is Charles Rogers Bordley's theory, which is unexpected, to say the least of it. He maintains that the master's best paintings are the work of Snyders (cf *Rubens ou Snyders*, Edition La Nef, Paris).

It is, of course, probable that a certain number of works attributed to Rubens are not in fact by him, and possible that some of these may be the work of Snyders. But it seems risky, to say the least of it, to maintain that Snyders was a sort of 'ghost-artist' of genius, working in obscurity to the greater glory of his master, whereas in actual fact this painter enjoyed during his lifetime an enviable reputation in his own right.

I

THE PROMISED LAND

The father of the family was dead, after a long illness. He had complained for years of his shattered health, which dated, he said, from the time of his misfortunes. But the mother had cherished him tenderly, never letting him speak of those days. He had been buried not far from his home, in the church of St Peter. Many people were present, for he was well known and had many friends.

It was natural to grieve, but life must go on. Simple enough words—but the mother well knew what toil and struggle they represented. The children knew too; the two eldest, Jan-Baptist and Blandina, better than anyone, and the two youngest, Philip and Peter Paul, probably rather less. But they all knew the terrible importance of money. As far back as they could remember they had watched their parents struggle to acquire a little of that indispensable commodity. Prison, banishment, confiscation of property, were all familiar terms to them. Their father had used them every day and no one had taken fright at them, except perhaps at an already far-distant period when the words seemed to hang like a mysterious threat over the house.

The mother was no weakling. It was not her habit to complain. She had loved her husband, but she still had four children, and life must go on. What then, was she to do? Her husband had been a lawyer and his income died with him. Her family was far away, and so was what little property she had left. In spite of the long years spent in Cologne she was still a foreigner there. And her own country was at last fairly peaceful. Like all exiles, she felt that things would be easier at home. She quickly made up her mind to return to Antwerp.

No other name could ever wake so many echoes in the children's minds. It had always been the *leit-motif* of all their conversations. Their parents, grandparents and great-grand-parents all came from there. Their father had been one of its magistrates and Jan-Baptist and Blandina were born there. The friends who came to the house were constantly referring to the town, and it was the birthplace of a large number of them. Their mother went there on several occasions to settle family business. In every possible circumstance, its name was contrasted with that of Cologne. And yet Cologne was a great city. It was the fief of an archbishop and elector, and its university dated from the fourteenth century. A large number of artists, both painters and sculptors, had contributed to its fame. Its buildings were beautiful, from the severe lines of the ancient church of St Maria im Kapitol to the recently finished Town Hall, built in the new style imported from Italy. It was a Hanseatic town and an important commercial centre. But all this mattered little. For the admirers of the great city by the Scheldt, Cologne was a mere village, and the Scheldt itself far superior to the Rhine, with more ships and more prosperous trade. Of course the town of Antwerp had had its misfortunes of late. Trade, it was said, had suffered greatly, and there were few sea-going ships in its port. But now that peace had come, the proud city was about to regain its old splendour.

Antwerp! For the children, the name was an invitation to dream. The elder ones had been born there, it is true, but no very precise image of those far-off times remained in their memories. When they left, Jan-Baptist was six and Blandina four, and almost twenty years had passed since then. They might well wonder why they had stayed so long away from such an enchanted city. The elder ones never spoke of it, but Philip and Peter Paul were less easily satisfied. Over and over again they returned to the attack with their questions. The answer was the same every time. In those days there had been great disasters in Flanders. The King of Spain had delegated his authority to the terrible Duke of Alva, and since then no one had been safe. Everyone suspected of sympathy with the Protestants was per-secuted. The Reformation was not a new religion. The members of its churches were still Christians, but they disputed certain points in the dogma of the Roman Church. Like the Catholics, they believed in Jesus Christ, but claimed to have entered into a new relationship with him. The result was catastrophic. Both sides were guilty of terrible excesses. People whose ideas appeared heretical to their fellow Christians were burnt on every side. What is more, the Protestants did not always agree among themselves; Lutherans and Calvinists both had their own ideas. There is nothing more tragic than a country torn by religious quarrels.

The father of the family had been a scholar, and had studied law in Rome and other Italian cities. On his return to his own country he had been made a magistrate of his native city, and held this important office for several years to the satisfaction of all concerned. When the fateful troubles broke out, he was greatly distressed, for he had friends on both sides, and both sides were acting like madmen. To a scholar whose only aim was a quiet life, there was only one course open. He decided on voluntary exile and when the troubles were at their height he left Antwerp with his wife and four children. These were first of all Jan-Baptist and Blandina, and then Clara, barely three years old, who died in 1580 at the home of her grandparents at Lierre, and Henry who died in Cologne at the age of sixteen. And then came war, the worst calamity of all. It raged in the Netherlands for many years, the Spaniards on one side, and on the other the United Provinces fighting for their independence. It is a sorry tale of sieges, battles, pillage, extortions of every kind, and suffering beyond description. In 1576, one year before the birth of Peter Paul, their beloved Antwerp fell a prey to the rebellious Spanish garrison. Whole districts were burnt down, and people butchered by the thousand. The general horror at this savagery found expression in the well-deserved name of the 'Spanish Fury'. And there were other disgraceful episodes. Antwerp, the beloved city, suffered further attacks. It was besieged by the valorous Duke of Parma, and had to surrender in 1585 after a heroic defence. Later, peace returned. Was it not better to live with one's family in a land where all was tranquil? And yet even that was no protection against the blows of fate, Clara died, Henry died, and so did the last-born, little Bartholomew. And now their father too was dead.

Why should they have waited till the father's death before thinking of returning? He had spoken of it from time to time, but never felt well enough to make the effort. That was indeed one reason, but why did the mother sometimes go to Flanders and the father never? Peter Paul was only ten and Philip thirteen; it was natural for them to ask such questions. Their mother would answer that their father was a scholar and a man of peace, to whom a tranquil life counted above all things. In order that there should be no doubt of this, she affirmed it upon his tombstone in the church of St Peter: 'When civil war at last broke out, his need for peace and his desire to live far from all unrest led him voluntarily to leave the fatherland in which his services in the administration of the commune and his zeal for justice had gained him so much love.' She adds: 'His wife, who bore him seven children and with whom he lived in harmony for twenty-six years without giving her any cause for complaint, erected this tomb in honour of an excellent and most dearly loved husband.'

Finally, since nothing will stop a child's questions, and reasoning cannot erase the memories of the young, Maria Pypelincx may well have said to her younger children, as she must have done to her elder ones: 'You must accept what I tell you. We have lived in Cologne for almost twenty years. Philip and Peter Paul were born there and we have friends in the town. But we live in troubled times. The things which on the surface seem simplest may sometimes cause the worst disaster. Let us speak as little as possible about all this. Please do this in memory of your father, for love of me and in your own interests. Above all, when we go back to Antwerp, be careful not to stir the ashes of the past. Do you understand, children?'

And the children understood. But how can we stop our thoughts from beating stubbornly against a wall which we know is hiding something from us? Legend can spread its wings and be lost in the distant heavens; but history, gnawing its patient way, is not far behind.

Despite all the clever concealment of Maria Pypelincx, the romantic story of Rubens' father was bound sooner or later to see the light.

II

THE FATHER'S STORY

Until he was thirty-eight years old, life seemed to smile on him. He was the only son of an apothecary, and the first of his family to have a really good education. Apart from the apothecary grandfather, all his family were tanners by trade and were already known as citizens of Antwerp in the fourteenth century. When his father died, his mother married a widower, Jan de Lantmeter. This worthy grocer was a real father to his stepson, who studied at Louvain, Padua and Rome. At twenty-two he gained his doctorate in civil and canon law at the college of La Sapienza in Rome. At thirty-one he returned to his native country and soon after married Maria Pypelincx. The following year he was made a magistrate of the city of Antwerp. In this capacity he sat on the *Vierschare* or magistrates' bench and was responsible for putting many a prisoner to the question. He was among those present at the interrogation of the famous Lutherans Fabricius and Bockius; and although he already passed for a Protestant, Rubens acquiesced in his colleagues' sentence, and Fabricius was executed.

In 1567 things took a turn for the worse. The Iconoclasts, in a wild frenzy, had ravaged all the Catholic places of worship. The highest ranking lord in the land, William of Nassau, Prince of Orange, had not yet broken with the government. He was still a member of the Council of State and was trying hard to restore peace. His main idea was to settle religious differences in order to further the struggle against the policy of Spain. At one point he employed John Rubens as mediator between the magistracy of Antwerp and the Calvinists. On her side, the regent, Margaret of Parma, was demanding from the burgomasters and magistrates an explanation of their attitude during the upheavals. They complied, but remained on tenterhooks. In order to bring the Netherlands to heel, Philip II sent a new captain-general, the Duke of Alva. This man enjoyed his master's complete trust, and was resolved to deserve it. When the regent saw him she asked and obtained permission to resign. When Egmont saw him, he spent sleepless nights and talked of shutting himself up in his castle at Gaesbeeck—and Lamoral of Egmont was one of the bravest soldiers of his time. A brooding anxiety hung over the country. The Duke of Alva took his time; he knew what he wanted and nothing could distract him from his mission. This soldier, cold, fanatical and uncouth, seemed to have no room for any human feeling. He was simply a weapon in the hands of the King, striking ceaselessly and remorselessly until his master was obliged to recall him.

On September 9th, Egmont and Horn were arrested at Brussels and the burgomaster Van Straelen at Antwerp. William of Orange had been more far-seeing and had gone into exile. Terror and stupefaction fell upon the people. The Duke of Alva visited Antwerp and demanded a fresh justification in writing. As it was rather slower in coming than he would have liked, he called his *Tres-chiers et bons amys* to order in so forceful a manner that the municipal authorities decided to reply at once. John Rubens was uneasy. He drew up a statement in his own defence and sent it to John Gillis, pensionary of the city of Antwerp, for transmission to a member of the sinister Council of Troubles, Ludovico del Rio, whose duty it was to try the case of the people of Antwerp.

In his statement Rubens placed his relations with the Prince of Orange on a purely administrative footing and gave assurance of his strictly Catholic views. In the meantime there came to light a list of those inhabitants of Antwerp who had shown favour towards the new ideas, and it included the name of John Rubens. Feeling rose high. The executions began : 84 on January 4, 1568, 37 on February 20th, 71 on February 21st, 55 on March 20th; and so it continued. On May 28th the Duke of Alva had the Culemborg Palace razed to the ground for the sole reason that the signatories of the Compromise had met there two years earlier. On June 5th he added the crowning terror with the beheading, after nine months' imprisonment, of Counts Egmont and Horn. Anthony van Straelen, a former colleague of John

Rubens, fell in his turn. On September 24th he was beheaded at Vilvoorde after having been tortured. His sufferings had so weakened him that he had to be seated in a chair so that the executioner could give him the finishing stroke. John Rubens could stand it no longer. On the intervention of the Spaniards his appointment as magistrate had not been renewed. Armed with a certificate testifying to his services to the city, he fled with his wife and four children. It was not a moment too soon. He had scarcely left when his name appeared on the proscribed list.

First of all, Rubens and his family went to Limburg, in the territory of the Prince-Bishop, in the neighbourhood of Curingen, where Maria Pypelincx had relatives. Then they continued their journey towards Cologne, where many fugitives from Flanders were finding asylum. They were barely settled when they became the target of a hail of insults. As they lived opposite a presbytery, there were jeers for this former Antwerp magistrate who never went to church. In May 1569, Rubens was given eight days to leave the district with his family. He replied by asking the Antwerp magistracy to get various prominent persons to certify that he left the town of his own free will, solely for the purpose of transacting private business in Cologne. A good lawyer is never short of arguments. Nevertheless, the local authorities did not look kindly upon him; but as he claimed the protection of the Prince of Orange, they dared not say anything. John Rubens had in fact made contact with the prince.

The Princess of Orange, born Anna of Saxony, had settled in Cologne a short time earlier, and was seeking means to save the estates belonging to her dowry from the confiscation to which all the property of William the Silent was subject. Her legal adviser was an emigré named Jan Bets, of Malines. John Rubens soon became assistant to this lawyer, and when the latter had to be absent for some time his assistant stepped into his shoes and was made the princess's *chargé d'affaires*. John Rubens was a very clever man. It did not take him long to achieve this position of trust even in exile, and thus to make sure of his family's future. Anna of Saxony received her adviser at her own table. When she moved from place to place, he went with her. Finally she entrusted to him her children and all her worldly goods. She was twenty-five years old, and her husband, to whom she had borne four children, was continually absent, either fighting wars or discussing treaties. Like so many princesses, she felt that real life was passing her by. People said she was capricious and spiteful, and accused her of a lack of affection for William, which was perfectly true. When, after his unfortunate expedition to the Netherlands, he returned, beaten and broken, to his native country, she refused to meet him despite all his pleadings. John Rubens was a fine-looking man, fluent in speech and charming in manner. She admitted him, not only to her house, but to her bed.

For two years the lovers, drunk with delight, must have forgotten the world and all its possible stumbling-blocks. A lawyer needs to discuss his client's affairs, and that was sufficient pretext for any number of interviews. But towards the end of 1570 the Princess became pregnant. The power of fleshly desire knows no bounds. How otherwise is it conceivable that these two beings should have been so utterly unheeding of the consequences of their association? They stayed where they were, and did nothing to avert the catastrophe. The Princess had not even the last resource of fathering the child upon the Prince, for it was a long time since she had last seen him. We may wonder by what impossible miracle they expected to be extricated from this terrible situation. Soon the scandal broke, perhaps not in public, but at least in the Princess's own household, since her swelling figure made further concealment impossible. However, when Count John of Nassau tackled his sister-in-law, her only reply was a brazen denial. One day in March 1571 John Rubens was about to join the Princess at her house in Siegen when he was arrested by the Count's men. He was taken to Dillenburg, where he made a full confession. According to German law, as he well knew, he could expect the gallows; and the only favour he begged was that he should be beheaded.

While he awaited the death he fully expected, his family were in the grip of anxiety. For three weeks his wife had been writing letters and sending messengers in all directions. Finally she received a letter in which the culprit confessed everything and begged her forgiveness. She forgave him without hesitation. She did not even let herself be downcast; since her husband was

alive, the only thing that mattered was to save him. She began at
once to organize his defence. She knew very well that before her
reply was read to the prisoner, it would be read by the appro-
priate official. So she wrote: 'I am sure that if these good gentlemen saw my tears they would pity me, even if they were wood
or stone; so when no other course is left to me, that is the one I
shall follow, even though you have written to me not to resort
to entreaties.' In that way she was proclaiming her intentions
and at the same time shifting the responsibility from the
shoulders of the culprit. She calls on God himself to help her:
'You do not desire the death of a sinner, but rather that he
should turn from his wickedness and live. Imbue the souls of
these good gentlemen, whose anger we have provoked, with your
own spirit of mercy, that we may shortly be delivered from all
this terror and desolation.' And she ends: 'I will offer my most
heartfelt prayers for you, and our children will copy me; these
poor little ones send you their love and long to see you—and so
do I, God knows! Written on the first day of April, between
midnight and one in the morning. And you must not write
"your unworthy husband" for I have forgiven you everything.'

The Nassau family were in a very difficult position. To punish
the criminal would be to make public the insult their house had
suffered. On the other hand they shrank from ordering an execution without observing the correct legal procedure; it would in
fact be a crime. These vacillations worked to John Rubens'
advantage. His wife wasted no time. She wrote letter after letter
to Count John of Nassau. For a short time she even allied herself
with her rival, who was delivered of a little girl in August 1571.
She went to Dillenburg in the hope of seeing her husband; and
shortly afterwards she was at Siegen visiting Anna in childbed.
She appealed to her family, and Philip de Lantmeter, John
Rubens' half-brother, came post-haste from Antwerp. They went
together to try to see the prisoner, but in vain. These were not
the only disappointments suffered by this worthy woman. At
Cologne she found herself threatened with expulsion and had to
seek refuge with one of her relatives, the apothecary Raymond
Ringott.

After trying for two years, she finally obtained permission to
visit her husband. She sold up everything at Cologne and went

to Siegen hoping to settle there. New difficulties arose. She could not find a house to let, and John Rubens begged Count John to come to the help of his wife, who was lodging at the inn. But Maria Pypelincx had the kind of temperament which never gives up. She had not even a roof over her head, but she 'rented a plot of ground near the walls and sowed there, for household use, all kinds of useful herbs for which she went to the Netherlands' for if she had waited longer the season would have been too far advanced and her kitchen garden would have produced nothing. In the meantime she negotiated for her husband's release. On May 9th a messenger informed her that John Rubens would arrive in Siegen next day. Victory at last! They had, it was true, to pay a deposit of 6,000 thalers, which was to be confiscated at the slightest slip. The criminal's release was subject to several conditions; he could not show himself in the town nor attend church; he was to return to his cell at the first summons; and he was to be kept under observation by an agent of the Nassau family who could resume the trial at any moment. The only privilege allowed him was that of walking in the country immediately around the town. But nevertheless it was a victory. To leave prison safe and sound after twenty-six months, and after coming so near to being hanged, could scarcely be called anything else!

However, life at Siegen was by no means carefree. It was no joke to live in a little gossip-ridden town, shunned like the plague, the target of every kind of suspicion, with no other resources but the interest from the sum they had paid over as security, which came to them only as a trickle of irregular payments. Not to mention the threats. One day John Rubens was advised, if he valued his life, to take no more country walks. Another day he was accused of having shown himself in the town and having spoken ill of his masters. He had to clear himself, dispute every inch of the ground, and even struggle to regain tiny advantages. Maria Pypelincx was always the chief advocate of the family, and she made a much better showing than her husband, who was a mere logician, quite devoid of brilliance. For the moment, the most pressing needs had to be dealt with. John Rubens must have permission to seek consolation in long country walks, and also to attend church. On the

26

first point John of Nassau yielded, but on the second he remained adamant. Rubens claimed to be bitterly hurt by this refusal. Could his religious feelings, which were rather lukewarm, have suddenly become more intense? Or did he simply loathe the thought of being the sinner to whom the church doors were closed? He took advantage of an epidemic to seek, for the first time, permission temporarily to leave the Nassau dominions with his wife and children. Here we see, taking tentative shape, the idea of departure, which was to dominate the thoughts of the Rubens family.

On April 24, 1574, their son Philip was born. A new life was beginning. We may suppose that it was then that the idea of wiping out the memory of her husband's lapse took root in the mind of Maria Pypelincx. Anna of Saxony had just been sent back to her uncle, the Elector Augustus who had brought her up. And so, little by little, a plan took shape. If they could escape the clutches of the Nassau family, the first step would have been taken. But they were nowhere near that point. John Rubens was forbidden even to go out. They had to struggle to regain by dint of pleading the privileges which had been granted to them much earlier.

We can imagine how passionately the Rubens followed events in their own country. The 'Spanish Fury' was a cruel blow to them because of all their ties with Antwerp, but the proclamation of the edict of Marche-en-Famenne filled them with excitement: all property confiscated from those who had risen against Spain was to be restored! To the Rubens family it meant the end of their material worries. John Rubens obtained permission to go to Cologne to sign a document conferring power of attorney on his wife. With their feet set on so fair a road it would be a shame to stop. Letters and applications came thick and fast. The mother of Maria Pypelincx made the journey to Germany in order to add her prayers to those of her daughter. They boldly asked that John Rubens might be allowed to retire to some town in Brabant, and suggested Lierre. But the Nassau family remained inflexible. Philip de Marnix informed John Rubens that patience was absolutely essential.

On June 28, 1577, Maria Pypelincx was delivered of her sixth child, whom they named Peter Paul. Anna of Saxony died a few months later, aged barely thirty-three. The following year John Rubens was finally authorized to leave the territory of the Counts of Nassau, but was forbidden to set foot on that of the Prince of Orange. He had in addition to give up half of the 6,000 thalers which his wife had put down as security. Without his wife's knowledge he sacrificed a further 1,400 thalers. He would have signed anything in the world just to be allowed to leave Siegen. The Rubens family went to settle in Cologne in a house belonging to Burgomaster Pyll. The second step towards freedom had been taken. The Rubens had friends in Cologne, and the father worked hard to build up his practice again. The mother was not in the habit of wasting her time, and she carried on a business. Life was still difficult, but here at least they were not treated like pariahs.

At the end of 1580, their daughter Clara died at Lierre, at the home of her maternal grandparents. And shortly afterwards, grandfather Pypelincx died in his turn. The Rubens' faith in life does not seem to have been weakened by these blows of fate; they replied to death by creating new life. Their seventh child, Bartholomew, was born in 1581. John Rubens was gradually fighting his way back, and his finances were improving. His wife opened a boarding-house and made business deals with borrowed money. By working night and day, as we learn from their letters, they were managing to scrape a living, borne up by hope for a happier future. The children were growing up; Blandina, already a big girl of seventeen, was engaged.

But their trials, alas, were not over. In September 1582, an emissary of Count John, the lawyer Andreas Christianus, called upon John Rubens and gave him notice to be at Siegen by the first of November. To the anxious questions fired at him he replied frankly that Rubens' life appeared to be in danger. The intention was, in fact, to reimburse the balance of Rubens' deposit; Christianus understood that the landgrave wished to settle once for all the question of the little girl born to Anna of Saxony at the castle of Dietz. Rubens was horror-stricken. He wrote to Count John, and the chancellery at Dillenburg confirmed the decision. He tried again; his wife, more eloquent in writing than he, entered the fray. The date was drawing near and Nassau remained adamant. Poor Rubens begged for a few months' grace; he wanted to settle his affairs so that his family should not be plunged into destitution.

This terrible threat finally boiled down to a sordid question of money. Rubens was given to understand that the decision would be reversed if he gave up his deposit and the interest due on it, and if he repaid in addition the interest already received. Faced with such demands, the poor man asked for a horse and a servant to be sent to him; he would appear. He felt he had not the right to ruin his wife and children. There was much arguing and haggling. The Count's negotiators offered 700 thalers to settle the matter. Rubens demanded a thousand. A settlement was reached at 800, about one-tenth of what the Rubens family were actually owed. They were not only compelled to give a receipt as though the whole sum had been repaid to them, but they also had to express their gratitude to Count John. On January 5, 1583, the couple signed this false statement. These four months had been among the most terrible of their eventful life, for although they had already experienced dreadful moments, these had all occurred in periods when they were without hope, when suffering was their daily portion. This last misfortune had burst upon them suddenly, when their ship had almost come home. Nevertheless, they came out on the other side, poor and nearly ruined, but their struggle with the house of Nassau was over; it had lasted almost twelve years and cost John Rubens his health. And now they had to put their shoulders to the wheel once more.

Blandina's engagement was broken off, and Henry died at the age of sixteen. Still, life had to go on. Then they lost little Bartholomew; but there were still the others left to provide for. Maria Pypelincx went alone to Antwerp to settle some family business, as her mother and her husband's stepfather were both dead, and she had to appear before the magistrates and sign various documents. Despite the dire poverty of the time, the deceased had left some property. The mother of the family went on doggedly with all that had to be done. Then after leaving her interests in the hands of an agent, she set out once more for Cologne.

The arrival of Alexander Farnese in Flanders struck terror to the exiles' hearts. Antwerp was soon surrounded. The vicissitudes of the siege and the respective chances of each side formed the theme of every conversation. The assassination of the Prince of Orange came as a horrible interlude in the drama. Months went by. One day favoured Antwerp and its citizens, the next Farnese. Miracles were expected of the Dutch, and talk was all of bridges, fireships and infernal machines. And finally, Farnese won. On August 17, 1585, Marnix de Sainte-Aldegonde surrendered the town. The conditions of the treaty were lenient towards both residents and exiles. The way was open at last.

The Rubens family, like so many others, could go back to Antwerp. Even John Rubens, since the man whose territory he had sworn to avoid was now dead. But the former rival of William the Silent was sick, worn out and old. He almost certainly told his wife and children that they would go back soon, when his health was better. He had taken all the necessary precautions, including a return to the Catholic church. He hoped people would forget that his youngest children had been baptized in the Lutheran faith. Persistently and with enthusiasm, the mother built up the legend. Philip and Peter Paul, she said, were born in Cologne, a Catholic town, which gave them an affinity with the local religion. For greater certainty she let it be assumed that the Rubens family had always lived in Cologne. The children were growing up and it was important that they should make no mistakes. The older children would have to be coached, but the little ones would accept the legend. Everything must be put in order ready for the return to Antwerp, and their father's sorry tale must be completely wiped out.

This return was to be the last act of the drama, the final victory. But alas, the principal actor was not to play his part. In March 1587, John Rubens died at the age of 57. Maria Pypelincx had to return to Antwerp alone, after nineteen years' absence. But she took with her four of her children; and thus all was not lost.

III

THE YEARS
OF APPRENTICESHIP

1587–1600

Almost four months had passed since the father's death, and it had taken all that time to settle their affairs. Finally, on June 27th, Maria Pypelincx and her children left the city by the Rhine, bidding a last farewell to the old house in the Sternengasse which had been their refuge for the last nine years. They looked for the last time on the rather impressive façade with its six windows, the main doorway opening on to a peristyle, the monumental staircase and the pocket-handkerchief of a garden where the children used to play. It was goodbye to the familiar twisting streets huddled round the old churches: St Gereon, St Pantaleon, St Maria im Kapitol, St Martin and so many others. The most beloved was St Peter, where John Rubens lay; the most beautiful was the cathedral, which seemed to keep its holy vigil over the whole town.

The stage-coach took five days to reach Antwerp, passing the province of Liège with its green hills, the plain of Hesbaye with scarcely a ripple to break its flat surface, and the Campine with its dunes and fir-woods, and going through many villages and several towns. Their eyes were dazzled by these enthralling sights, but they were preparing to see a vision to eclipse all else—the town whose name had been constantly on the lips of their parents and friends. At last the tower of Notre-Dame appeared on the horizon, and as it grew, other towers took shape around it: St James, the abbey of St Michael, St Andrew, St George, St Walburga.

Five of Antwerp's children were returning home; and though

31

the two youngest had been born far away, it was to Antwerp
that their hearts and minds belonged. For them it was something
better than a mere birthplace; it was the city veiled in legend
that had haunted their childish dreams. We may wonder what
they thought of this city now that they were within its walls.
Could they have been so bewitched that the magic stayed in
spite of that reality which always makes so poor a showing in
comparison with escapist dreams? It is true that many a building
in Antwerp was still suffused with the glow of past splendours,
and there were sumptuous mansions in plenty; luxury and
elegance were combined in the guild houses, and some private
homes were regular palaces. But was that enough to hide the
real poverty? Famine had reigned for two years. Supplies were
hard to come by and their price prohibitive, since public distress
always offers a fruitful ground for profiteers. A third of the
houses were empty. As soon as darkness fell, people dressed in
silk and velvet began to beg for alms. Starving wretches searched
every festering rubbish heap for bones, vegetable peelings or dis-
carded cabbage leaves. Wolves prowled around the city walls,
and it was said that in the nearby Campine whole villages were
uninhabited. Bandits infested the countryside. Was this the
promised land? Was this the proud city which had been—or so
it was said—the richest in the world? The trouble had begun
through oppression and religious intolerance, and spontaneous
revolt had led to interminable war. The land had been ravaged
for years; arson, theft, murder were rife. And the children,
though they had heard of such things, were now seeing them for
the first time. But they had courage, and they had hope, despite
everything.

Maria Pypelincx and her sister Susanna were joint owners of
a house on the Meir which they had inherited from their
parents. Maria went to live there with her children. Philip and
Peter Paul were sent to school with Romuldus Verdonck, *'maistre
d'escolle sur le cimiterre de nostre dame'*. Among their fellow-
pupils was a lad of thirteen who became their friend. He had a
lively mind which made up for his physical shortcomings: the
poor boy was paralyzed down the right side, and his health was
delicate. But he put a bold face on his misfortunes. He wrote
beautifully with his left hand and his activity was such that few

Archduke Albert and his patron saint, Saint Albert of Louvain; Archduchess abella and her patron saint, Saint Clara. Volets from the retable of St Ildefonso by P. Rubens. (Vienna, Museum of Fine Arts—Photo A.C.L.)

1598.

[Handwritten manuscript in 16th-century Flemish cursive. Best readings below.]

Int jaer Alsmen schreef duijsent vijf hondert
ende tacht in Negentich. Soo waerd Regeerder
van S. Lucas Gulde Adam van Noort. oppe
Deck. ende thins. ende Deck was Pieter Bom ...
Hier na volghen die meesters. ende meesters sone
die dit ontfangen heeft. Binnen zijne Jaere.

Marcil Coris Bouwduerwercker vrij meester
Heyndrick ... Bouwduerwercker meester sone
Pieter Loetkint. meester sone. ende
Anthoni Loetkint. meester sone — 2 gebroeders.
Cornelis Olivier Beeldsnnder. meester sone
Pieter de Cater, Borduerwercker vrij meester
Lucas floquet vrij meester schilder
Bertholomeus Wolckint schilder vrij meester
Hans van Herentals vrij meester. tafereelmaker
Marcil Symon gontslager. meester sone
Hans Meulenaer. schilder meester sone
Pieter Rubbens vrij meester. schilder
Anthoni Surra, schilder vrij meester
Heynart ... schilder meester sone
Cornelis van ... gelatmaker vrij meester
Cornelis ..., Bouwduerwercker meester sone
Mathijs Willekens. schilder vrij meester
Huijbrecht vande ven vrij meester. ...

3. Reproduction of folio 159 verso of the manuscript 'Liggere van de St Lucasgilde'. Enrolment of P. P. Rubens in the Guild of Saint Luke. (Antwerp, Académie Royale des Beaux-Arts)

would have guessed that half his body was useless. Balthasar Moretus was the grandson of Christopher Plantin, the famous printer who had settled in Antwerp in 1549—'a cornucopia of knowledge and worth', he was called—and founded a workshop which soon became famous. It was still there, and despite the misfortune of the times it remained a cultural and artistic centre. And there, too, remained the old master, of whom it had been said that there was nothing material in him. He had known exile and ruin, and it mattered nothing. Had he not himself shown the way to triumph over all adversities?

> 'Let humble toil, constant from day to day,
> And simple patience arm thee for the fray.'

Two of his sons-in-law—'my two other selves at the two main points of my realm'—helped him as best they could; they were Raphelengius and Jan Moerentorf, known as Moretus. Young Balthasar was the latter's son.

Romuldus Verdonck was a Greek and Latin specialist. He loved children, and those in his school had not discouraged him from having a quiverful of his own; his offspring numbered thirteen. Like their friend Moretus, the Rubens boys remained with him until 1590. In August of that year, their sister Blandina married Simeon du Parcq. As this nobleman had an income of 400 florins to offer, he had no intention of taking the girl empty-handed. Maria Pypelincx had to make heroic efforts to get together a dowry for her daughter, which she could only do bit by bit. Philip was sent to Louvain University, because she wanted him to become a lawyer like his father, then she tried to find a career for Peter Paul. Did she, one wonders, really try to make him a page? She may or may not have actually sounded on this subject the Countess of Lalaing whom she had met earlier when in exile.

As far as Peter Paul himself was concerned, the whole thing was very simple. He wanted to become a painter. It was a strange choice for a child of thirteen; and there had never been a painter in the family. Maria Pypelincx, who was ambitious for her children, was probably not very enthusiastic. She called a family council. What arguments could they possibly bring against so

C   33

clearly expressed a wish? And if Peter Paul entered into an apprenticeship he would ease the financial burden on his mother a little; so his request was granted, and a master sought who would agree to have him. The man they found was Tobias Verhaecht, and Peter Paul went to live with him and was initiated into the noble art of painting. This meant that he was allowed to clean the brushes, grind the colours and tidy the studio. He also watched his master at work and tried to imitate him. Tobias Verhaecht was a man of less than thirty who did not appear to be consumed by any very fierce flame of inspiration. He painted landscapes in the style of Josse de Momper. Breaking with the subtle analytical manner dear to the elder Bruegel, and with the fantastic style of composition practised by Patinir, de Momper had a more untrammelled vision, based on direct observation. But Tobias Verhaecht was much more arid than his colleague, and his fussy manner was ill adapted to the new style. He painted uninspired Towers of Babel and other Biblical scenes.

Two years later Peter Paul entered the studio of Adam Van Noort. We do not know what motives led the young apprentice to change his master. Van Noort was older than Verhaecht and enjoyed a greater reputation among his fellow-painters. He painted figure compositions, which may well be the explanation, as Verhaecht was primarily a landscape painter. Artists still believed in a kind of hierarchy of types of painting. We may quite justly consider this a completely wrong idea, but at that time it had every appearance of truth. The Flemish painters were hypnotized by the monumental works of the Italian masters; and those who dreamed of following in the footsteps of Michelangelo or Raphael needed vast knowledge combined with great talent. Adam Van Noort happened to be one of those most capable of putting into practice the lessons of Italy.

While his brother Philip and Balthasar Moretus were studying at the University of Louvain under the guidance of the great scholar Justus Lipsius, Peter Paul was attempting more and more complicated work. He worked with Van Noort for four years. In the meantime his mother was still struggling with financial worries. Her son-in-law was nagging at her relentlessly for Blandina's dowry which was still unpaid. Her business agent was drawing money in her name without accounting for it, and she was compelled to bring a lawsuit against him.

At the age of nineteen, Peter Paul changed masters again, leaving Van Noort for Otto Vaenius. It was a godsend for the young painter to be admitted to the studio of the most famous artist in Antwerp. Otto Vaenius was thirty-eight years old, a man of lordly demeanour, who was in fact of noble origin and had all the charm of the enlightened amateur. He dabbled in Latin verse and had been page to Bishop Ernest of Bavaria before becoming 'engineer to the royal armies' at the Farnese court. When Archduke Ernest made his triumphal entry, he had been entrusted with the decoration of the town. He painted religious and historical pictures, and also portraits. Like most of his fellow-painters, he was a fervent adept of the new style from Italy which excited the painters of the Netherlands to such a degree that they lost many of their innate qualities. He avoided bad taste, but not cold correctness. His composition always showed more technique than inspiration, and his colouring lacked depth. But could a young man who had never seen the great masters for himself have been expected to judge all that? It takes time for the eyes to be opened. Above all, a great deal of hard work is necessary in order to understand the possibilities and the limits of other people's work, and to acquire that inner light which makes a wider vision possible.

Otto Vaenius was a man of culture with a wide field of knowledge. His conversation, brilliant and varied, returned constantly, by whatever secret and tortuous paths, to one single theme: Italy. For this man of the North had lived on the other side of the Alps for five years, and was still dazzled by what he had seen there. He had been the pupil in Rome of Federigo Zuccaro, an artist of great renown, who had had the honour of finishing a picture by Michelangelo, of decorating the great dome of Santa Maria del Fiore in Florence, and of working at the Escorial for Philip II. It mattered little to Otto Vaenius that Zuccaro's painting was mediocre; he was probably not even aware of the fact. There was no disputing the genius of a painter who had been appointed President of the Academy of St Luke at Rome. The painters of the Netherlands were convinced that all enlightenment came from Italy and that it was there that the true secrets of art must be sought. They all felt it their duty to cross the Alps. The lessons of the old Flemish masters were repudiated as invalid. Neither Van Eyck, Van der Weyden nor Memlinc found favour with these enthusiasts for all things Italian. Mabuse and Van Orley set an example; they returned fired with zeal for the new style. The others—almost all the others—followed: Michael Cocxie, Peter Coecke, Lambert Lombard, Frans Floris, Antonio Moro, Martin de Vos, Bartholomew Spranger, the Franckens, to quote only the most important. Denis Calvaert even stayed there and founded a school at Bologna.

All their admiration was drawn ceaselessly towards two centres of attraction, Michaelangelo and Raphael. And these two, though the finest models they could have found, were dangerous to imitate; those who followed in their footsteps were far quicker to reproduce externals than to penetrate to the real underlying feeling of a work. Michaelangelo, who drew magnificently, but whose colouring was weak, impressed them by his knowledge of anatomy and by that amazing gift of conveying movement which rose to dramatic heights with such perfect ease. They did not understand that this was the reflection of the tragic soul of this proud, shy Florentine with his admiration for Dante and Savonarola. Imitation of his forms without his inspiration was, alas, bound to end in turgidity and hollow eloquence . . . It is easy enough to understand how the Flemish painters could make the mistake of letting themselves be captivated by Michelangelo, but how can we explain their admiration for Raphael, that gentle genius, full of moderation and quiet charm? Raphael's technique is hidden beneath an apparent simplicity; we can gaze at any number of his Madonnas without becoming aware of the triangular framework on which they are built. His colouring is so subtle that to the untutored eye it may seem almost banal. His quest for ideal beauty is handled in so masterly a way that the unlearned may well take it for insipidity. His art imperceptibly transfigures and turns to poetry everything it touches. The Flemish painters are realists, patiently striving to express their model in terms of paint; Raphael is a poet, giving not the reality, but the essence in idealized form. On one side analysis, on the other synthesis; on one side faithful reproduction of a strongly characterized individual, and on the other the individual transcended and replaced by the eternal image of man. In Flanders, ever since Van Eyck, the Mother of God had been a sweet Flemish girl whom you might meet any day. Raphael's Madonna is not an Italian woman; she is a creature of dreams with scarcely a thread binding her to the earth . . . The Flemish painters strove in vain; genius is not to be imitated. They dreamed of giving wings to their drawing, but all they achieved was gesticulation. They would have loved to free colour from its fetters, but remained faithful to their own style, carefully detailed like works in enamel. And if, as happened very occasionally, one of them preferred Venice to Rome, the result was no less sterile; Martin de Vos remained blandly unaffected by all the fire and vehemence of his master Tintoretto.

Rubens was too young and too much of a beginner to have any suspicion of all this. And anyway none of his elders suspected it either. At the age of twenty-one, Peter Paul was admitted as master-painter to the guild of St Luke, of which his former master, Adam Van Noort, was the dean. He could now practise his art on an equal footing with such fashionable painters as Jan Snellinck, Wenceslas Cobergher or Otto Vaenius. But was that really what he wanted? No—he felt he must go further and do something quite different. He decided that it was time he too crossed the Alps and met the real masters. For in Italy there was not only Raphael, the idol of the Flemish school, and Michelangelo; there was also Titian, and Tintoretto, and Paul Veronese, and Leonardo and Correggio. There was Giulio Romano and Parmigiano; there was Giorgione, Andrea del Sarto, Fra Bartolomeo, Sebastiano del Piombo, Sodoma, Bronzino, Palma, Bordone . . . So many of them! And then, there were sculptors too. A Fleming, Giovanni da Bologna, had become a famous artist there. Architects like Bramante, Palladio and Sansovino had scattered their masterpieces throughout Italy. For a century all the Flemish painters had been fervently reproducing the elements of this new architecture. In Antwerp itself the new Town Hall built by Cornelius de Vriendt—a firm devotee of the Italian manner—bore witness to the beauty of this style. There were also engravers like Marcantonio, goldsmiths like Benvenuto Cellini, who was at the same time a sculptor, a medal-maker, and a writer. It was indeed an infinite variety of genius that allowed a sculptor to paint and to work as an architect, an architect to carve stone, and a painter to achieve miracles of engineering. Some painters produced learned treatises, others wrote poems. Nothing could hinder the soaring flight of these wonderful men. They had only to wish to do something—anything of which man is capable—and they succeeded, not only with ease, but with perfect mastery and consummate grace. It was enough to make anyone's head spin. Can we wonder that an inexhaustible flood of travellers made their way to Italy, or that the journey came to be considered an absolute necessity for anyone wishing to practise an art?

Unfortunately Maria Pypelincx was still struggling with financial difficulties. Her son-in-law Simeon du Parcq was still insistently claiming the remainder of the dowry. She had owned two little houses at Borgerhout, but they had gone up in flames. Debtors declared themselves insolvent, rents remained unpaid. Still, she was not the type of woman to be easily disheartened. With great generosity, she decided to break into the small capital she had left and sell some share certificates, and also a house she owned on St Catharine's Wall. She did not wish her son to be deprived of something which appeared indispensable to his education. She already possessed several paintings of his which she thought very beautiful, and she had no doubt that after he had crossed the Alps he would return more skilful still.

They had one last diversion. Archduke Albert and his wife Isabella made their triumphal entry into Antwerp. For eight days the town forgot the anxieties caused by the closure of the Scheldt to shipping and the slump in business. The civic heads did their best to receive their Highnesses in a fitting manner, anxious not to be outdone in splendour by noblemen and courtiers. Otto Vaenius was in charge of the decoration of the town. He designed triumphal arches, pavilions, theatres and floats, with a great array of allegorical and mythological figures. Even though it was December, processions, State visits and ceremonies took place in brilliant sunshine. It was wonderful for a northern clime, but imagine what a similar festival would be like under an Italian sky!

Italy! John Rubens had won his doctorate there, and Philip was soon to go and win his. Peter Paul was taking the same road in search of fame and fortune. He was twenty-three, handsome, intelligent and talented. Fortune could not help but smile on him.

On May 8, 1600, Peter Paul received his passport. The next day he mounted his horse and bade farewell to Antwerp, that city of drab, commonplace reality, of familiar faces in familiar streets, of a dull existence beneath a dull sky.

IV

BEYOND THE ALPS

1600–1608

Peter Paul was only ten when he went on his first journey, which
was from Cologne to Antwerp. He would probably have found
it very difficult to dredge from his memory even a few images
garnered on the way. At that age the journey is unimportant,
and only the objective counts. When one is obsessed, before even
leaving, with the idea of arriving at one's destination, it is too
easy to ignore the beauty of the countryside and to live only for
that moment, so soon to come, when an unknown yet beloved
place will at last be revealed to the sight. Today he was leaving
that place, now grown familiar, and embarking upon another
journey upon which his whole future was to depend. Before
starting out he had had to wait till he was twenty-three, for
travel was expensive and his mother had to watch every penny.
The essential thing was that he was free to go, and the rest was
up to him.

This was the classic journey which artists from the Netherlands made only once in a lifetime, but which they prolonged
sometimes for years, simply because they had so much to gain
from it. Rubens knew the names of all those who had made the
journey, and also of those who were still living there.

It was a long journey, but that mattered little to anyone
trained to observe, whose gaze was always alert as he looked at
the ever-changing landscapes of plain, hills or mountains. There
were blue distances such as he had seen only in the paintings of
the masters. Soon after came hillsides clothed with vines.
Gradually the sky became more serene and the air warmer.
Unknown scents rose from the earth. Then the mountains
appeared, their snowy crests clear-cut against the blue. In the

warm valleys the old familiar plants were gone, and gayer flowers held sway. This was Italy! Even the sun, it seemed, was not the same sun that shone on Flanders. Here it transfigured everything, a shining demigod blessing the land. It was the sun that gave meaning to every being and every object. Like an enchanter, it transformed every beggar to a prince, every hovel to a palace. Even the voices of the people flowed like a golden stream.

Peter Paul was free. In what direction should he turn? People from the North always went to Rome. His master had lived there for five years, and his friend and teacher Zuccaro was still there. It was the city of the Popes—the Vatican, St Peter's, St John Lateran — grafted on to the city of the Caesars, with the Pantheon, the Coliseum and the Forum; or the fusion of two worlds in Hadrian's mausoleum which became the Castel Sant 'Angelo. It was the spiritual capital of the Christian world, and also, since Bramante, Michelangelo and Raphael had worked there, the capital city of the world of art. But there were at least twenty other towns whose glorious reputation was a lure to attract any artist. There was Florence, the glowing heart of Tuscany, melting-pot for all the wildest passions, the home of a long line of eminent men—painters, architects, sculptors and poets — all of whose works have the same intellectual tinge. There was Venice, almost an Eastern city, full of splendour and sensuality. There was Siena, Urbino, Ferrara, Padua, Parma, Pisa, Mantua, Milan, Vicenza, Piacenza, Verona, Perugia, and finally Bologna where, under the influence of Denis Calvaert, painting was experiencing a new resurgence which carried it to awe-inspiring heights.

All these names of towns passed in a confused medley through the mind, because most people's knowledge of them was purely theoretical, born of some picture or the memories of some fortunate traveller. The visitor needed to see Italy with his own eyes, breathe its air, feel its ground beneath his feet, rub shoulders with its people, gaze at its sky and its horizon. He had to discover the country, step by step, before he could begin to study its art. And anyway, all effort in that direction would have been superfluous. Art everywhere was so completely a part of life, so inextricably mingled with it, that it was impossible not to be imbued with it willy-nilly. In palaces, in churches, and on the common highway, art boldly asserted itself, but in order to understand it, time, and perhaps some hidden affinity, were needed. It was not enough to be there in its midst, even to drink it all in greedily; it was the spirit which must be caught, for a form the spirit of which eludes us is nothing but an empty symbol. The foreigner must take off his old familiar clothing and put on fresh garments. He must change his soul as he changed his surroundings. The Athenians used to laugh at the dull heavy Boeotians, though they were Greeks like themselves. What place, then, had a northerner, a Fleming from the land of mist and rain, among these passionate Italians? To paint great clusters of human figures, as Frans Floris did, was not enough to put him on a level with Michelangelo, and the careful charm of Cocxie was never Raphael. Martin de Vos and the Franckens strove in vain; they could only imitate the form, while the spirit eluded them. And for that reason their forms are stiff and theatrical, and their colours brassy and strident. They kept their realist view of the world and the meticulous technique arising from it; and they shouted themselves hoarse in pseudo-heroic epics.

For those faced with the magnificent flowering of Italian art, there were only two possible attitudes: to surrender to it, body and soul, or to turn away from it altogether. The elder Bruegel had understood that. He too crossed the Alps, but he came back to his country without changing his style at all; or, to be more precise, he kept out of sight, as it were, the valuable gains he had made. The cult of antiquity so dear to the Italian masters left him cold, and he could contemplate their work without being shaken to the core as his fellow-northerners were. Was this indifference? Indeed not. Bruegel had a quick eye and a clear mind. If he disdained the art of Italy, he gazed with rapture upon her natural beauties. And if, in his glorious landscapes, the allusions to Italy were so subtle as to be almost imperceptible, this only went to show the independence of his nature.

Rubens chose the other road, with enthusiasm. He knew, of course, that the study of painting alone was not enough. He had to enter into the life of this nation which, for more than a century, had been living a stupendous kind of adventure story of mad passions, secret intrigues, crimes, wars and rebellions, and was producing an incomparable wealth of poets and artists, princes and condottieri, scholars and churchmen, dazzling women and passionate lovers. It was the triumph of Man. The gold of corruption, the murderer's dagger and poison, were no more than the reaction of man's violence to a hostile Fate; while the artist and the scholar, blending past and present in an all-embracing synthesis, were seeking to express the universal nature of man; the one creating an entirely new art in which the pagan and the Christian mingled in one vision of beauty, and the other garnering in his mind the sum total of all human knowledge. The end result of all this outpouring of vitality and emotion was seen in the buildings which sprang up almost miraculously all over Italy, bearing eloquent witness to the overflowing life which gave them birth: imposing churches and splendid palaces, conclusive evidence of the new style which embodied in its forms a return to the Rome of the Caesars. Every city bore this magnificent signature, giving it in each case its own individual aspect. And this was not all. Within the orbit of the builders, the sculptors and painters had vied with each other in fervour and in genius. Every dwelling—whether of man or God—was above all a temple dedicated to art. Side by side with the bronze or marble statues, the painter's craft rose to unprecedented heights. It reigned over high altars and retables, adorned halls and galleries, graced walls and ceilings. All subjects were acceptable, all stimulated the inexhaustible energy of the painters—Bible stories, mythology, fable, allegory or portrait. The history of every nation has its peaks when time and evolution seem to stand still, and every creative force is heightened and concentrated so as to fix for all time the indelible image of the world as it then exists. Italy had just lived through one of these glorious moments, and that was why artists from other countries came as pilgrims paying devoted homage. For one sceptic like Bruegel there were a hundred others conquered once and for all by the irresistible magic of Italian art. And of these Rubens was one.

But for all its heady enchantment, a man cannot live on beauty. When money troubles have formed the chief topic of family conversation since childhood, it becomes a matter of course to shift for oneself. Peter Paul was armed with a handsome passport in Latin, in which the Magistracy of Antwerp certified that the shores of the Scheldt were free from plague and that the holder was not likely to spread any dangerous infection. One assumes that he was also provided with more immediately useful documents. It is not known what they were, but they were obviously effective. On October 5, 1600, Marie de Medici was married at Florence, and towards the end of the same year Rubens obtained employment at the court of Mantua. It was a sure sign.

Mantua had been for three centuries the fief of the Gonzaga family. The reigning duke, Vincenzo I, engaged the young artist to copy paintings for him. Ardent collectors were not content with seeking out works of art; some were unattainable, jealously guarded by their owners. No one knew this better than Vincenzo, who had once offered a marquisate for the chance of possessing a certain madonna of Raphael. Since every collector had these unsatisfied cravings, custom decreed the exchange of copies; failing the work itself, they could gaze on its reflection. Copying pictures is not a glorious task, but it is not a sterile one either for anyone who knows how to approach it; there is no finer means of initiation to the technique of the masters. In the last analysis, everything depends on talent; when Titian copied Raphael's portrait of Giulio II, it was hard to tell which was the more admirable of the two. Mantua was an excellent place for the study of painting. Churches such as San Pietro or San Andrea were rich in frescoes and pictures. The ducal palace, the Castello di Corte and the Palazzo del Te were overflowing with master-pieces. The Gonzaga collection was one of the most famous in Italy, containing works by Bellini, Titian, the elder Palma, Tintoretto, Paolo Veronese, Mantegna, Leonardo da Vinci, Andrea del Sarto, Raphael, Pordenone, Correggio, and Giulio Romano. Peter Paul could take his fill. Beside these giants, his colleagues the Flemish painters, Frans Floris, Martin de Vos, the Franckens, Spranger or Vaenius, seemed so wretchedly poor. And he himself, despite his masters' praise and the waves of ambition that sometimes rose within him, seemed small, miserable and almost non-existent.

The Gonzaga family were not content to be ardent collectors; they had always desired to have artists about them. Mantegna had spent the last forty years of his life at Mantua, where he had been summoned by the marquis Ludovico III. He completed many great works there, including the frescoes in the 'Camera degli Spozi' in the ducal palace, and the 'Triumphs of Caesar' for the Palace of San Sebastian. He was an excellent draughtsman, and, as Vasari says, 'demonstrated in a most wonderful way that it was possible to show in painting the foreshortening of figures seen from below; this was indeed a rare and original invention'. Before him painters had decorated walls, often successfully, but always keeping to two dimensions. With great firmness, Mantegna added depth to length and breadth, thus opening up new possibilities in mural painting. That attractive genius Ariosto, who was his younger contemporary, placed him among the three greatest: 'Leonardo, Andrea Mantegna, Gian Bellino'.

Thanks to Mantegna, the capital city of the Gonzagas became an important artistic centre — and also thanks to a woman, Isabella d'Este, wife of Giovanni Francesco III. She was a passionate devotee of art and had fruitful relationships with Giovanni Bellini, Leonardo da Vinci and Michelangelo. After her husband's death it was she who invited Giulio Romano to Mantua. Giulio Romano, who had been condemned to death and burnt in effigy in the papal city, was glad to yield to the pleas of Count Baldassari Castiglione, the ambassador of the Gonzaga family. He never had cause to regret it. During the sixteen years he spent at the Gonzaga court, he lavished his talents in all directions. As a military engineer, he completed the fortification of the town; as a civil engineer, he canalized the Mincio; as an architect he built the famous Palazzo del Te and the Palazzo Colleredo and restored the cathedral; as superintendent of works he earned this praise from Vasari: 'Mantua, once so dirty and marshy as to be almost uninhabitable, became both healthy and beautiful thanks to Giulio Romano; to him the city owed most of its attractions: chapels, houses, gardens and façades.' And as a painter he adorned the Palazzo del Te with works that were remarkable for their movement, somewhat confused in composition, but full of mythological beauties, daringly naked.

The reigning duke followed the tradition of his ancestors. He loved everything rare and beautiful. He had agents everywhere; Europe was not enough for him, and his collections were fed from America and Asia as well. His love for painting was tinged with a certain Epicurean flavour; he dreamed of a collection embodying the image of the most beautiful women of his time. He had recently engaged a portrait-painter, a Fleming, Frans Pourbus the Younger; it could well have been with this charming gallery in mind. He could turn a pretty sonnet, and did not underrate his literary colleagues. When Tasso was under close surveillance in Ferrara, Vincenzo interceded with his brother-in-law and succeeded in taking the unhappy author of *Jerusalem Delivered* back to Mantua with him. This generous gesture gave Tasso, who always suffered from persecution mania, the chance to live quietly for a while and regain the will to work. Nor did the Duke neglect the sciences; he corresponded with a scholar upon whom all Europe had fixed its attention: Galileo, who was teaching mathematics at the University of Padua.

But greatly as he admired science, the Duke of Mantua was eclectic enough to be infatuated with astrologers, alchemists and other charlatans. Above all he loved display, pleasure, and a gay life. His company of actors was famed far beyond his own frontiers. A troupe of dwarfs lived in his palace. His stables held a hundred and fifty horses of a world-famous native breed, and his kennels were full of valuable animals. His *maestro di capella*, Claudio Monteverdi, was a bold innovator. After a long period as violinist and singer, this composer of madrigals and 'can-zonette' replaced the rather dull Florentine recitative with an expressive type of declamation, and did not shrink from the use of dissonance; and he was in consequence bitterly attacked. My lord of Mantua loved to shock people, and he must have been delighted with this musician who set tongues wagging all round. He was, after all, a collector of wild beasts. He loved travel and never set out without a huge retinue, in order to dazzle the populace who came out to watch him pass. He went so far as to make war, learning to his cost that fine sight though it may be, it is something rather more than a theatrical display. In spite of being a hunchback's son, the Duke was a handsome gentleman, said to be very fond of the fair sex. He thought nothing of emptying the State coffers in order to satisfy his whims and his taste for luxury. He was on friendly terms with the most power-ful rulers. His one purpose in life was to dazzle the world; all that mattered was that the name of Gonzaga of Mantua should eclipse that of Medici of Florence, Farnese of Parma, and Este of Ferrara.

Compared with the careworn existence in the mist-shrouded North, this life was like a fairy-tale. For a painter there was no need to weave dreams, no spur to the imagination was necessary; he had only to open his eyes. Not only were the incomparable treasures of art spread around him; life itself was an Aladdin's cave. What subjects there were, what models! Here the human fauna was as varied as the animal. And all this swarming, quivering life was going on for the benefit of a man not yet forty, who could bestow good fortune or inflict disgrace by one gesture of his all-powerful hand. But Peter Paul knew, by hearsay if not by experience, how thankless dealings with the great could be. Failing the prince, it would be a good thing to win the minister's favour. So he approached the Secretary of State, Annibale Chieppio, an old and worthy civil servant who did his best to introduce some semblance of logic into the whims of his gracious master. As it happened, in July 1601 the Duke was preparing to go off to war, to fight the Turks in company with the emperor Rudolph II; but he had given orders that the work of improvement was not to cease. Carrying a letter of introduction to Cardinal Montalto, Peter Paul was sent to Rome to copy several pictures there. This cardinal was a person of considerable importance; it was to him that Clement VIII, who was then Pope, and two or three of his predecessors owed their tiaras, for Montalto was the most powerful elector in the conclaves. This shrewd diplomat scattered wealth with a munificence for which his proteges frequently paid. He was said to be very susceptible to the charms of the fair ladies of Rome. One day in the distant past he had professed his willingness 'to sell his soul for the Marchesa d'Aucisa, and the tiara for Contessa Scotti'. He speculated on the popes whose election he favoured; and he took an interest in the arts. The Cardinal received Peter Paul very kindly, but the mercenary task with which the Fleming was entrusted could not claim more than a passing attention on his part. Montalto, powerful as he was, did nothing more for the painter than to make his task a little easier by providing him with the necessary introductions.

At last Peter Paul could experience the boundless delight of coming into contact with the great masters who had made Rome into a place of pilgrimage for every artist—Raphael and Michelangelo. It was not Raphael who won his heart. Of course, in the Vatican Raphael appeared in a different light from those works of his seen in churches and in princely collections. Here, he was obviously in his own home; the rooms which he covered with frescoes from floor to ceiling were entirely his; the Stanza d'Eliodoro, the Stanza dell'Incendio, and the most important of all, the Stanza della Segnatura, were not rooms which had offered hospitality to an artist; it was the artist who had taken them for his own, and stood there like a conquering hero to receive an endless procession of homage. But a little further on was the Sistine Chapel, all aglow with the titanic genius of Michelangelo. What was the charm of Raphael, what, even, was his strength, compared with this tremendous revelation? No draughtsman had ever juggled like this with the human form. His knowledge of anatomy was prodigious. Figures like these, spawned by some Apocalyptic genius, were never thus dominated by a man. Only a superman or demigod could cover a vast wall with clustering, swarming bodies until the brain reels, as he did in that stupendous fresco of the Last Judgment. And what a personality! When he heard that Pope Paul IV had decided that the naked bodies in the Last Judgment went too far and must be covered, he replied 'Tell the Pope he can do more than that; let him reform the world, and then we can reform the paintings.'

Obviously Titian's drawing must seem timid in comparison with this giant. Michelangelo admired his colouring, but thought, according to Vasari, 'that it was a great pity that at Venice they did not pay attention at the very beginning to good drawing and more careful study; if, he added, this man had been aided by art and draughtsmanship to the extent that he had been favoured by Nature, especially in the portrayal of living subjects, nobody could have done better nor achieved more than he, for he has a fine feeling and a vivid and brilliant style'. It may have seemed almost possible that Titian, the shining light of the Venetian school, might pale into dimness before this wild genius. But Titian had his own treasure—his magic palette. Michelangelo

Isabella Brant by P. P. Rubens. (Uffizi Gallery, Florence—Photo Alinari)

5. Sketch for the sign of the Plantin printing shop. (Plantin-Moretus Mus
Antwerp)

The Port of Antwerp in 1644, from the 'Werfpoot' to Saint Michael's Abbe
Bonaventura Peeters. Etching by Joseph Linnig. (Prints Department, Antwerp)

was a very great artist, but no colourist. His colour is dead. Titian's colour sings. Its charm is intoxicating, but delicately so. Besides his magnificent natural gifts, the Venetian painter was an innovator. The Tuscans and their disciples saw only antiquity as the source of all knowledge, while Titian, following Giorgione, preferred to look at Nature; but that is not in itself enough to differentiate them. Titian carried out, in the course of his career, an absolute revolution; he widened the scope of painting and made touch of primary importance. In his work, design and colour are inseparable. Colour is no longer merely complementary to the drawing as it was with all his predecessors. He designed while painting, and consequently colour at last became more active, playing, in fact, the dominant role. Helped by the Venetian's persuasive brush-strokes, colour triumphed to such an extent that from that moment onwards painters—all of them —were faced with a choice on which would depend the direction which painting was eventually to take. Which was to predominate, design or colour? Unless—though this seemed an impossible dream—they could try to fuse the two; Titian's colouring and the drawing of Michelangelo . . . The artist who could blend within himself those two supreme qualities would indeed be the God of Painting.

Young men are presumptuous. Rubens may quite possibly have dreamed this wonderful dream. Others had dreamed it before him; Jacopo Robusti, called Tintoretto, had in his youth written this profession of faith on the walls of his room : 'Michelangelo's drawing and the colouring of Titian'. But Tintoretto, who had, as Vasari says, 'the most original, capricious, quick and decisive, or in one word the most awe-inspiring mind painting has ever known', never achieved this supreme synthesis. His nature was too stormy, too dramatic for him to be other than Tintoretto, a wild, disorganized, nightmare force lit spasmodically by a flash of genius. Michelangelo may have let loose a tumult, but his struggling bodies were really ordered by a master hand, while Titian's sensuality blossomed into warm colour-harmonies. Tintoretto alone was fighting like a madman against the monsters that raged in his unconscious. 'Michelangelo's drawing and the colour of Titian' . . . It was a goal still to be reached.

Gazing at other people's works of art or even copying them is all very well for someone who cares only to dream, but anyone wishing to chance his luck must work for himself. A painter needs commissions, and they do not fall from heaven. It is as well that people who have the power to help should occasionally be reminded of one's existence. Far away in Rubens' homeland, his brother Philip was attached to the departmental staff of Jean Richardot, the president of the Privy Council.

This eminent personage, whom Peter Paul had glimpsed on the occasion of the Archduke's triumphal entry into Antwerp, was the most outstanding member of the Flemish government. Before marrying, under a dispensation from the Pope, the eldest daughter of Philip II, Archduke Albert had been a cardinal, Archbishop of Toledo and Viceroy of Portugal: so he remembered, at a very opportune moment, that he was titulary Dean of the church of Sant Croce di Gerusalemme in Rome. The chapel of St Helena in this church needed decorating; the Archduke's envoy in Rome was asked to attend to it, and this envoy was none other than the son of Richardot. By a fortunate coincidence, Peter Paul happened to be working in Rome, and was commissioned to paint a triptych. As he was in Vincenzo's pay, however, he needed his employer's authorization; Richardot saw to this. The central panel, showing St Helena embracing the Cross, was scarcely finished when Rubens was recalled to Mantua. Richardot intervened to ask that the painter be permitted to finish the volets. Fortunately the Duke made no objection and Rubens painted 'The Crowning with Thorns' and 'The Son of Man on the Cross'. In the spring he returned to Mantua.

He might well think himself fortunate. For the first time he could make direct use of his youthful experience in Italy. He was clearly still hesitating, dreaming of the powerful drawing of Michelangelo and the dramatic colouring of Tintoretto. The Carracci family, those masters of eclecticism, came to his aid, apart from the fact that his Flemish tradition still weighed heavily upon him. The somewhat stiff figures, and the treatment of light, together with a certain frigidity, recall Otto Vaenius. The resultant whole is rather chaotic, with contradictory tendencies coming face to face without any real fusion. Despite these weaknesses, the work is by no means negligible. Rubens had passed in one bound the stage reached by the Flemish imitators of Rome, which seems to prove that although his execution fell short of its mark, he had already understood the lessons of Italy better than most.

V

SUCCESS

1603–1608

The Duke had for some time been considering sending some presents to the King of Spain, probably bearing in mind the old adage which says that small gifts keep friendship alive. The King of Spain owned Milan, the Two Sicilies and Sardinia, and for a small potentate it was no bad thing to be on good terms with a prince with so many interests in Italy. Vincenzo I was on the best of terms with his neighbours, the Venetians and the Piedmontese. Henry IV, who had married his wife's sister, was full of attentions towards him. But with the King of Spain there were ups and downs, which was yet another reason for a conscious effort to counteract these sudden changes of mood. The Duke, true to his reputation, had every intention of making a display. He decided to present the King with a small travelling coach drawn by six horses, eleven arquebuses of a new type, and a rock-crystal vase filled with perfumes. His gifts for the all-powerful Duke of Lerma were sixteen paintings, a large silver vase and two gold vases. The paintings were copies made specially for the occasion by Pietro Facchetti. Two rock-crystal candlesticks and a cross were to be sent to the Countess of Lemos, the Prime Minister's sister and the King's favourite. Finally the secretary Don Pedro Franqueza, Lerma's confidential agent, was to receive two rock-crystal vases and a damask wall-hanging bordered with cloth of gold.

When he had collected all these gifts together, the Duke felt it would be a good idea to have them accompanied by a member of his household, and Rubens was chosen. Duke Vincenzo saw a double advantage in this. With regard to the pictures to be presented to the Duke of Lerma, 'Peter Paul will say what is necessary, like the well-informed man he is'. Mindful of his gallery of famous beauties, Vincenzo instructed his resident in Spain, Annibale Iberti: 'And as this same Peter Paul is an admirable painter and skilled in portraiture, we desire you, if there are other ladies of quality besides those whose portrait Count Vincenzo obtained for us, to take advantage of his presence and of his skill.' A sum for expenses was allocated to Peter Paul, the Duke added a bonus payment, and the courtiers declared that he was feathering his nest most successfully.

For a young ambitious painter it was manna from heaven to be able to hand over gifts from an Italian duke to the powerful Spanish King and his Prime Minister. It would have been an entirely honourable mission if he had not been obliged at the same time to act as a sort of attendant; still, someone in a subordinate position like himself could not expect any choice. As his employers had allowed him to hope that he might accompany them on their next journey to France, Rubens decided to do his best not to forfeit their esteem.

At the beginning of March 1603, after personally supervising the packing of pictures and other precious objects, he set out with his coach, horses and parcels. He had been advised to embark at Leghorn; whereas the best way, as he learnt on arrival at Florence, would have been to make for Genoa. One wonders whether he was misdirected through ignorance or malice. Ferdinand I, Grand Duke of Tuscany, summoned him to his court, where he received yet another surprise. The Grand Duke talked to him about his masters, his art, and—in great detail— about the presents he was carrying. 'I was utterly dumbfounded,' Rubens wrote to Chieppio, 'I can only suspect that one of my friends has played me false, or that I have been the object of careful scrutiny by observers, not to say spies, living at His Highness's court. In fact there can be no other explanation, because I have given no details of the contents of my luggage, either at the Customs or anywhere else.' When he reached Leghorn at the beginning of April he was lucky enough to meet the captain of a vessel from Hamburg, who was willing to take horses, men and luggage on board. The first part of the journey was thus accomplished without a hitch. Nevertheless, Peter Paul was horrified to realize how much he had spent, and felt in duty bound to send an explanation to the Secretary of State.

On arrival at Alicante he learned that the court was at Valladolid, and set out without delay. It was an appalling journey; the rain fell in torrents for twenty-five days. His troubles were not at an end; at Valladolid, the Mantuan resident declared that he had no orders and knew nothing about this mission. Fortunately this was simply a pose intended to increase his own importance, for Signor Iberti very soon looked after his master's envoy. He provided him with money—Peter Paul had not a penny — had him dressed Spanish fashion so that he would appear to greater advantage, and prepared for the handing over of the presents. But when the canvases were unpacked they were found to be in an incredibly dilapidated state caused by the rain. Peter Paul was plunged into despair, but it would have taken more than that to worry Annibale Iberti. He suggested that Rubens should hastily paint several canvases with the help of Spanish painters, and patch up the others. Peter Paul was up in arms at once, saying he could not accept the help of Spanish painters owing to differences in technique. Besides, the Duke of Lerma, who was a connoisseur, would detect the fraud. He declared, naïvely, that he could not risk his reputation 'which is not unknown in Spain' by signing works unworthy of his name. These arguments made very little impression on the Mantuan diplomat, for whom Rubens was no match, however hard he tried.

Fortunately the court had just left for the castle of Aranjuez, and was going from there to Burgos. The King would not be back in Valladolid before the beginning of July. Two months in which to repair the damage had simply fallen into Rubens' lap. He patched up Facchetti's canvases as best he could, and replaced the works spoiled beyond repair with two works by his own hand. As the choice of subject had been left to him, he painted a 'Heraclitus' and a 'Democrites' in order to have a contrast. Iberti was pleased with him.

When the King returned, the pictures were handed over to their proper recipients. For this purpose two ceremonies were organized. Peter Paul was present, but did not play the part he had hoped, for the Duke of Mantua had ordered Iberti to present

Rubens to the King. Iberti had indeed drawn up a plan and handed out parts, but when Philip III appeared, he threw it all to the winds and presented the coach and horses by himself. Peter Paul did not even have the chance to make his bow! When it came to the Duke of Lerma, his luck was better, for he was a member of the delegation presenting the canvases. The Prime Minister thought them very fine, and despite his reputation as an expert, took the Raphaels copied by Facchetti for originals. As for Rubens' works, they pleased him so much that he was anxious to commission something from him. Peter Paul was so delighted at this reception that he quite forgot all that he had said a few months earlier. He also learnt that the Duke of Mantua was pleased with him. Annibale Iberti, for his part, did his best to exploit the painter's presence. Soon Rubens began an equestrian portrait of the Duke of Lerma.

The Prime Minister was forty-eight years old, and at the height of his power. Since the accession of Philip III he had been the real ruler of the kingdom. The King was a likeable man, very devout, but lacking in energy; his father, at first delighted by his extreme docility, had in the end been horrified by it. Ever since his accession, Philip III had entrusted the government to his favourite, declaring that henceforward Lerma's signature would be as valid as his own. This man's influence over the King was so great that it was said at court to be founded on witchcraft. The Duke was a frigid, intelligent man, with a certain love of finery. He achieved the most successful effects with an art dear to Spanish hearts: that of ceremonial. Under his influence, ceremonial became of capital importance. For the minister it was an excellent way of winning the allegiance of the grandees of Spain by playing on their vanity. Their role was no longer any more than nominal, but they were very proud of their right to keep their heads covered in the presence of the King or to oblige the queen to rise from her seat for them. The King was the natural summit of this hierarchical pyramid, and Philip was content to be a mere figure-head. Every action of his life, public or private, was governed by ceremonial. He could not move a step without setting in motion a complicated machinery of regulations and formalities.

No other country showed so clearly the aim of the Roman

Church to restore order to the Christian religion by means of outward display. Spain, of all countries, proclaimed most eloquently her adhesion to the counter-Reformation. Her reply to the provocations of the iconoclasts was to impose a new style, richer and more splendid than all preceding forms of art. The Church's triumph was thus manifest in the splendour of its buildings and ceremonies, equally as much as in the dialectics of its learned men. The new unity of the Church, which was given fixed form by the Council of Trent, was finding aesthetic expression. A new type of sacred art was coming into flower, compounded of both painting and the plastic arts, and very near to the theatre. Ceremonies overflowed from the Church buildings and took their place in public life. A kind of street art was being born, with processions and masquerades, triumphal entries, giants, travelling theatres and fireworks. In these manifestations sacred and profane were mingled. As if by one powerful impulse, all forms of life became merged in the eternal myth of Unity, which had for a moment been restored to youth and vigour. On the death of Philip II, Juan de Orviedo, the architect of Seville Cathedral, had already built a huge catafalque, decorated by Montanes. Since then, other artists, both painters, sculptors and architects, had contributed to the development of this new art. That docile monarch Philip III was dragged into an endless succession of journeys and junketings, ordered according to strict rules, while Lerma reigned. An Italian nobleman, whom the King was trying to pass on to his minister, is said to have replied: 'If I could have obtained an audience of the Duke, I would not have come to see Your Majesty.'

The Duke of Lerma distributed prebends and benefices to his friends and relations and helped himself generously at the same time. He had recently been widowed, and assumed a grief he did not really feel. All the court was busy trying to marry him off again, and prognostications were rife.

Rubens had the good luck to be summoned to the castle of Ventosiglia to paint the portrait of the powerful man. Ever since painters had existed, portraiture had been the most popular art. It was not easy for a young artist to succeed in a branch of his craft distinguished by so many great masters. Rubens did not hesitate; he put the Duke of Lerma on horseback. It was a great novelty. It is true that Donatello and Verrocchio had seated Gattamelata and Colleoni on unforgettable bronze horses. But who had ever painted an equestrian portrait? Titian had; but that was for an emperor; Rubens intended to do it for the Duke of Lerma. It was a wonderful chance to show that he could paint a spirited, elegant, ideally beautiful horse. When the portrait was finished, the painter was delighted to realize that it was an unqualified success. He had, however, other worries. He was uneasy about his journey to France, and protested about it in advance. It was not worth while, he said, to send him there at great expense, just to 'paint a few miserable portraits'. A task like that would give his talent 'a most unworthy goal'. He would certainly agree to paint portraits as a step towards obtaining 'much more important work'. If there was no chance of that, he asked for permission to return to Mantua. He won his point, and was back by the end of April, 1604.

Shortly afterwards, the Duke allowed him to carry out an original work; he commissioned a retable for the Church of the Trinity. Even though this work was not destined to take its place in the ducal collection—a faint shade of meaning which Peter Paul could not have missed—he set to work joyfully. He painted a triptych of impressive size, of which the central panel showed the Holy Trinity, the left-hand volet the baptism of Christ by John the Baptist, and the right-hand volet the Transfiguration. Rubens also contrived to introduce the portraits of Vincenzo, the Duchess and their father and mother. Was he hoping by this to win for himself the favour of a master who set no great store by him? Once he had made this concession, he gave himself over entirely to the joy of painting, and to his own particular tastes. The Romanists, fortunately, were forgotten : the stiff attitudes and strident colours were gone. The composition was better arranged, but the colouring had become completely Italian. The work is full of echoes and reminiscences, such as rounded musculatures like those of Michelangelo, bronzed skins, shades of bluish green, and earthy colours. Sometimes there is a very definite echo, such as the figure of Christ baptized in the Jordan, which, apart from the fair hair, is oddly like a Christ by Cesaro da Sesto, which appears in the church of St John Lateran. After all these contradictory tendencies, one remained predominant — that of Italy. But that was of little importance; what mattered was that in following this road Rubens was taking the work of the great masters and making it his own.

Before long, Rubens was once more taken up with his mercenary tasks. In April 1605, the colourless Emperor Rudolph II asked for copies of two works by Correggio in the collection of Vincenzo I. It would have been churlish to refuse a fellow-collector so small a service. The work was entrusted to Peter Paul, and the imitations despatched at the end of September.

A man without power must, if he wishes to succeed, use ingenuity instead; and Peter Paul was scheming to get himself to Rome. While he was in Spain, his brother Philip had gone to Rome to gain his diploma as doctor of laws, and at that time he was there for the second time, attached to the staff of Cardinal Ascanio Colonna, and occupied in archaeological research. Peter Paul also knew that he would find there quite a large colony of his compatriots, not only artists, but also craftsmen, officials of the Papal court, and businessmen. Most of them were living there permanently. Some of them held influential positions, like the Pescatore family of powerful bankers and patrons of the arts, who came from Audenaerde, and a century earlier had still been called Visscher. All these men, whether their Roman citizenship was longstanding or recent, kept a great love for their fatherland. They had their own churches, even their own cemetery, the 'Campo-santo dei Tedeschi e Fiamminghi', and they maintained two houses from their own funds — San Giuliano dei Fiamminghi and Santa Maria dell'Anima — in which they received poor pilgrims coming from Flanders or from the Empire.

The necessary authorization was granted, and Peter Paul could go to the Eternal City 'for the purposes of study'. The first step was taken; he was released from the court of my lord of Mantua, where he felt he was not getting the recognition he deserved, and plunged headlong into the whirlpool of the artistic life of Rome, the only one that counted in the world.

The echoes of the passionate quarrels between the followers of Annibale Carracci and those of Caravaggio were still resounding. There was no hiding the fact that art was passing through a crisis. The great masters were dead, and living artists were content to rest on their laurels without making any new contribution whatsoever.

They gave free rein to their deplorable facility, and painted everything from memory, so that the reaction of the Carracci family was favourably received. Their teaching, begun at Bologna and continued at Rome, was on the study of models and of the art of antiquity, not forgetting the lessons of their famous predecessors. The Carracci themselves set the example by painting pictures inspired by Raphael, Titian, Tintoretto, Correggio, Veronese and Parmigiano. Their formula consisted in modelling every detail on the master who had showed himself superior to the others in that particular subject. In order to give impetus to this emulation, the literary men of Rome would come along to recount historical episodes to the pupils of the Carracci, who would make drawings inspired by these stories; and several cardinals offered prizes for the most skilful.

But the initial success of the Carracci was soon challenged by a fanatic who, after having worked for the Cavaliere d'Arpino, decided to dispense with all the rules, condemning Raphael and the painters of antiquity equally, and declaring that only first hand observation of life could be a valid source of inspiration. This was Michelangelo Merigi, called Caravaggio. At first he painted figures, with the single purpose of coming as near to reality as possible, but gradually he began to eschew his open-air effects, and ended by painting violent contrasts of light and shade. It was not enough for him to declare that vermilion and azure were poisons; in the end he painted only dark backgrounds against which a pale figure stood out eerily. He painted his models as he saw them, refusing to improve them. On the contrary, the most depressing sights attracted and fascinated him. His clients, appalled by the horrifying visions he offered them, sometimes refused to accept works they had commissioned.

Annibale Carracci, on the other hand, was always correct, even charming. Cardinal Farnese sent for him to Rome to decorate his magnificent palace which Sangallo and Michelangelo had built the century before 'with stones taken from the Coliseum and the Theatre of Marcellus', and Carracci had been working on it for five years without finishing his task. His brother Agostino had helped him until professional rivalry caused a split between them. Because the Roman public showed more favour towards his brother's work, Annibale had forced him to leave Rome. To help Agostino, Cardinal Farnese had him engaged at Parma by the Duke, his brother, while Annibale continued his work with the help of younger painters like Dominichino and Lanfranc, who constituted no threat to his reputation.

The Cavaliere d'Arpino, known as Giuseppino, reconciled the two factions by decrying both Carracci and his former collaborator Caravaggio. So when in the same year, 1605, Guido Reni came from Bologna to settle in Rome, the Cavaliere hastened to offer him his patronage and to get commissions for him; this was a blow against Annibale, who had a great deal to fear from the man who had been, at Bologna, the most brilliant student in the school. Giuseppino had not the patience to paint directly from nature, and he knew that his facile, insipid style could not stand up against Caravaggio's brutality. It seemed to him that the only way to bring to heel this hated rival, this insolent fellow who wielded brush or dagger with equal fire, was to set up against him another successful painter. The way to hold in check this accursed Caravaggio was for Guido Reni to abandon his blue skies and his serenity; he too must emphasize the shadows. The Cavaliere d'Arpino showed himself to be an excellent psychologist; faced with a choice between the charming things painted by Annibale Carracci and Caravaggio's horrors, a man of refinement would probably incline towards the former, but youth must also be reckoned with, and young people would certainly have more sympathy with this outburst of harsh reality than with the conventional prettiness of a style that was all too familiar to them. Annibale Carracci was already distressed by the successes of Caravaggio, whom he considered incompetent; and now he had to look on helplessly while a new rival was enthroned. He could only retaliate with spiteful remarks; but these had no effect. Even before he had produced anything in his newly adopted city, all Rome was acclaiming Guido Reni. The Cavaliere d'Arpino had done his work well.

When Pope Clement VIII died, the conclave elected Leon XI on April 1st, after a fierce struggle which lasted for days and was by no means free from scandal. After reigning for twenty-six days, the new pope died, and the tiara fell to Cardinal Borghese. It was whispered that there were fisticuffs in the conclave and that the Conti ladies had something to do with the victor's success. They had even circumvented the old fox Montalto, whose influence was still enormous. Borghese, who took the name of Paul V, was an imposing, dignified man, utterly self-absorbed. He was only fifty-three and dreamed of doing great things. He had been in power since May when Peter Paul settled in Rome. Work on St Peter's was going on busily. Flaminio Ponzio was finishing the Borghese palace. The cardinals were ceaselessly embellishing their magnificent houses. The one aim of them all was to dazzle their colleagues and the fair ladies of Rome. Intrigues were going on as usual; plots were being hatched and foiled, and mad risks taken. Scandal was often inevitable. Half a century earlier, Joachim du Bellay had written:

'Would'st thou know, Duthier, what manner of thing is Rome? Rome is a public stage where all the world appears, a theatre, a show from which no action that man can perform is missing.

'Here is seen Fortune's wheel, and how her hand can raise us up or cast us down; here everyone stands exposed, and cannot, for all his care, avoid being named by the people for what he is.

'Here rumour tells truth and falsehood alike; here courtiers carry favour and make love; here is ambition and guile in plenty. Here licence makes the humble bold; here idleness makes good men vicious; here the lowest ruffian can give his opinion on the actions of the world.'

A pleasant permissiveness reigned, making life sweet for anyone who was sufficiently clever and adaptable. This was the society on which Rubens intended to make his mark.

He was living with his brother, and he had good friends, among whom were Deodate del Monte, a Fleming of good family who, like so many of his compatriots, had come to beg from the Italian masters the secret of their art; and Adam Elsheimer, the German painter who set his biblical or mythological scenes in spacious landscapes. The realism practised by Elsheimer, even purified as it was by his entirely classical conception, was a

61

novelty in the Italian school. Coming as it did from a man of the North, it found an immediate response only in another northerner, Paul Bril from Antwerp, who had been living in Rome for twenty years.

While Philip Rubens, thanks to the intervention of Justus Lipsius, was working in the library of Cardinal Ascanio Colonna, Peter Paul was able to devote himself to the study nearest his heart; he steeped himself in the spirit of the great masters. Michelangelo was an inexhaustible fountain of inspiration, and there were also the marble and bronze statues of antiquity which were scattered throughout Rome. And there were remarkable medals, too. Pen and pencil drawings, sketches in red chalk, wash-drawings, gouaches; every possible medium was pressed into service in order to fix the image in a few swift strokes—not a servile copy, but a lively interpretation, giving the substance of the work filtered through the artist's own personality.

Art, gold and passion turned life in Rome into a perpetual ecstasy. One day a work of art turned every head; another day, a great drama. Even the earth, which still held many a fragment of imperial Rome, fed this wild rapture by now and then giving up some unknown treasure to the admiration of the people. Thus a magnificent fresco showing a marriage ceremony had just been found near the arch of Gallienus on the Esquiline Hill. It went to enrich the collection of Cardinal Aldobrandini, the same man who, a few years before, had arranged the murder of the Cavaliere Girolamo Longobardi because he kept a young girl as his mistress; the same, too, who had had the governor of Rome beheaded for having censured him; and who had twice been leader of the conclave and twice been outwitted by the wily Montalto. The fresco, which everyone, including Rubens, flocked to see, was placed in the delightful Villa Aldobrandini and from then on was known as the 'Aldobrandini Wedding'.

In this atmosphere of ardent enthusiasm Peter Paul scarcely thought of Mantua, except to claim his salary, which the Duke was slow in paying him. 'I should then be able to continue my studies', he wrote to Chieppio, 'without being compelled to support myself by other means, although actually that would not be difficult in Rome.' He was soon to prove that this was no idle boast.

At the end of 1606 he obtained a commission from the fathers of the Oratory; to decorate the high altar of a new church, Santa Maria in Vallicella. Several artists had come forward as candidates, including Guido Reni and Pomerancio. The fact that he could win such a success in Rome itself, and against a person of importance like Guido Reni, proves that he had made real progress in human relationships. He did not trouble, moreover, to ask the permission of his master, who brought himself to Rubens' attention in the most unfortunate way—by recalling him. Peter Paul at once resisted the order, and asked for an extension of time, admitting to having undertaken the work: 'I have yielded to necessity as I could not have kept up my position in Rome, and had a house and two servants for the past year, on the 140 crowns which are all I have had from Mantua since I left.' The painting was not yet begun, 'but so many people of quality have taken an interest in it that I could not, without deserving the greatest censure, give up this commission which I won gloriously, in competition with the great masters of Rome'.

It was excellent diplomacy to involve third parties in the affair and to show off his own abilities into the bargain. Finally he played his trump card; he made a final appeal to the Secretary of State, his protector Chieppio; if this failed, he said, he would easily gain the support of Cardinal Borghese. It was a superb piece of name-dropping — Scipio Cafarelli-Borghese, the all-powerful nephew of the Pope—this was the man whom Rubens was flinging into the scales on his side. Naturally he got his way; Vincenzo granted him a three months' extension. Six months later, Peter Paul was still in Rome. This time he received a formal summons. The Duke was planning a visit to Flanders and wanted to take his painter with him. Rubens obeyed, but made sure at the same time of being able to return to Rome when the journey was over, by getting Cardinal Borghese to ask that favour on his behalf. He had an excellent excuse; the painting was not yet installed and still needed a few touches.

Towards the end of June 1607, Peter Paul arrived in Mantua. In the meantime the Duke had changed his mind, and decided that what he needed was not the waters of Spa, but sea air. So instead of Flanders he went to Genoa. If this was a 'cure' it was an unorthodox one. It was a succession of receptions, banquets, shows, concerts, excursions and a variety of ceremonies well supplied with 'fair nymphs'. Cardinal Doria proved to be as frenzied a gambler as the Duke himself. The Doge, the Senate and such wealthy notabilities as the Pallavicini and Spinola families, vied with each other in magnificently entertaining the prince and his entourage. Genoa was trying to live up to its longstanding reputation for hospitality.

Peter Paul was present on the fringe of these sumptuous entertainments, but he did not forget that he was a painter. To be strong, one must be well-armed. He took an interest in architecture, as Michelangelo, Leonardo, Raphael and Giulio Romano had done. Genoa was full of remarkable houses: the Lercari Parodi palace, built by Galeazzo Alessi; the Roggio Poddesta palace, by Gianbattista Castello; the famous Doria-Tursi palace designed by Rocco Lurago, and the palaces of the Via Balbi and the Via Nova, with their rich sculpture and polychrome façades. Peter Paul was never tired of drawing elevations, cross-sections and plans. He was painting, too; he had the chance to paint the portrait of the Marchesa Brigitta Spinola, betrothed to the Doge.

When the Duke of Mantua returned to his capital he found a letter from Archduke Albert which irritated him considerably. The ruler of the Spanish Netherlands asked for leave of absence for one of his subjects who was needed in Flanders to settle some family business. The subject in question was no other than Peter Paul Rubens. What was this pressing business at home? The letter does not say precisely, and Peter Paul would have been at a loss to explain. His brother Philip had returned to Antwerp, and was on friendly terms with people of high rank there. Could he have been responsible for the letter having been sent? Did the two brothers hatch this plot in Rome? Peter Paul, true to his usual policy, remained impenetrable. Whatever happened, he was still his courteous, smiling self. He was in the weaker position and knew it. At least he kept his inmost thoughts strictly to himself. He probably realized that he had nothing to hope from Vincenzo. The great ones of this world show consideration only to their equals or to those who seem so to them; this explains the Borghese letter, and now the letter from the Archduke. But if this was to be the game, Peter Paul had played the wrong card. The Duke was no fool, and the malice of this letter struck him as somewhat blatant. He hastened therefore to reply to his princely colleague, in a distinctly off-hand manner, that he could not accede to his request. Would Rubens consider leaving his service? 'The intention of the said Peter Paul is quite otherwise, since he wishes to remain, and so is mine, since I wish to keep him.' The battle was lost, and there was nothing for it but to start at the beginning again.

Towards the middle of December Peter Paul was able to return to Rome. When his painting was installed he saw that reflected light on the high altar had a disastrous effect. It was impossible to see anything at all! Rubens, who set great store by his reputation, did not intend to be judged on a work shown in such unfavourable conditions. The Oratory fathers were very pleased with this canvas, and were not willing for Peter Paul to remove it without undertaking to make a copy on slate or some other material which would absorb the colours. What was to be done? Peter Paul was willing to start afresh, but he hoped to profit in some way by his mischance. He thought of his master, the Duke of Mantua. Suppose he were to buy the picture? He immediately wrote to Chieppio for his support. This, he declared, was his best work, greatly admired by those who had seen it; it would certainly not disgrace the Mantuan collection. As far as the price was concerned he left it to Vincenzo's discretion, saying that he would be satisfied with a small payment on account, and the rest could be paid at the Duke's convenience. As for the copy, two months would be time enough to finish it, for he would not 'take such pains' with it as with the original. Peter Paul had great hopes of this approach. Had he not just been asked by the Duchess to negotiate with Pomerancio for the purchase of a painting to adorn her private chapel? Unfortunately his offer was turned down. It arrived in the middle of the festive season, at the moment when Vincenzo was preparing to set out for Turin 'with the largest and most brilliant company I have ever seen' as the worthy Chieppio declared—and he must have seen a few of these impressive departures! And, without bothering too much about logic, the Secretary of State explained the refusal: 'In the matter of expense we are now proceeding with great reserve.' Even though his motives in saying it may not have been disinterested, Rubens was not exaggerating when he declared that this painting was his best work. This 'Virgin adored by the Saints' was in fact a glorification of St Gregory the Great treated by the painter with a breadth of vision that was entirely new. The lessons of Italy had borne fruit. The Italian influence could indeed still be seen, but a new touch had been added—that of eloquence. It was not the majestic tumult of Michelangelo, nor the disorder of Giulio Romano, nor the dramatic fire of Tintoretto, nor the insidious charm of Correggio. It was eloquence pure and simple, as far from glandiloquence as it was from rhetoric. Both style and colour showed complete mastery and perfect power.

Most decidedly the Mantuan court was no good to Peter Paul, and Philip, he felt, had been right to warn him against it. He was furious, and perhaps for the first time, without seeming to drop his exquisite politeness for a moment, he showed the claws beneath the velvet glove. The painting had, after all, 'been seen and admired by all Rome', and Rubens was 'certain of finding a serious buyer in Rome'. That, he obviously meant, would be far better than those useless customers in Mantua; he did not say it as crudely as that, but he clearly thought it, since he speaks of 'the expenses incurred by all the festivals' and the trouble he would have had in getting his money as a result. He then moves in to the attack: 'The treasury of Mantua would scarcely have been in a hurry to give me satisfaction; it is certainly in no hurry to pay me the salary I have been owed for a long time.' In conclusion: 'For that reason I have finally begun to consider the failure of my proposition as a stroke of good fortune.'

He could not have been more insolent. Finally he recalled his misadventure with Pomerancio, who had dropped all his other work to please the Duchess, and had not been paid what was due to him, namely four hundred gold crowns, when his original price had been five hundred: 'This sum appeared exorbitant to the Duchess, who doubtless does not understand how Roman masters conduct their affairs, and imagines that they can be treated in the fashion of Mantua.' Peter Paul could certainly be rude, and proud into the bargain: 'I earnestly beg Your Excellency to do me the kindness of insisting that the Duchess pays this debt without delay; otherwise I shall be humiliated in everyone's eyes, and I certainly should not take the risk in future of accepting a mission of this kind.'

On that date—February 23, 1608—he was as impertinent as any great lord; he had dared for once to take off the mask of almost servile politeness which he had worn ever since he began to live in the shadow of the great. He had ceased for a moment to weigh the consequences of his act, and given free rein to his inmost reactions; he had been helpless perhaps, but not beaten, and his arrogance was splendid. We could almost cry 'Bravo, Peter Paul!'

He went back to work, and as the fathers allowed him to modify his subject, he divided his original composition into three parts. He expected it to take him only three months, but after six months the work was still not unveiled.

On October 28th Rubens wrote to Chieppio from Rome: Although His Highness is not at Mantua, I think I ought to explain to Your Excellency the necessity which obliges me to commit what is almost an act of incivility towards the Duke, by extending an already long absence by a journey abroad. I hope that it will at least be a short one. The day before yesterday I received very bad news of my mother who is suffering from a serious attack of asthma; this added to the weight of her seventy-two years leaves us little to hope, alas, but that end which is common to all humanity.'

The Duke of Mantua, who had just travelled to the Netherlands without taking his Flemish painter, was on the way back. After spending more than two weeks in Brussels and visiting Antwerp, he had been received by Henri IV at the French court. He had left Fontainebleau on October 22nd. Rubens said he would endeavour to 'meet His Highness somewhere on the way'; he had not time to go to Mantua, for he wished to take, 'in all haste, the most direct road'. He did not know when he would be back, but promised on his return to go straight to Mantua, for his work in Rome was finished. His master's will would be 'always and everywhere his strictest rule'. At least that is what he wrote to Secretary Chieppio.

VI

RETURN TO THE FATHERLAND

1608–1610

'I am driven by frantic haste' . . .

Peter Paul galloped along the highroads of Italy and France, tortured by the fear that he might never see again the woman who had been the living symbol of his family. She was not one of those timid women whom motherhood makes egotistical and demanding. She was a strong woman like the matrons of antiquity, knowing suffering and struggle, always watchful, never giving up whatever her trials. It was now more than eight years since he had left the country, and his mother had never flinched, never claimed her share of peace and protection. She had, of course, Philip; and Philip was still there. But on two occasions he too had gone away across the mountains, first to gain his diploma and then to carry on his archaeological research. She had said nothing. She realized that it was no use setting herself against her son's destiny. And yet life had always treated her cruelly. Death had struck her family twice more: in 1601 it was her eldest, Jan-Baptist, and in 1606 her daughter Blandina. And there were always the same money worries that had gone on all her life. She had defended her property, disputing every inch of the ground. She still had a few bonds and several houses. Time and again she had been forced to sell. Thus the beautiful house 'St Arnold' on the Meir had to go, as well as other smaller ones. A debtor might declare himself insolvent—no matter, she made other investments, and saved what she could from the wreck.

'I am driven by frantic haste,' said Rubens.

But the way was long, and Peter Paul had all the time in the world to think of his mother, his family, and his own destiny.

68

Towards the end of November he arrived in Flanders. In a few days he would be in the city of his ancestors. His speed, alas, was in vain; Maria Pypelincx, widow of John Rubens, was no more. She had died on October 19th, and was laid to rest, according to her own wish, in the Abbey of St Michael. She died fighting to the last for the defence of her interests; in April she had appeared once again before the city magistrates for the ratification of a legal document. She died as she had lived, concerned for her family, loving justice above all things. She was dead, but her will was not. More than two years before, sound in body and mind, but 'considering the frailty of human nature, and that nothing is more certain than death and nothing more uncertain than the hour at which it comes' she had taken the pen which had served her so well; and alone and in her own hand made provision for her end, since she did not want her nearest and dearest to quarrel because of her. Calmly, she wrote down the list of losses suffered in the course of the last few years, then made an inventory of all that was left and proceeded to share it out. Among her surviving relatives were Philip, Peter Paul, and Blandina's children. She recalled how much Blandina had cost her while her sons were earning their own living, and decided that they must each receive a share equal to that of her daughter, for she had no intention of favouring some to the detriment of others. She offered no moral precept, doubtless thinking that her children's minds were sufficiently well-tempered to take them safely through life. But she knew how harsh material considerations could be; her last thought was concerned with her account-book.

The house Peter Paul entered was quite unknown to him. He recognized a few of his own early works, and one or two objects brought back memories. But the decoration was strange to him. When he had left, there were still five of them in the old house called 'St Arnold'. Now only Philip and himself were left. A work by Philip on the costumes of the ancients, *Electorum libri duo*, had just been published, thanks to the good offices of their friend Balthasar Moretus. This book was illustrated with drawings which Peter Paul had made especially for this purpose during his stay in Rome. Philip was a person of considerable status. On the death of one of the four municipal secretaries he was chosen to take his place. Among his new colleagues was

Henri de Moy, a respectable old gentleman with a daughter of twenty-three who made a great impression on the new secretary. He married her in March.

These family events kept Peter Paul at home. Was this to be permanent? Nobody knew. It seemed hardly likely that the grey sky of Flanders could ever make him forget the glorious skies he had left. And the dreary existence of the Spanish Netherlands could never come anywhere near the splendour of life in the Italian cities. There princes and cardinals vied with each other in magnificence. Here the country was making a slow, painful recovery from a terrible war. And yet there were those who did not despair of the future of Flanders, and they pointed out that calm had returned two years before; it was the prelude, they said, to a more lasting peace. And they prophesied well; on April 9, 1609, a twelve-year truce was signed in Antwerp.

It had taken no less than two years of negotiations to reach that point, the reason being that for one of the parties the matter at issue was much more serious than the conclusion of an armistice. After a struggle lasting more than a quarter of a century, Spain had been forced to recognize the independence of the United Provinces. Her representatives, and in particular the most stubborn of them, Father John Neyer, had tried in vain to save face by demanding that the King of Spain should keep the titles, arms and distinguishing marks of his sovereignty over the lost provinces; the Dutch plenipotentiaries, led by Oldenbarneveldt, remained adamant, and finally won the day. This truce was a real peace treaty, and a great victory, both political and economic, for the young republic. The southern provinces gained nothing. As a final touch to the ruin of Antwerp, the Scheldt was still blocked by the Dutch, but everyone was so war-weary that the truce was welcomed joyfully. And all the benefit went to the rulers of the loyal provinces, a country which the humanists, in their high-flown style, called Belgium.

The Archduke Albert and his wife Isabella, promoted to sovereignty by the last will of Philip II, were in fact kept in complete dependence. Albert's military failures had gained for him in Madrid a firm reputation for inefficiency. In 1605 he was deprived of the command of the troops, which passed into the hands of the Marquis Ambrose Spinola, who was raised to the rank of captain-general. The Archduke, a serious, reserved, slow, diligent and very pious man, showed great dignity in these painful circumstances. So far from picking a quarrel with the brilliant general who had supplanted him, he tried to come to terms with him, and succeeded too, resigning himself to being a mere figurehead. He delighted in the official ceremonies to which the rigid Spanish etiquette gave an air of austere magnificence. He was full of benevolence towards his subjects, even if he did not understand them; and he overcame his ignorance of the language of the country by a rather original method: if spoken to in French, he replied in Spanish, and when addressed in Flemish he replied in German.

Albert and Isabella did their best to keep up the appearance of independent sovereigns, and to that end had themselves surrounded by the highest-ranking nobility of the country. Among these new dignitaries were the Count von Buren, son of that stubborn William of Orange murdered by order of Philip II, and Count Louis of Egmont, son of Lamorel of Egmont, whose head had fallen in the Great Square in Brussels under the eye of the terrible Duke of Alva. The Archduke and his wife were even more Catholic than Spanish, and it is not surprising that under their care a gentle breeze of devotion blew over the country. Catholics persecuted for their religion's sake came from all over to Brussels where they were sure of finding help and protection. Chapels were to be inaugurated, churches built. Urged by the powerful impetus given by the Jesuits, guilds and burghers were to wipe out the traces of the iconoclasts. There was to be work for architects, sculptors and painters. The ducal couple were prompted by the best intentions. Had they not just commissioned Rubens to paint their portrait?

The court of Brussels was not without prestige. The great powers accredited ambassadors there, for the palace of Coudenberg was an important centre of European diplomacy. It was like a crossroads where men of every nationality rubbed shoulders. And two top-ranking personages even brought a little of Italy to the scene—Ambrose Spinola and Cardinal Bentivoglio.

The Marquis Spinola was more than a brilliant general. This wily Genoese was an excellent politician, as he had proved some years before when Henry IV asked him about his military projects. He revealed his whole plan, rightly surmising that the King would not believe him. That was exactly what happened. Believing that it was a trick, Henry advised Maurice of Nassau to take precautions against completely different strategies. The King, realizing that he had been tricked, exclaimed: 'Others deceive by telling lies, but Spinola has deceived me by telling the truth.' Since his victory at Ostend, Spinola's prestige had been immense. One wonders what would have been said if people had realized what no one knew—that the Captain-General carried secret orders empowering him to imprison the unfortunate Albert if he should ever happen to show himself recalcitrant in certain circumstances.

As for Cardinal Guido Bentivoglio, as Papal Nuncio he played an important political role. It was he who bore witness that Brussels was one of the liveliest and most cosmopolitan places of the period. He was a shrewd observer, and became the chronicler of the events in which he was involved.

What was Peter Paul to do—to leave, or to remain? If he had only his own personal tastes to consider, the choice would not have been difficult. He had not lived for nothing in a country which passed for one of the most beautiful in the world. He never for a moment considered returning to the Gonzaga court, despite the assurances he had given to Chieppio; it was Rome alone that attracted him. The magnificence of the cardinals put that of princelings into the shade. He was fascinated, too, by the rivalry between artists, the intrigues, calumnies and malicious gossip. But in Rome it was not easy to reach the top rank, and in Flanders it would be absurd to expect such brilliance. There was, it is true, the Archduke's court, where the outstanding figure for several years had been Otto Vaenius, official painter to Their Highnesses and Master of the Mint. There was Antwerp, the town of Rubens' ancestors, the proud city of the time of the Emperor Charles V. Although the Scheldt was still closed, the life of the town was not extinct. Various industries were still carried on; silk was made there, and lace, and glass in the Venetian manner. Goldsmiths and engravers were very active. A large number of painters also lived there, but their worth was rather doubtful.

Peter Paul had a lucid mind, and he had lived eight years in

Italy. It would have been useless to extol these colourless imitators to him. Even Otto Vaenius did not escape his criticism. Should he go or stay? Mantua, no. Brussels, no. But Rome or Antwerp? 'I do not know whether I shall remain in my native land or whether I shall go and live permanently in Rome, where I am offered excellent conditions. Here too, moreover, great efforts are being made to keep me. The Archduke and Her Highness the Infanta have written to ask me to remain in the country and enter their service. Their offers were generous, but I have no intention of becoming a courtier again. Antwerp will be a perfect retreat for me the day I decide to leave Rome for ever.'

But Rome was Annibale Carracci, Guido Reni, Dominichino and Albano. Antwerp was Marten Pepyn, Henry van Balen, Abraham Janssens and the older painters. That, correctly interpreted, meant on one hand the prospect of a merciless struggle against talented men with powerful protectors, and on the other an easy victory. As Caesar said, 'I would rather be first in a village than second in Rome'.

The choice was made, and Antwerp won.

More and more people began to take an interest in Peter Paul. He was known to have worked for the Duke of Lerma in Spain, for one of the Spinola ladies in Genoa, for the Fathers of the Oratory in Rome, and for the archducal family. He had been on friendly terms with princes, cardinals and archdukes, and few on the banks of the Scheldt could make that boast. The Archduke and his wife sent him a gold chain and appointed him official painter to their house. He was admitted to the Society of Romanists, of which Jan Bruegel was the dean. He met again his old school friend, Balthasar Moretus, who was his father's deputy at the head of Plantin's famous printing works. He made friends with Nicholas Rockox, the burgomaster of Antwerp. This man, descended from an aristocratic family, is an important figure in the history of the town. He was both rich and cultured, and had in addition a taste for art, being an enthusiastic collector of coins and medals. Peter Paul became acquainted also with Philip's brother-in-law, Joannes Brant, the Town Clerk, a scholar and author of several works, who had studied at Louvain and Bourges and spent long periods abroad. His eighteen-year-old daughter Isabella delighted Peter Paul by her modest charm.

Peter Paul was thirty-two and everything seemed set fair for him; he could now think about founding a family. In October 1609 he married Isabella. The ceremony took place in the Abbey of St Michael, not far from his home, for he still lived in his mother's old house in the Kloosterstraat. At Philip's wedding, Peter Paul had, as he tells us himself, acted as master of ceremonies. At Peter Paul's wedding, Philip became a poet, celebrating the happy couple in Latin verse. And Peter Paul added a tribute of his own, by showing himself and his young wife in a painting full of tenderness. In a setting of greenery and flowers Isabella Brant, richly dressed, is seated at her husband's feet, her hand laid confidingly on his. He is bending slightly towards her, in a gentle protective attitude; his other hand is resting on a sword. Had he the right to carry this symbol of nobility? The matter is open to question.

There followed a period of peace, of work, and of happy contentment.

There was no lack of commissions. The painter enjoyed a high reputation with everyone. Pupils flocked to him. The whole country was calm and trying to come to life again. There was peace at home and abroad. Rubens divided himself between work and family life. In April 1610 he stood godfather at the baptism of little Clara, his brother Philip's daughter. He had the opportunity to paint the portrait of the Archduke and Archduchess, and worked hard at it, which is to say that he idealized as best he could these two people whose faces and characters were equally uninspiring. The Infanta looks more like a healthy Flemish peasant than a Habsburg of Spain, and her husband is like a worthy and not very intelligent bourgeois; but their robes are magnificent and their attitudes are undeniably intended to be majestic.

At the instance of Nicholas Rockox, the Antwerp magistracy decided to improve the appearance of the Town Hall. Commissions for the decoration of the newly restored State Room were given to two artists, Rubens and Abraham Janssens. Rubens painted an 'Adoration of the Magi'. It was a fine opportunity to show his fellow-citizens what he had learned during his long stay in a foreign country. Fortunately the dimensions called for were large, and there was plenty of scope for the scene of the adoration. Splendidly costumed characters, horses and camels, rich gifts, nudes with rippling muscles, smoking torches, all combine to make a brilliantly glowing work, in which the dark background throws up the luminous parts in powerful contrasts. It is incontestably an echo of Rome, or, to be more precise, of Caravaggio. In his preliminary sketch Rubens even drew elongated, almost slender figures, but when it came to the actual painting he corrected himself and rejected this idealization in the Italian manner. This picture made a great impression, as the style was one that had never yet been used by a Flemish painter. But, most surprisingly, the painting of Abraham Janssens made no less impression. In the allegorical composition, 'Scaldis et Antverpia', this painter imitated his colleague in every way. The movement of the design, the powerful muscles, the contrast of light and shade in the manner of Caravaggio, made it appear as if the two men were acting together to prove that Italian painting held another and far more lively lesson than that followed for almost a century by the poor Romanists of the Netherlands. If they were rivals, so much the better. Rubens was ready to prove his point as soon as other work was entrusted to him. He soon got his wish.

On the intervention of his friend Cornelius van der Geest, the vicar and churchwardens of St Walburga's church commissioned him to paint a large retable and three small compositions to adorn the high altar. The price agreed on was enough to support a family in comfort for several years. Now he had the opportunity to show his capabilities in full; and he painted an 'Erection of the Cross' which caused a sensation. Here he had a better means of proving himself than in the 'Adoration of the Magi' which was greater in width than in height. Poetic feeling needs an upward movement. In the 'Adoration' the movement was reduced to a secondary plane; by the very nature of the subject the scene was static. In the 'Erection of the Cross', on the other hand, action is the subject. It is useless to look for movement in cleverly studied poses or in robes draped in an arbitrary manner. Horizontal and vertical lines are static, but diagonals are dynamic. This fiery work is all movement and joy. Yes, joy—the joy of strenuous effort bravely made, the joy of healthy bodies and well-controlled muscles, joy even in the body of

Christ, firm and strong like that of Zeus on Olympus; the joy of Rubens himself, lost in an intoxicating ecstasy, almost forgetting his central theme; and the joy of immortal life in triumphant reply to Death, the love of life that transfigures even the theme of death. Such was doubtless not Rubens' intention. His brush, breaking the bounds of reason, betrayed the secrets of his soul, the soul born of generations of Rubens and Pypelincx ancestors, a soul clinging passionately to life, tempered by trials, touched by death and arising again each time from the darkness to spring towards the light. But those who admired the 'Erection of the Cross' did not think of all that, the painter apparently less than anyone. They saw before them a work which surpassed all the paintings in their churches by its boldly conceived play of forms. And the most perceptive must have said to themselves that in all probability a great artist had been born to them.

VII

FAME AND FORTUNE

1611–1618

Life was good. In March 1611 Peter Paul became the father of a daughter, Clara Serena. Philip was her godfather. Pupils flocked from all directions, and many had to be refused, which was a certain way to be even more in demand. There was no lack of work. Everything was going well.

But the triumphant moments of this life are short-lived, and, as Maria Pypelincx had said, 'though we are certain to die, nothing is more uncertain than the hour of our death'. The Rubens family had always been sorely tried by sudden and premature deaths. In the last days of August, without even an illness, Philip Rubens died at barely thirty-eight. Peter Paul mourned his greatest friend, discreetly, as befitted a man who prided himself on his stoicism. This was the fashionable doctrine; Justus Lipsius swore only by Seneca, and Justus Lipsius, although he died in 1606, still reigned over the humanists of 'Belgium'—which was the name they had brought into honour again to designate their country. For the epitaph Peter Paul, who was insufficiently sure of his own command of Latin, called upon Balthasar Moretus, who asked for the help of Woverius, who in his turn consulted Jan Brant and Hemelarius. Custom demanded that an epitaph should be high-sounding in the classical battle manner. For his contribution Peter Paul did more—he added a painting by his own hand. He was already the guardian of Blandina's children, and took over Philip's two offspring on the same basis. Exactly as in the days of Maria Pypelincx, all efforts had to be concentrated on the living, and the battle had to go on. Philip left an unpublished work: *S. Asterii Episcopi Amascae Homiliae Graece et Latine*, a scholarly work which was indeed worthy to honour his memory. It was decided to publish it, thanks to the good offices of Jan Brant, brother-in-law of the deceased, and Peter Paul's father-in-law. Rubens was to do the drawings, which were to be engraved by Cornelius Gallus the elder.

At the beginning of September the Brotherhood of Arque-busiers, the leader of which was Nicholas Rockox, commissioned Rubens to paint a great triptych for their altar in the cathedral; the work was to glorify their patron St Christopher. Besides a grant of 2,400 florins, Rubens was to receive a piece of land adjoining his new property on the Wapper. When the members of the brotherhood visited the painter to judge his work for themselves, they had a great surprise. The central panel showed 'The Descent from the Cross', and on the volets they saw 'The Visitation' and 'The Presentation in the Temple'. They looked for their patron saint in vain; except on the outside edges of the volets, he was not to be seen. The worthy arquebusiers were all ready to protest at this exclusion, but Rubens explained to them that all the characters shown were 'bearers of Christ'—which is the meaning of Christopher in Greek!

These plays on words delighted their inventors quite as much as they did the ignorant people to whom they were offered. Rubens loved this language of 'emblems' and used it in painting as well as in the many sketches he provided for Balthasar Moretus. The ignorant may imagine that the owl is a sign of contempt, according to the pejorative significance which the Flemings gave it, but the painter replies that this bird is the symbol of wisdom. An eagle and a peacock, adorned with a torch, stars and a rainbow, indicate a marriage. An altar represents piety, a vase religion, and a plate the sacraments. Poetry is a lyre surrounded by ivy. War becomes a lightning streak, and peace a wand of Mercury. A chain of medals means ancestors. By subtle combinations of these various elements a whole language can be built up. Here, for instance, is the spirit of Art. He is offering a pen and brushes to Mercury and stretching out his hand to Nature, which means that practice and natural gifts combined make the artist; it could not be clearer.

Rubens had already made a great impression when he painted an 'Adoration of the Magi' for the Town Hall. He determined to strike a decisive blow with the 'Erection of the Cross'. In both cases he played his trump card—movement. But he had come to understand that even movement must be disciplined. Instead of the somewhat chaotic tumult of the first of these works, he carried out in the second a composition on a diagonal plane. That cluster of swollen, tense muscles around the Cross is something which no one else in Flanders could have done, and its success came up to all expectations. From then on no one dreamed of contesting his obvious supremacy. He therefore permitted himself to soften the movement in the 'Descent from the Cross'. The diagonal line of the 'Erection of the Cross' curved into a supple S-shape. The composition is less tumultuous, and the harmony more ordered. But movement is still the guiding spirit of his painting. Every character is moving; every gesture, every fold of cloth continues the flow of movement around the shining central motif which stamps its own lofty rhythm on the whole. Despite the tragic subject, it is a work full of health and life. There may be sombre pools of colour in the shadows, but this is because the influence of Caravaggio had not entirely faded. All the figures are strong-muscled athletes, and despite the livid flesh, Christ is the most powerful of all. Whatever anyone may say, it is not a sorrowful work. It does indeed evoke the cruel scene of Golgotha, but at the same time it makes great concessions to the new spirit of Counter-Reformation which stressed beauty of form and the splendour of religious ceremony.

The success of the 'Descent from the Cross' was even greater, if that were possible, than that of the 'Erection of the Cross'. Commissions flowed in. Everywhere altars were being re-erected and churches and chapels rebuilt or repaired. Everywhere brilliant images were seen, catching the eye with the intensity of their life, yet not repelling it by a pathos exaggerated to the point of utter gloom. The Counter-Reformation sent a wind of optimism blowing over the Church. Rubens, an optimist if ever there was one, became the prime mover of this new conception.

The Archduke did not forget the painter of Antwerp. In 1603 he commissioned an 'Assumption' for the church of La Chapelle in Brussels. The following year, when Isabella Brant gave birth to a son, the Archduke consented to be godfather to the child who was christened Albert. The feast day of his patron saints coincided in that same year with the end of his deanship of the fraternity of Romanists, a function he had performed for a year to his entire satisfaction, declaring that he had 'perfectly accomplished all ceremonies pertaining to it, such as sung Mass, evening service, Requiem Mass for deceased brothers, and a banquet given in my house, and as the expenses considerably exceed the receipts, I feel there is no need for me to give a detailed account, for I make a present to the guild of anything it owes me'. He also offers 'two large effigies painted by his own hand on panels, representing the above-named saints Peter and Paul'.

Work went on. He accumulated paintings, created life, built, and thought himself immortal. Since 1610 Rubens had owned a house situated in a street running along the 'Wapper' canal, near the Meir. He had waited some four years before beginning the building of this house of his dreams. The original house, which he kept, was simple; the ground floor had a wide doorway and five mullioned windows, and the upper floor six identical windows; the roof had two dormer windows and a stepped gable. Rubens added a wing of a completely different character: five high windows surmounted by five smaller ones, overtopping the original wing by one floor. This new building was surmounted by a roof with a wide cornice adorned with a sundial.

Although he loved an abundance of decoration, Rubens made little effort to adorn the outside of this imposing building. Was it because of the Wapper, that dirty canal which made it impossible to move back to the right distance for seeing it, and so would have rendered useless any effort in that direction? Or was it a piece of deception? The modesty of the outside may well have contributed to the surprise of the visitor once he had crossed the threshold. For let us make no mistake—Rubens remembered Rome, Venice and Genoa. He wanted to build a palace in no way inferior to these splendid examples. His visitors must be open-mouthed with admiration from the very beginning. The front door opened into a great vestibule. On the right, a monumental staircase by the sculptor Hans van Mildert led to the upper floor of the new building.

The courtyard was shut off by a portico joining the old and new buildings, and looked very like a triumphal arch. On the balustrade which surmounted it stood statues of Minerva and a

AL ILLVSTRISS. SIGNOR

E T

PADRON MIO COLENDISS.

IL SIGNOR

DON CARLO GRIMALDO.

LLVSTRISSIMO SIGNORE, mi parerebbe di far torto à V. S. Illustrissima, se mandando io in luce questa poca racolta d'alcuni Palazzi più famosi della bellissima città di Genoua sua Patria, ciò non facessi sotto il Titolo i drocinio di V. S. Illustrissima, ch'è tanto vniuersale curiosa d'ogni sorte de virtù e scienza, ch'à punto pare ella habbia vna capacità d'ingegno tanto felice che sola possa intendere, quanto tutti gli altri bei spiriti sieme. I perciò la supplico, sia seruita d'agradire que-mia diuotione verso lei, & di dare mediante il fauor o qualque reputatione à questa operetta: la quale an-r che minima, ha però questo à proposito ch'ella trat-di cose concernenti à l'honor della sua Patria; & farà de al mondo della singolar affettion mia verso di quel-. Alla qual in genere, si come à V. S. Illustrissima in rticolare, mi professo per sempre

D'Anuersa, alli 29. di Maggio, 1622.

Humilissimo seruitore

Pietro Paolo Rubens.

tle-page of the album 'Palazzi Antichi di Genova Raccolti e Deignati da Pietro Rubens'. (Prints Department, Antwerp)

7. The Battle of Ivry. Sketch by P. P. Rubens for the Henry IV Gallery. (Musée Bonnat, Bayonne)

symbolic figure representing Painting, and two huge urns. Two tablets show two quotations from Juvenal:

'*Permittes ipsis expendere numinibus, quid Conveniat nobis, rebusque sit utile nostris. Carior est illis homo, quam sibi.*'
(Let the Gods themselves decide what is good for us and useful for our affairs. Man is dearer to them than he is to himself.)

and

'*Orandum est, ut sit mens sena in corpore sano, Fortem posce animum, et mortis terrore carentem . . . Nesciat irasci, cupiat nihil.*'
(We should pray for a healthy mind in a healthy body. Ask for a brave spirit, with no fear of death . . . let it know no anger and covet nothing.)

At the bottom of the garden, in the direct line of vision from the courtyard, was a little pavilion decorated with a statue of Hercules; between the columns were Bacchus and Ceres, and in a niche above the entrance, the goddess of Plenty. Finally, on the left, between the courtyard and the garden, was 'a hall circular in shape like the temple of the Pantheon in Rome, into which daylight penetrates only from above and through one single opening which is in the centre of the dome'. This room contained busts, statues from antiquity, pictures brought from Italy and other rare and precious objects, as an eye-witness informs us.

It was a magnificent setting. Sculpture reached from the ground to the cornice; bas-reliefs, high reliefs, carving in the round, festoons and garlands. Columns and niches, pediments and balustrades, consoles and vases, busts and statues combined to give a heavy yet rich effect. This was not all. Behind the house, the garden stretched the whole width of the building and even extended a little beyond it on the right-hand side. It was, of course, laid out in the Italian manner. The flower-beds were sectors and segments of circles, cunningly arranged. Orange trees were indispensable to a convincing evocation of Italy, but the local flowers were represented too, by wallflowers and tulips.

This was Rubens' dream—a clear, precise dream which he

carried out in every detail. After drawing the plans he supervised the work and directed his various collaborators so that they would act exactly according to his calculations. This was the way he always worked.

The engravers reproducing his works had to comply with his wishes, for he would have nothing to do with the meticulous technique made famous by whole families of well-known engravers with such names as Collaert, Gallus and Wierix. He wanted interpretations more worthy of a painter, and if graving-tools were not enough, he would have recourse to acid. He cared little that he was imposing a bondage on the noble art of engraving that amounted almost to treason. He wanted all the subtle shades on his palette to be reproduced by cunning transpositions of lines. This was not easy. Of all the many members of the Gallus family to wield the burin, only old Cornelius found favour in his eyes, and even he did not succeed in satisfying him completely. In order to put his theories into practice he even turned to foreign countries; several artists in Holland worked for him, including Willem Swanenburg, Jan Muller and Jakob Matham.

He had formed in the same way the painters he employed in his home. He guided the sculptors, too, for their art had to follow the general direction. Michelangelo showed the way; he had been able to translate movement better than either Donatello or Verrocchio. With less power and more grace, a Fleming with a well-deserved reputation in Italy had followed in his footsteps. This was Giovanni da Bologna who had just died in Florence in 1608. Rubens was only waiting for the opportunity to impose upon his compatriots the new style in this field.

He had earned a great deal of money, but he needed more. Money was the means by which he could assert himself and win power. He had not forgotten his childhood and his parents' constant anxieties. The poor man is pitied, but often despised as well; what is needed in life is success. There must first be money, for the sake of the opportunities it gives. But he had to go further; he had to climb every step of the ladder. To begin with he sought to dominate his colleagues the painters, not only by his undisputed mastery of his craft, but also by the splendour and magnificence of his life; for he knew that though good painters are impressed by the aesthetic success of one of their number, mediocre ones are hypnotised by his social conquests. He knew too that a man who wants to succeed can afford to neglect no one, and mediocre artists are legion no matter where. And so he had to rise and keep on rising until he reached the level of those who dominated the world by virtue of their origins, and could treat them as equals—since after all a man is only a man and a title makes no real difference. Rubens had not far to seek if he wished to know what a commoner could suffer from being at the mercy of the great; the ghost of John Rubens must have risen to remind him.

Work on the princely dwelling went on for three years, and during that time Rubens worked as he knew so well how. For his friend Moretus he pencilled title-pages to be engraved by Theodore Gallus. He sketched with the tip of his brush innumerable compositions for his assistants to reproduce on a larger scale. His specialized collaborators dealt with the parts which were their particular field, and he touched up the whole picture before delivering it to the customer. He also painted himself, sometimes a figure, and very occasionally a whole canvas, as though to prove that he was still the undisputed master. For although he practised division of labour in his studio, making use of the services of Jan Bruegel, Frans Snyders and many others, he remained the one who summed them all up, easily surpassing them all, even in their own speciality.

Princes, prelates, great lords and wealthy notabilities all begged for works by his own hand and often had to be satisfied with a work done in the studio from the master's sketch and simply revised by him. There was a new 'Adoration of the Magi', less imposing and also less brilliant than the first; it went to Malines to adorn the church of St John. There was a gigantic 'Last Judgment', destined for the high altar of the Jesuits' church at Neuburg; it was commissioned by Wolfgang Wilhelm of Bavaria, Duke of Neuburg. This newly converted Catholic had recently been extricated, thanks to Spinola, from a very critical situation, and had begun to embellish the churches throughout his lands. The 'Last Judgment' is a hymn to the glory of the human body. Nudes appear one upon the other in tangled heaps, and the elect are scarcely less tumultuous than the group of the damned. Up to now we have seen muscular male bodies, but here there are nude women, heavily fleshed. But the image of God lacks breadth and does not dominate. It is only one figure among many around an empty space in the centre. Though the whole effect is one of splendid verve, there is a lack of order. It is all very well to echo Michelangelo, but not everyone can achieve his genius for composition.

For the same duke, Rubens painted a 'Lion-hunt'. Strictly speaking it is less a hunt than a battle, with lions biting and clawing, horses madly rearing, swords, arrows and stakes; the landscape is reduced to a fragment of horizon. Rubens adored this subject and repeated it again and again without tiring of it; he could give free rein to his love for movement and splendour, and to his knowledge of anatomy and perspective. It certainly contains echoes of a work fragments of which he had copied in Italy : the Battle of Anghiani, by the great Leonardo; but no one before him had painted lions, wolves and leopards, in attitudes as difficult as they were unexpected. As for horses, he had long been their most faithful admirer; he had created a type of ideal horse, with a delicate head and wide hindquarters, sinewy legs, long floating manes, and tails like plumes, flaring nostrils and fiery eyes. This horse appears in portraits, in hunts, battles, and religious scenes; and he was about to devote to it one of his most lyrical and harmoniously balanced works, despite the tumultuous nature of the subject: 'The Battle of the Amazons'.

On occasions Rubens also painted fishes as in the 'Miraculous Draught of Fishes' commissioned by the Corporation of Fishmongers for their altar in the church of Our-Lady-beyond-the-Dyle at Malines. It is a magnificently robust work, in which the bronzed bodies of the fishermen, tense with effort, are in powerful contrast with the calm figure of Christ. But side by side with the ever-recurring and ever-increasing number of religious paintings—'Lamentation over the dead Christ', 'The Woman taken in Adultery', 'The Flight into Egypt', 'The Incredulity of St Thomas', 'The Descent from the Cross', 'The Adoration of the Magi', 'The Entombment', 'Christ in the Manger' and 'St Peter receiving the Keys'—Rubens was taking more and more pleasure in the painting of mythological subjects. He may have supplied paintings in plenty to the Counter-Reformation, but he was too imbued with paganism for the gods of Olympus not to mingle in brotherhood with the heroes of the Old and New Testaments. It was a fine opportunity to glorify the nude female body in the same way as Titian or Correggio.

Against the male nude, bronzed and powerfully muscled, he set the shining plump whiteness of the northern women. The Italians preferred golden-brown skin and shapes that were softened and subtly idealized. Rubens had his own kind of idealization, and evolved a type of woman which is his alone, with long legs, a rounded stomach, large buttocks, a plump back and rather small breasts. To make the flesh look really transparent, he painted his masses in pale blue and the shadows in pure carmine. This woman was called Venus, Diana or Cybele; she could be seen at the Bacchanalia or beside the drunken Silenus. Sometimes, as in the 'Daughters of Leucippus', he achieved, by a subtle balance of forms and colours, one of the most perfect successes in decorative painting. We may look in vain for any touch of drama in that harmonious picture in which the beauty of men and horses serves only to throw into relief the radiant bodies of the two naked women. It matters little that Van Dyck collaborated in that masterly painting. That astounding pupil is, after all, said to have done one of the famous 'Bacchanalia' almost on his own. But the master always led the way. The conception was his, and his inimitable style drew the others after him. This is clearly seen in the portrait.

Since his return from Antwerp he had painted a quantity of portraits, and their success was immediate. Here too he reversed all the accepted ideas. The Dutch and Flemish masters had always been excellent portraitists; during the preceding century, Mabuse, Key, Moro and Pourbus had made contributions to this branch of painting which were remarkable both for their style and their psychological insight. Rubens extended it in the direction of pure decorativeness. There was doubtless a loss of depth, but the vigour of the execution made this detail seem comparatively unimportant. The models were brilliantly portrayed, idealized as much as they could wish, and the background against which they were painted gave a clear indication of their social position, which must have pleased them more than too accurate a psychological study. Rubens did not invent this decorative style, but he made admirable use of it. The sheen of rich stuffs and the glitter of jewels, with ruffs, collars, plumes and other accessories, allowed him to pass more quickly over the face, not that he disdained it, but because it was only one element among many others. Even in self-portraits he felt it unnecessary to make a very searching study. Twice he painted himself hatless, first in the 'Four Philosophers' in company with Justus Lipsius, Woverius and his brother Philip, then alone. After this, since his hair was beginning to recede, he sheltered under a huge felt hat. He was less interested in individuals than in man—universal man, hardly to be distinguished from life itself, since Life is but a presentation of man. That explains his love for *putti*, which is everywhere obvious, in religious scenes as well as in mythological ones. His *putti* throng the heavens or mingle with the larger characters, and sometimes are themselves the central figures as in the enchanting 'Garland of fruits'. What could be more delightful than seven chubby, rosy cherubs carrying fruit? It is a hymn of joy and confidence, the work of a man who meets all possible trials with the same unshakeable faith in life.

Greedy for every source of satisfaction, great or small : genius, power, money, as well as all the little things tht appealed to his vanity—that is the kind of man Rubens was.

'The four Philosophers' . . . As a matter of fact there was not a single philosopher among them. Despite his pretensions to stoicism, Justus Lipsius, the learned philologist, who was by turn Catholic, Lutheran, Calvinist and then Catholic again, was really a very weak sort of man. Philip Rubens and Jan Woverius were two examples of that northern brand of humanism which is reduced merely to textual explanations of authors. Peter Paul too conformed to this trend, although he was less well versed than these exponents of the Latin epistle, and contented himself with filling his letters with quotations. The only philosopher present, if we may venture to say so, is the bust of Seneca, who was the idol of these gentlemen. Even so, Seneca was a wealthy courtier and a moneylender, and his stoicism was no more than a façade. It has even been claimed that this figure was not Seneca at all, but Philetas of Cos. It scarcely matters. To err is human (or we should rather say : *Errare humanum est*), and 'The Four

Philosophers' sounds well. Rubens supplied portraits at fourteen florins each, but he asked 1,600 florins for a triptych and 3,500 for the 'Last Judgment'. He painted portraits, hunting scenes, religious or mythological pictures—every possible subject, every possible size, and almost every possible price.

With the help of Van Dyck he painted for the Genoese merchants the seven tapestry cartoons telling the tragic story of the consul Decius Mus. Artists painting cartoons for tapestry were serving a very old tradition and contributing to what had become, in the Netherlands, an aristocrat among crafts. The weavers of Brussels, superseding those of Arras, had become the most famous in Christendom. It was to them that Raphael entrusted the carrying out of his series 'The Acts of the Apostles', giving the task of supervising the work to Bernard van Orley, who shortly afterwards showed himself to be a talented designer, with 'Hunts of Maximilian' and 'The Story of Abraham'. Raphael, in his cartoons, reversed all the accepted ideas by stressing the subject to the detriment of the decoration which was moved out to the borders. His predecessors had always treated the subject in a purely decorative manner, but with him it told a story in the same way as a fresco. It was perhaps not a happy innovation, but Raphael's prestige was enough to make it universal. Bernard van Orley was not the only one to follow his example. Rubens even went one better; his work told a story in the same way as Raphael's, and he made in addition great use of movement. The general effect might be rather chaotic and the balance between the various cartoons not very certain, but this mattered little to him; it was enough for him that he had been able to make his mark in a branch of art which he had not hitherto attempted, and had thus won a new victory. And it was the craftsmen of Brussels who wove it for him, cunningly mixing threads of wool and silk, gold and silver.

Rubens was working to his full extent and money was pouring in, which was all to the good, since he needed a great deal to finish his luxurious home. When the building was completed, there was the interior decoration to be done. Marble fireplaces, Spanish leather, chandeliers, carpets and carved furniture must all combine to produce an effect of opulence and grandeur.

Rubens' house was probably the finest in Antwerp; its only

rival was that of his friend Balthasar Moretus, who had been the director of the famous printing works since 1610. The spirit of old Plantin seemed to be reborn in him. Like his grandfather, he loved to be surrounded by scholars and artists. Rubens painted a whole series of portraits for him: Plantin and his wife Jeanne Riviere, *comere Jehanne*, as the 'Chief Printer'[1] affectionately called her; John Moretus and his wife Martine; John's parents; James Moerentorf and his wife Adrienne Gras; the learned humanist Justus Lipsius; the Hellenist and Latinist theologian Pantinus; the eminent geographer Abraham Ortelius, and Montanus, the Spanish theologian. All of these had in their various ways contributed to the glory of the printing-works, and justified, by their friendship, Plantin's lines:

> 'Ne pouvant etre
> Poete, ecrivain ne maistre
> J'ay voulu poursuivir
> Le trac, chemin ou trace
> Par ou leur bonne grace
> Je pourrais acquerir.'[2]

Moretus was a cultured man with an acute mind, whose tastes lay rather in the past, as he proved when he enlarged his old house. Rubens' taste was more modern, and not satisfied with providing his friend with designs, he imposed an entirely new style on him. The severe arrangement of sixteenth century publications was cast aside in favour of the baroque style, expensive and often pompous. Moretus was under the spell of his brilliant collaborator, whom he invariably called 'our Apelles', and on all aesthetic questions he trusted his judgment completely; he was always ready to call upon his authority to settle some difference in such matters.

When Theodorus Gallus had engraved his first designs on copper, it became known that Rubens had touched up the plates. He was the leader in everything. Thanks to him the Plantin printing-press created the majestic book of the seventeenth

---

[1] This title of 'Chief Printer' had been officially bestowed on Plantin by Philip II.
[2] 'As I could be neither poet, writer nor master, I resolved to follow the track, road or traces by which I could win their approval.'

century, the contents of which were unfortunately scarcely in keeping with its splendid outward appearance. In the reign of the Archduke literature seemed to have died. Books treated only of learned or pious subjects under a veneer of humanism that was by now behind the times. These works, which were pedantic but rather futile despite their serious approach, gave Rubens the opportunity to introduce a multiplicity of frequently obscure allegorical motifs, laid on so thickly that the space reserved for the titles was often reduced to one-eighth of the whole page. Over the years he varied the arrangement of his designs, but never gave any more space to the type. His ornamentation was always of first importance. Is this not significant? The books of men, like the stories of gods and saints, were only pretexts, allowing himself to express himself as he wished and obtain a just reward for doing so.

In March 1618 Isabella Brant gave birth to a second son, Nicholas. He was held at the font by Andrea Picheneotti, representing the godfather, the marquis Nicholas Pallavicini, a Genoese nobleman for whom Rubens had already worked. Peter Paul probably considered that no possible asset should be neglected. Relations between Genoa and Antwerp had always been excellent, and there could be no harm in enlisting a wealthy marquis on his side. In the history of Antwerp friendship and good business usually went hand in hand, and Rubens was one of Antwerp's most faithful sons. The Virgin Mary may have presided in effigy over its Town Hall, but it was the god Mercury who flourished in its inhabitants' hearts.

It was apparently the god Mercury who incited Rubens to get in touch with Sir Dudley Carleton in order to obtain ancient marbles in return for a few canvases. He had already made an exchange with this English diplomat the year before, when he bartered a hunting picture for a diamond necklace. The arrangement must have pleased him, and he may have felt that a few antiques would look well in his new home, and make a happy addition to the pieces he had brought back from Italy. Besides, the prospect of acquiring them without spending a penny was most attractive. Sir Dudley Carleton was the English ambassador at the Hague. He had been *chargé d'affaires* in Venice and was said to be a friend of the powerful Marquess of Buckingham, the favourite of James I. He was a very important person, and a patron of the arts of a type that is always with us; buying, exchanging, reselling and always remaining, after all his liberality, involuntarily in pocket. During his stay in Italy, Sir Dudley was seized with passion for ancient marbles, but not to such an extent that he could not part with them; he always agreed to do so to oblige his friends, and in return for a little profit. For the moment this pleasure was being sadly thwarted; the worthy burghers of Holland were interested only in painting. The English diplomat was quite ready to let such sculptures as remained to him go in exchange for good pictures. The Dutch painters were little known, but the name of Rubens was famous . . . and that made two interests in perfect agreement!

To begin the negotiations, Peter Paul appointed as his agent a painter from Haarlem, Frans Pieterssen de Grebber, whom Rubens warmly recommended: 'He is a completely honourable man, and we can have absolute confidence in his sincerity.' It is a somewhat surprising tribute, since this Grebber was not a very estimable person. But it is, of course, possible to sin through ignorance, and it is a rare man who has never passed wrong judgments on his contemporaries.

Negotiations went on apace. Rubens offered twenty-four pictures, several of which were very large; he estimated their total value at 6,000 florins. Sir Dudley Carleton, who was not born yesterday, carefully checked the list, and rejected the canvases which were not by the master's hand, plus a large painting he considered too cumbersome, all of which reduced Rubens' account to 3,000 florins; upon which the Englishman proposed a new solution—that payment should be made partly in pictures and partly in Brussels tapestries. Rubens was somewhat surprised, since he had expected to acquire the collection without drawing upon his own funds. It was really no use for the wily Carleton to claim that the bargain was in no way altered; as Rubens wrote, 'one is always more generous with fruit from one's own garden than with fruit bought in the market'. Tapestries were most certainly 'fruit from the market', and the painter said regretfully: 'I have spent in one year several thousand florins in the adornment of my house.' The other, unmoved, assured him that he would have 'the most beautiful and precious collection of ancient marbles that anyone—prince or collector—possesses this side of the Alps'. Enough to make one's mouth water! Peter Paul was not so easily beaten; he offered to add a few of his own canvases and spend 2,000 florins on the tapestries. His practical sense never failed him; he claimed 'the cases used to bring the marbles from Italy to Holland'. No gain was too small! This time, agreement was reached.

At the beginning of June, Rubens took possession of his antiques. Carleton's collection consisted of no less than a hundred and forty-two pieces: heads, busts, torsos and fragments of statues. They were perhaps not first-class pieces. Sir Dudley had cried his wares somewhat over-enthusiastically ('on the word of a gentleman!'), but Peter Paul had not lagged far behind ('on the word of a man of property!'), and to hesitate now would be ungracious. Besides, the market value of the collection was by no means negligible. Everyone knew it, and it was talked about everywhere. Rubens could scatter marble statues throughout his home, the walls of which were already covered with paintings. His house was without equal; and here at last was a setting worthy of the man whom Balthasar Moretus, echoing Baudius, called 'the Apelles of our age'.

VIII

RUBENS' WORKSHOP

1618–1622

The workshop was in full swing.

Numerous satellites gravitated around the master. Side by side with the apprentices, the office boys of painting, we find several finished artists. First of all there was Jan Bruegel, nicknamed 'Velvet Bruegel' because, it is said, of his love for that material. After a long stay in Italy and travel in Germany, he had lived in Antwerp since 1597. His works were eagerly sought after and fetched high prices, so that he was sufficiently comfortably off to be able to satisfy his taste for collecting. He was the only descendent of the great Bruegel to show real talent and originality; he painted figures, animals, flowers and landscapes with equal mastery. He was always ready to collaborate with other painters; he furnished the landscapes of Paul Bril and Josse de Momper with figures, animals and flowers, but on the other hand he asked Van Balen, one of the Franckens or Robbenhammer to paint figures in his own landscapes! As a flower painter he shared with Ambrose Bosschaert the honour of having created this branch of the art, but his vision was richer and more sensual than that of his rival. With Gillis van Conincxloo, Paul Bril and Josse de Momper he shared the honour of having created a new kind of landscape, to which realism and the play of light gave a more lively aspect, both poetic and familiar at the same time.

He had been closely associated with Rubens since 1609, and was the elder by nine years. He was glad to wed his subtle gifts to the fiery genius of his brilliant friend; and this sometimes produced an unexpected masterpiece like 'Adam and Eve in Paradise' in which Rubens, with all the craft at his command, painted two nudes slender enough not to clash with his friend's delicate landscape. When a letter had to be written in Italian, Peter Paul acted as his colleague's unpaid secretary, and he probably wrote the letter in which Bruegel told an Italian correspondent that Frans Snyders had painted some miraculous things —*cose miracolose*—for this painter of still life and animals was a friend of both of them and an eminent collaborator in the work of the studio.

He was a charming, gentle man with a pale delicate face enhanced by dark brown hair, a pointed beard and a thin moustache. He was two years younger than Peter Paul. He continued the trend begun by Pieter Aertsen and Joachim Beuckelaer, those designers of monumental still-lives, but his manner had softened on contact with the Italians, and he had reached his full flowering under the protection of Rubens. He countered the lush but entirely material richness of his forerunners with a conception that was more poetic, livelier and more decorative at one and the same time. It seems almost sacrilege to apply the name of still life to these canvases, which transform ordinary produce like fruit, fish, poultry or game into fragments of a great heroic poem. His chief rival was his brother-in-law, Paul de Vos, a jovial fellow full of health and high spirits, who painted the same type of picture and strove to achieve the same style.

As for Deodate del Monte, he was 'skilled in painting and in other arts', as Rubens, with some exaggeration, declared. This old comrade, who had lived with him in Italy, was a wealthy and greatly respected man. The master could acknowledge his collaboration without any loss of face; and in society that did very well instead of talent. There were also two talented landscape painters, Jan Wildens, who travelled for five years in Italy before joining Rubens, and Lucas van Uden; they were both skilled at filling in backgrounds with cleverly composed landscapes. Above all, there was the most brilliant of them, the most richly gifted and most precocious, the wonder of the studio, Anthony Van Dyck.

With his delicate profile and his cloud of light brown hair he was as handsome as any page, and his full lips under the small moustache told of a voracious love of life. His parents were well off, and everything came easily to this spoilt child of Fortune. At the age of eleven he had been apprenticed to Van Balen, but at seventeen he was already working as an independent master. Even before his admission to the guild of St Luke, Rubens took him under his wing and gave him the most important work. He did not specialize in any branch of painting for the simple reason that he practised them all with equal virtuosity. It was said that one day a number of collaborators, anxious to see the master's own work, found their way into his private room, where one of them accidentally damaged a painting in progress. Van Dyck alone was considered capable of repairing the damage, which he did so efficiently that Rubens, although he was not taken in, said not a word about it, as a silent tribute to the skill of the collaborator.

These were the men—or at least some of them—who formed a magnificent phalanx around their leader. Some specialized in one particular branch of painting, others carried out the master's sketches on a larger scale. The sketches were his particular concern. On wooden panels, rarely measuring more than four feet by three, he painted the essential elements of his compositions with amazing sureness and fire. He drew and painted at the same time, outlining the design in sepia with the point of the brush. A few rapid strokes were enough to bring out the large masses; a few highlights—pink, blue-grey, white—indicated the gradations of shade. Looking at the panel there appeared to be practically nothing on it, but, potentially, everything was there. Rubens occasionally took his sketches further and indicated the colours as they were to be in the finished painting. Then it was no longer a sketch but the work itself, foreshadowed and as it were summarized, with a freshness which was not always to be found in the final version.

His passion for movement shows itself most clearly of all in those bewildering compositions in which men, animals, heaven and earth are drawn together into a fierce whirlpool of motion. But this dynamic play of shapes was not enough for him. There had to be music too—light falling in a singing stream, and little bright comma-shapes like organ notes, while here and there red highlights kept the shadows at bay. It was a triumph of poetry in colour. Collaborators and pupils gazed at these panels, wondering. Rubens, whose versatility was astonishing, sometimes adapted his style to theirs; but he almost always carried them along with him. We have seen how he checked his usual fire and delicately painted an Adam and an Eve in the elegant Paradise of his friend Bruegel; he later worked up his natural ardour to the point of brutality in order to be in tune with the young Van Dyck, who was obsessed at the beginning of his career by a type of naturalism similar to that of Caravaggio.

Rubens was not only the vigilant leader who assigned the tasks and saw that they were carried out. It was all very well to ensure the output of the factory, but he also had to dispose of the merchandise and protect production. As far as the paintings were concerned, nothing could have been easier. Commissions poured in and collectors' agents besieged the studio, always on the look-out for an honest penny in commission; they were excellent at fanning enthusiasm and whetting the curiosity and self-esteem of their employers.

The engravings needed more care. They formed an invaluable sideline, as they were the best source of information available to anyone with a thirst for knowledge of the work and discoveries of the world. They were more useful in that respect than the weekly gazette *Nieuwe Tydinghe* which Abraham Verhoeven had been issuing since 1620, for Verhoeven, as an innovator, was timid, and cautiously ended every report with '*Of het waer is, sal den tijdt leeren*' (time will tell whether that is true), whereas with an engraving all that is necessary is to look at it. There is no better proof of this than the success of the print-sellers, who were often engravers themselves, like the families of Gallus and de Jode. Dürer acquired celebrity through his engravings, and Marcantonio made Raphael's name popular. Engravings spread the fame of an artist and won a vast public for him—not forgetting that they provided an honest source of income if, of course, a copyright was first obtained which enabled the holder to sue any imitators. A favour like this was not easy to achieve, especially in foreign countries; patience and per-severance were needed, and the helpful effect of a few presents could not be overlooked. Success was accompanied by the pros-pect of having to begin all over again before very long because copyright was granted only on a short-term basis. For Rubens, however, that was no obstacle; he pulled so many strings and so effectively, that he ended by having his way.

It was not enough for him merely to organize the sale of his prints. Engraving had always interested him for its own sake. As in everything he touched, he had his own ideas and imposed them on everyone else. He had not engraved much himself, but he had paid critical attention to the work of others and was not very satisfied with it. Neither old Cornelius Gallus, nor those who worked with him in Holland, had succeeded in getting the effect he wanted. He finally took an engraver into his studio in order to mould him better to his requirements. This man, Peter Soutman, attempted to convey the effects of light and movement, the two dominant aspects of Rubens' painting, by means of a cunning mixture of hand-engraving and the use of acid. But he exaggerated the contrasts and his outlines were too strongly marked. It was still not what Rubens wanted.

Finally he found in Luke Vorsterman someone who could give him complete satisfaction. This young artist had a strong, adaptable personality, and his interpretations were bright, warm and luminous. As soon as he had given the young man a series of sketches, Rubens applied for copyright in Holland. He wrote to Peter van Veen, a lawyer at the Hague and the brother of his former master Otto Vaenius: 'The engravings are not yet completely finished, but they will not be long delayed, and I think it would be to our advantage to start negotiations, basing them on a properly drawn up list, with the subjects they represent all down in writing—it would save time.' He was always as expeditious as that, and practical into the bargain. Further on he added a few lines: 'To tell the truth, I would very much like to show in my list a few pieces which will not be finished for some time. In that way we would avoid the bother of negotiating all over again.'

While he was trying to circumvent the States-General of the United Provinces — after Peter van Veen he appealed to Sir Dudley Carleton—he did not neglect his painting. He supplied pictures to the Archduke Leopold, bishop of Passau and Strasbourg, to Wolfgang Wilhelm of Bavaria, Prince of Neuburg, to his friend Van der Geest, a collector from Antwerp, to the Marquis Nicholas Pallavicini, his son's godfather, and very many others. For one of them St Ignatius worked miracles, the Amazons waged war for another, while a third received 'The Nativity' and 'The Holy Ghost'; and so on.

Philip IV by Velasquez. (National Gallery, London—Photo Anderson-Giraudon)

9. Gaspar Gevartius by P. P. Rubens. (Antwerp, Musée Royal des Beaux-Arts—PH
A.C.L.)

For Jaspar Charles he painted 'The Last Communion of St Francis' to be hung in the Church of the Recollects in Antwerp, and many of his admirers proclaimed it a miracle. The work is not in the usual style of the master. Although the upward movement is present, Rubens has not attempted this time to cover the whole of his canvas with a crowd of figures. The scene, on the contrary, is all on one plane without any arrangement in depth and the upper part is left comparatively empty. Is this because he seems to have been inspired by 'The Last Communion of St Jerome' by Dominichino? There is practically no movement, and the religious feeling appears more expressive than usual. Even his colouring is more muted. It is an exceptional work but not a representative one.

The vigorous nature of the artist is better expressed in a huge canvas painted soon after with the help of Van Dyck for the same church: 'The Spear-Thrust'. This is a Calvary scene, dramatic without being really poignant. The body of Christ still has an athletic vigour, as have also those of the two thieves. The sad group composed of Mary and John, to which we may add the touching Magdalene, is balanced by horsemen full of life and colour. Behind the body of Christ Crucified, the dark sky provides a contrast, and a few touches of black again recall the Italian masters.

One day Rubens delivered 'The Three Crosses'; another day, 'The Assumption'. He repeated 'The Last Judgment' on a smaller scale, and succeeded in achieving a composition which was more restless and better balanced at the same time. And as if he still had not enough to satisfy his virtuosity, he began once more to juggle with groups of naked bodies in 'The Fall of the Damned'. This did not prevent him from lovingly painting three female nudes for a flowery landscape by Jan Bruegel. Then there was his studio work. Rubens passed serenely from the sacred to the profane. A few swift strokes on a panel were enough to set his collaborators to work. And after all, he retouched everything with his own hands. He was amazed that his customers sometimes protested, and insisted on having a work done entirely by him. Those clients! Some even had their own ideas about the pictures they commissioned, such as those the Duke of Bavaria had on a certain 'Saint Michael'. It was a conception, said the painter, 'as beautiful as it is difficult to carry out'. And he added, 'I do not think I shall be able to find among my pupils a man capable of successfully attempting such a task, even on one of my sketches; and in any case I shall find myself obliged to retouch it entirely personally'.

Relations with the great are not always easy, and it is a good thing to be able to protect oneself. What could he reply to Sir Dudley Carleton, who was always fond of bargains and negotiations, and who wanted freshly painted works in exchange for a Bassano belonging to Lord Henry Danvers? New works were worth their weight in gold, and what was he to do with a Bassano? But Sir Dudley Carleton, especially with Lord Henry Danvers behind him, had to be handled carefully. Rubens finally accepted, and asked for the Bassano to be sent. As soon as he saw it he exclaimed in horror, and swore that the work was in a dreadful state. To oblige the ambassador, he said, he was willing to offer a little 'Wolf-hunt', done 'by his own hand'. As this brought protests, he declared that he was ready to enlarge the canvas and to replace the wolves with lions, which, according to the master, increased the value of the painting. And so he asked to be paid extra. And he won the day; Carleton gave in.

In March 1620, Rubens signed a contract with the rector of the Jesuit College in Brussels and with the superior of their professed house in Antwerp. For a fee of 7,000 florins he agreed to furnish the new Jesuit church with thirty-six ceilings and three paintings to adorn the retables, and he expressly undertook to make the thirty-nine drawings 'by his own hand, on a smaller scale'; however the execution was to be entrusted to 'Van Dyck and to others of his pupils'. This Van Dyck, though only twenty-one, already enjoyed such a reputation that the famous collector Thomas Howard, Earl of Arundel, was trying to entice him to London. Whether he would ever have succeeded seems doubtful when we read a certain letter from his representative: 'Van Dyck lives with Mr Rubens, and his work is beginning to be as highly considered as that of his master. He is a young man about twenty with very rich parents belonging to this town. For this reason it will be difficult to induce him to leave this country, especially as he can see what a fortune Rubens is amassing'.

For Rubens this was a magnificent windfall. This church was

to be the most sumptuous in Antwerp. Work on it had been going on since 1614. The plans were drawn by Father Francis Aguilon who died in 1617, and Brother Coadjutor Peter Huyssens who continued the work alone. Thanks to his excellent relations with the Jesuit Fathers, Rubens was able to put in his word, and to give occasional advice or information. The architects had drawn their inspiration from Vitruvius and from the theories of Da Vignola, giving the church the form of the ancient Roman basilicas and a façade in the Italian manner; but the style was more massive and florid than that of the Italian models. It was absolutely new to the Netherlands, and was henceforth known as the Jesuit style. There had already been a foretaste of it in the central building of the Town Hall, but here it asserted itself with real conviction. It was the style which served the new Catholicism brought into being by the Council of Trent. After the Inquisition and the Reformation with their train of misery and cruelty, the old faith was to find a new setting, the forms of which were more pleasing, and—dare one say it?—more human, to proclaim that religion binds and does not repel. It was impossible to be sparing of either pains or money if this result was to be attained. According to the traditions of Antwerp, things must be done on the grand scale. The most beautiful marbles imported from Tuscany covered the walls of the choir and the two lateral chapels; ophicalcite, brocatel, onyx, griotte, not forgetting the white Carrara marble for the columns. The vaulting was gilded. Finally, there were the thirty-six painted ceilings, and the pictures, and the sculpture!

Architecture, painting and sculpture all combined to make this 'marble temple' the wonder of Antwerp. The task which fell to Rubens was worthy of Michelangelo or Raphael. At last his painting was to find an adequate setting, and he was freed from the Gothic which he hated. Here indeed was an opportunity to enjoy himself to the full.

On September 12, 1621, the Bishop of Antwerp, Jan Malderus, solemnly consecrated the new church. It was dedicated to the founder of the Society of Jesus, Ignatius Loyola, who was to be canonised a few months later. For the high altar, Rubens painted 'The Miracles of St Ignatius and St Xavier', two magnificent works which were to be on view in turn, according to a new fashion. On the ceilings he opposed Old Testament to New Testament scenes, and added the four great doctors of the Eastern Church—Athanasius, Basil, Gregory of Nazianzus and Chrysostomus — and those of the Western Church — Jerome, Augustine, Ambrose and Gregory the Great—besides a whole litany of saints including the Infanta's three patron saints, Isabella, Clara and Eugenia—the whole drawn in a powerful sweep of movement, and with a knowledge of perspective worthy of the great Italians, which was, for Rubens, the true mark of the master.

But alas, building churches and pouring forth devotional works is not enough to ensure the safety of a country. At Antwerp in particular the situation was worsening. The closing of the Scheldt was slowly ruining the metropolis. The unhappy city saw the gradual departure of all the noble families which were the source of its wealth. In 1616 Bishop Jan Malderus had already complained to Brussels that more than two hundred and forty families had gone. A few years earlier the outlawing of the Jews had caused another exodus. The city's finances were so heavily burdened that in 1618 the government had to promulgate the 'Albertine Statute' in order to give the over-generous Antwerp magistracy a definite policy in financial matters. Not only had the budget to be balanced, but the municipal officials were forbidden to give presents, receptions or banquets. The people of Antwerp, who called themselves 'Sinjoren'—'lords'— were deeply grieved; ostentation had always been part of their life. To give an example—they had only one Rubens in the Town Hall, that 'Adoration of the Magi' of which they were so proud; and they offered this to a Spanish nobleman in order to smooth the way for some difficult negotiations. That was the kind of people they were.

Since the Spaniards who negotiated the truce had omitted to insist on the opening of the Scheldt, Antwerp had lost all contact with overseas. It was the end of all those visits of travellers from distant lands, bringing exciting news and carrying rich and curious merchandise. All this strange and wonderful life, with all its plenty, was dead. All that remained was the ruins of former splendour, and a few industries. Trade with India, which might have brought some profit, remained the prerogative of

Spain alone. Even the most pious would hardly have found compensation in the establishment in the country of numerous orders such as the Augustinians, the Minims, the Carmelites, the Discalced Carmelites, the Carthusians, the Carmelite nuns, the English Carmelite nuns, the Spanish order of St Theresa, the Sisters of the Annunciation, and the Franciscan and Dominican nuns—not forgetting those which were already there, such as the Recollects, the Cellite Friars, the Beghards, the Premonstratensians, the Capuchins, the Dominicans, and lastly the most influential of all under the new regime, the Jesuits.

As a measure against the excesses of the moneylenders, pawn offices were set up at Antwerp and Brussels, on the initiative of Wenceslas Cobergher who had studied the running of these organizations in Italy. They were palliatives, not true remedies. There were also external worries. King Philip III had just died, and his favourite, the powerful Duke of Lerma, had fallen into disgrace. The Archduchess had lost not only a devoted brother, but also the support of a minister who was friendly towards her.

With the accession of Philip IV, a nephew whom she did not know, there appeared a new favourite, the Count Olivarez. The poor woman did not know what to expect. And her troubles were not yet over. Shortly after the accession of the new King, Archduke Albert died. For several weeks the Archduchess, completely prostrated, remained in her apartments; and henceforward she only appeared dressed in the habit of a nun. She seemed to have no desire to remain in power. The situation was as critical as it could be.

The twelve-year truce had just expired, and the timid attempts at negotiations which had been undertaken in the hope of reaching a new agreement had either failed utterly or were dragging on hopelessly. Archduke Albert had lent credence to baseless rumours and allowed himself to be lured by a foolish hope—that of bringing the United Provinces under Spanish rule. It is not hard to imagine how successful his emissaries were likely to be. On his side, Maurice of Nassau threatened to break off negotiations if the King of France had any suspicion whatsoever. The impetuous son of William the Silent and that same Anna of Saxony who had a daughter by John Rubens, was now but a shadow of his former self. Twelve years ago he had shown himself hostile to the truce, but now, weakened by disease, he was anxious to come to terms with Spain. Everything had to be done in absolute secrecy, because there were unshakeable opinions to be reckoned with in both camps. At the court of Brussels one of the most uncompromising was the Spanish ambassador, Cardinal de la Cueva.

Alonso de la Cueva, Marquis of Besmar, was both energetic and unscrupulous. He was very devoted to his master, and had been obliged to leave Venice, where he had been ambassador, after being seriously involved in a plot to put the 'Most Serene Republic' at the mercy of Philip IV. In Brussels he had only the interests of Spain at heart, and for that reason he opposed Spinola, undermining his authority as far as lay in his power. He was very hostile to the States and derided their privileges, calling them 'the formalities and amusements of idiots'. With the Infanta his role was similar to that of Granvelle with Margaret of Parma, and his unpopularity, though less universal, was quite as great.

Since the death of her husband Isabella was no longer sovereign, but regent of the Netherlands. This is no mere exchange of titles; Spain had every intention of conducting the affairs of the Netherlands exactly as thought they belonged to the Crown, while leaving the Infanta an illusion of power. Thus Rubens found himself entrusted by Pecquius, the Chancellor of Brabant, with the task of opening negotiations, behind La Cueva's back, with a cousin of his, Jan Brant, who had settled in Holland. After the personal defeat of Pecquius, attempts were made to negotiate secretly, through the agency of individuals with no official standing. All these efforts were superfluous, because Spain, under the energetic leadership of Olivarez, had set her hopes on a decisive revenge for all past disappointments.

Hostilities soon began again. Spinola returned to the field, and the United Provinces engaged Ernst von Mansfeld, a general who had won his spurs in Germany.

Rubens may not have been fortunate in his mission, but as a painter he remained triumphant, though not without a few setbacks. The affair of the Bassano, for instance, had some very disagreeable repercussions for him. Carleton's agents, Matthew and Trumbull, had just despatched the canvas to England. In a report to his employer, Matthew wrote: 'The original was an excellent work, sold to the Duke of Bavaria for a hundred pounds sterling; but it was larger than this one. Rubens has told me in confidence that this second "Lion Hunt" is not all of his own doing, and I now thank him for this confession, for a man who has but half an eye may easily discern it. But he protests nevertheless that he has retouched it in all its parts.' As for the price, Matthew had spoken of it discreetly to the painter, 'but his demands are like the laws of the Medes and Persians which may not be altered'. Trumbull was no more sympathetic. He even suggested giving up the whole affair and approaching Van Dyck who had just arrived in England. 'I would venture', said Trumbull, 'to wager my two hands against a pair of gloves that Van Dyck will furnish us a better work than this, and for half the price that Rubens demands.'

When Lord Henry Danvers received the 'Lion Hunt' he apparently flew into a rage. He wished to present a Rubens to the Prince of Wales and had nothing but a bad copy. He therefore demanded an original work or the return of his Bassano. So Carleton wrote to the painter: 'We shall return your lions safely to you, and you shall send us tamer beasts better made.' Rubens was deeply grieved. The fact that the painting was destined for the Prince of Wales added to his contrition. He pleaded not guilty. Nobody had told him, he wrote, 'that this work was to be a true original, painted all by my hand, and by my hand alone', and he offered to replace the offending lions. Lord Danvers accepted, but no agreement was reached. The breach became complete, and finally the Bassano went back to London and the lions to Antwerp.

The field of engraving had its own worries. In 1619, after engaging Luke Vorsterman, Rubens had been able to write in good faith to Peter Van Veen: 'I always see that the engraver does not stray from the model, and I find I have less trouble if I have a willing young man working under my eye than if I entrust the work to eminent masters whose whims become law.' Vorsterman was twenty-four when his master gave him this testimonial. But unfortunately the young man did not continue in this happy frame of mind. Rubens complained: 'For two years we have published nothing worth mentioning, through the fault of my engraver.'

Vorsterman was, in fact, succumbing to megalomania, to such an extent that it was impossible to do anything constructive with him. He declared that the whole value of the engravings was due to his work alone, coupled, of course, with his personal reputation. Rubens was exasperated by such pretentiousness, and anxious to prove 'to no matter whom' that his designs were 'more careful and more detailed' than Vorsterman's engravings. The situation had a touch of comedy. The designs Rubens gave to his engravers are well known; they were rapid sketches merely indicating the composition and leaving the craftsman to make a detailed interpretation in the authentic Rubens style. It is quite understandable that Vorsterman, a talented artist but a man quick to take offence, should have been up in arms at the thought that his work, which gave the engravings their real value, should count for nothing in the eyes of the ignorant. For anyone who knows the slow, painstaking toil of the engraver, Vorsterman's pride is easily explained. Rubens would not admit this; his own dictates were all that mattered to him. And if he argued like any apprentice, trying to prove the impossible—that his designs were 'more careful and more detailed' than his assistant's engravings—it was because he could not bear to be disobeyed.

Poor wretched Vorsterman—with a nature like his, there was nothing he could do but become his own master. That, in fact, was what he did, not without uttering a few threats aimed at his former employer. Some of Rubens' friends were so excited by this that they asked the authorities to give special protection to the great artist. And even though Rockox refused this whereas the Archduchess Isabella granted it, that would not have been sufficient reason for accusing the Burgomaster of Antwerp of a lukewarm attitude towards his friend. The more discerning must have believed that Rockox, knowing the people concerned, did not attach great importance to Vorsterman's threats. Artists are not all sweetness and light, and though some may play the nobleman, many have remained real plebeians. The court of Brussels had taken seriously something which to a native of Antwerp was nothing but a quarrel between artists.

IX

THE NEW PASSION

1622–1626

Rubens may have had his troubles, but he was never short of compensations. In February 1622 he was called to Paris by the Baron de Vicq, the Archduchess's ambassador, who put him in touch with the Abbé de Saint Ambroise, treasurer to Marie de Medici. The Queen Mother had just become reconciled with her son, and had been able to return to the Luxembourg Palace which she had had built by Salomon de Brosse a few years earlier, and had been obliged to leave two years before. She wanted to adorn one long gallery with pictures retracing the episodes of her life; and later she intended to glorify the life of her illustrious husband, Henry IV, in another gallery. The honour of being picked out for this double task fell to Rubens.

And so he found himself in the presence of that same Marie de Medici whom he had glimpsed twenty-two years before, when he arrived in Italy. He had been among the bystanders at the wedding of the daughter of the Grand Duke of Tuscany to Henry IV; and, moreover, she was the sister-in-law of Vincenzo I, his former master. The Queen Mother was forty-nine years old. She was a plump matron with rather coarse features and an unintelligent expression. The contrast with her husband was remarkable; all his portraits show his bright malicious eve, and his air of pride coupled with cunning—half gallant, half fox.

Naturally the painter accepted the mission entrusted to him. It was a gigantic undertaking and the theme was a thankless one. All the better: 'I confess that a natural instinct makes me more fitted to paint very large pictures than little curiosities. Everyone has his own gifts; my talent is such that no undertaking, however immense in size and variety of subject, has ever daunted

me.' When he wrote those lines a few months earlier, he ha
surely not believed that he would have his wish so soon.

As soon as he was back in Antwerp, he set to work. What wa
there to say about the life of this Florentine woman who ha
become Queen of France because Henry IV was head over ear
in debt and the Medici were among his biggest creditors? Urge
on by his minister Sully, the King had accepted her withou
knowing her, in order to restore the fortunes of his house an
consolidate his power. Before marrying her, he had seen onl
her portrait. Though he did not take a strong aversion to her
she was far from winning his love. As soon as they were married
everything went wrong and their life became hell. On the deatl
of Henry IV, Marie de Medici became Regent. She was weak
scheming, vain, bad-tempered and superstitious; she surrounded
herself with foreigners and undid all the good done by the King'
wise policies. As for her intelligence, we have only to remembe
what her former confidante, the wife of the Marshal of Ancre
replied, when accused of sorcery, to the judges examining he
case. When they asked her what charms she had used to bewitcl
the queen, she replied, with some effrontery: 'Nothing but th
power which any clever woman has over a fool.' The Queer
Mother's encounters with her son were memorable. Arrest, exile
escape, even pitched battle—nothing was lacking. She had jus
ended by making her submission to the King, and it was saic
that Richelieu had something to do with this reconciliation.

Her life could have provided the subject-matter for some
dramatic scenes, but Rubens knew how much use he could make
of the truth; and he had to fall back upon allegory and
mythology. He began with the Fates, spinning the destiny of the
future queen; Jupiter and Juno had apparently joined the party
as well. For 'The Education of Marie de Medici' he brought in
Minerva, Apollo, Mercury and the three Graces. When Henry
IV is receiving the portrait of his wife-to-be, a helmeted France i
quite simply advising him to follow the dictates of his heart! At
Lyons, where he met his wife for the first time, the King i
transformed into Jupiter himself. Fertility and Health are pre-
siding at the 'Birth of Louis XIII'. France mourns at the 'Death
of Henry IV'. All the gods on Olympus are not too much to
glorify the 'Regency of the Queen'. The Virtues are present at

the 'Majority of Louis XIII'. Thrusting aside angry Discord and striking monsters with a thunderbolt, 'Mercury reconciles the young king and his mother'. Finally, in the 'Triumph of Truth', under the aegis of that divinity, Louis XIII offers his heart to Marie de Medici!

In these compositions, overflowing as they are with imagination, Rubens transformed into a kind of fairyland the not particularly edifying life of his heroine. He surrounded her with such a wealth of appurtenances that at every moment she was very nearly pushed into the background. Consider, for example, the 'Disembarkation at Marseilles', where everyone has eyes only for the voluptuous Naiads, to the disadvantage of the queen who is being received with open arms by France. Even in the 'Coronation', one of the few episodes treated without allegory, the foreground is occupied by two superb hounds—in the basilica of St Denis! Rubens was so kind to the queen, and adorned her with so many imaginary graces, that Marie de Medici was beside herself with delight. That, of course, is the way in which the great ones of this world want history to be written.

After a few months Rubens went back to Paris to submit his sketches to the Queen Mother. Apart from a few tiny details, she approved them, and the painter was able to return to Antwerp and get the work under way.

Van Dyck was no longer there to help him. This brilliant assistant of his had left Antwerp two years before. Thomas Howard, Earl of Arundel, the most influential of English art-lovers, had managed to induce him to come to England. King Charles I had given him a pension and leave to visit Italy, and since then the *pittore cavaleresco* had been enjoying ever-increasing success. Evil tongues, it is true, said that he was 'more skilled in kissing a woman's hand than holding a brush', but nevertheless he had created in Italy a new style of portrait, brilliant, facile and full of easy grace, yet at the same time psychologically penetrating.

However, Rubens still had a few loyal collaborators such as Snyders and Wildens, and he was able to draw upon some new recruits like Justus van Egmont, Theo van Thulden and Jacobus Moermans. The gallery, though a long-term project, was far from absorbing all his attention. He had just published his *Palazzi di Genova*, the fruit of his stay in Italy. It was a splendid opportunity to express some ideas on architecture and to give vent to the hope that he might 'see the old style, called *barbaric* or *Gothic*, gradually fall out of fashion and disappear altogether in Flanders, giving place to that order and symmetry, conforming to the rules of Greek and Roman antiquity, which men of taste have introduced to the great honour of this country'.

In March 1623 death struck a sudden and cruel blow at his household. His eldest child, little Clara Serena, died aged only twelve years; it was a sad reminder that, however irresistible his triumphant progress might seem, he was still subject to the strokes of fortune. He had to rise above his grief, gather the rest of his loved ones more closely around him, and bravely take up his task again.

Three months later, Rubens went to Paris to arrange for the hanging of his pictures; and there he had the pleasure of meeting Peiresc. He had already been corresponding for some time with this brilliant humanist, and on returning to Antwerp he continued with renewed enthusiasm. He talked to him about Latin epigrams, recent books, precious stones, and even imparted to him a plan for achieving perpetual motion. There was no subject that could not be discussed with Claude Fabri de Peiresc; the man knew something about everything. After many travels he was living in retirement at Aix, where he was acting as judge of the *Parlement*. His study was a museum, a cabinet of medallions, a library and a botanical garden. He lived surrounded by cats, not to mention goats, tortoises and birds. Five thousand volumes and two hundred manuscripts were piled around him. He was always ready to lend his books, and though he was horrified when anyone forgot to return them, he still could not bring himself to refuse to share his wealth. He was very proud of his portrait gallery; he wrote to a friend, 'I have some by Vouet, by the late Porbus, by Fr Apollodoro . . . and by some others. I am even expecting one by the hand of Mr Rubens.' And his expectations were to be fulfilled. He possessed ancient marbles, minerals, engravings, and curiosities, while he furnished his mind with every subject known to man.

While staying in Paris, Rubens also made the acquaintance of

Peiresc's brother, Palamede de Fabri de Valavez, a Parisian and a courtier, who was soon also corresponding with Rubens. They discussed science and contemporary gossip. When Theophile de Viau was sentenced, Rubens asked Valavez to send him the famous *Parnasse Satyrique*; for a humanist, even a pious one, cannot be indifferent to literary works, however licentious they may be.

A new spate of creativity began. For the high altar of the abbey church of St Michael, Rubens took up again one of his favourite themes, 'The Adoration of the Magi', and, without any assistance at all, achieved one of his most brilliant masterpieces. When Rubens worked alone, unhampered by pupils and assistants, his art became more poetic and more limpid. The last shreds of Caravaggio's influence had been swept away, and the luminous parts of his painting had gained the ascendancy over the dark ones. His drawing had become more flexible and his touch more ethereal.

This new 'Adoration of the Magi' with its larger-than-life-size figures, is enchanting in every way. The eye, at once charmed and amused, does not know where to rest first. Should it be on Balthazar, the Moorish king, dressed in green silk? Or else Melchior, the old man of giant stature, with the air of an old philosopher, whose gold-embroidered mantle is in itself an amazing feat? And then there is the kneeling king, draped in a full white surplice. The Virgin Mary is a healthy Flemish girl with very white skin. As for the baby Jesus, he goes almost unnoticed in all the wealth of detail. Everything is there: helmeted men, a fine horseman, camels with their riders and an ox. A Corinthian column stands, with perfect naturalness, by the threshold of this vast stable. A whole thesis could be written on the judicious choice of colours and on the skill of the composition, but to subject this work to a cold and technical appraisal would surely be to belittle it. True art is far beyond technique, as Rubens proves so well in this brilliant painting. He first made a sketch, as he always did, then carried it out; and at that point everything that might have been hesitant or confused fell into place as if by a miracle. Everything in this painting appears natural: it is the expression of a spirit which could rise above all earthly fortunes.

Towards the end of 1624, the Abbé de Saint-Ambroise warned him that the sister of the King of France was to marry the Prince of Wales, and that the gallery must be ready without further delay. Richelieu, whose part in the reconciliation of the King and the Queen Mother had won him his cardinal's hat and the position of Prime Minister, wanted a work by him. It was a perfect opportunity for Rubens to declare himself 'the busiest and most harassed man in the world', holding forth at the same time on a multiplicity of topics, and asserting, in passing, to his friend Valavez that 'there is nobody in the world less interested in public affairs than I am, except where my jewels and my own person are concerned'—this when he had only just written in great secrecy to Pecquius on the subject of Dutch affairs. A diplomat, even an occasional one, should be able to hide his thoughts. And this man, than whom 'nobody in the world' was 'less interested in public affairs', had a few months before asked for and been granted a patent of nobility following a favourable report from the Bishop of Segovia, president of the Council of Flanders in Madrid.

In February 1625 Rubens arrived in Paris, and his paintings were hung. A few were finished in the gallery itself. People of high rank came to judge the effect; but the only opinion that really counted was that of the chief minister. Armand du Plessis de Richelieu was forty years old. He had been in power for only one year, and was already known to all as 'The Cardinal', a man who, underneath his lordly air, hid an implacable will. He was the object of savage hatred or fanatical affection. He had become a bishop at nineteen, deceiving the Pope who is said to have declared 'This young man will be a great rogue'. His rise had the speed and force of lightning. At thirty he was a member of the Council and almoner to Anne of Austria, the young Queen, chief secretary to the Queen Mother, Secretary of State for war and for foreign affairs. At one point he had had to come to terms with Marie de Medici and her favourite, that sour woman Galigai, and this was then referred to as the 'government of the three robes'. But had he not professed that one must 'sacrifice even to unfavourable gods'? Now the die was cast. He held power and intended to make good use of it, and to leave nothing to chance. The statesman should 'sleep as the lion sleeps, without

osing his eyes'. And so he did not disdain to cast a nonchalant
ye over Rubens' canvases. Not a single cloud must shadow his
ork of reconciliation—and there, precisely, was 'The Queen
aving the Capital'. So many unpleasant memories — quick,
mething else must go in its place! Rubens complied. With the
elp of the gods of Olympus, he provided a stately allegorical
mposition vague enough to offend no one. Here, for all to see,
ere the splendours of the Regency, including 'The resurrection
f the arts and sciences thanks to the liberality and munificence
f her Majesty'. Rubens remarked 'This subject has nothing to
o with matters of state, and cannot be applied to anyone in
articular; it pleases everyone, and I am persuaded that if it had
een left entirely to me, the other subjects would not have pro-
oked either scandal or criticism'. The Queen Mother was
aturally delighted; and so was the Abbé de Saint-Ambroise.

Finally Louis XIII visited the gallery. It was, apparently, the
rst time he had ever been in this palace. Rubens was in bed,
aving been injured in the foot by a bad shot when hunting, but
ne Abbé de Saint-Ambroise gave a commentary on the pictures,
nodifying their meaning very cleverly when this was necessary'.
he King expressed great satisfaction; this was the virtue of the
llegorical style based on riddles. Others were less enthusiastic;
1 their opinion the painter had used the gods in a somewhat
avalier manner. These detractors did not realize the difficulty of
he task. The painter was to show, in 'The Life of Henry IV',
hat there was no need for all this mythological paraphernalia
hen he had a really worthwhile subject.

Meanwhile politics were not neglected. Rightly or wrongly, he
elieved that the Duke of Neuburg, whose arrival in Paris was
nnounced, was charged with a mission for the King of Spain:
He is accredited by the King and authorized to treat and to
onclude peace with the Dutch.' This did not suit Rubens' book;
e had vainly tried in 1623 to open negotiations with the United
rovinces, and the appearance of this new actor on the scene
vas a great embarrassment to him. He did not hesitate to point
o the culprit: 'All this is the work of the secretary de Bye' and
te stressed the disadvantages of the undertaking; he wrote from
'aris: 'The only result of the Duke of Neuburg's mission will be
o divulge our secrets, and give our enemies in France as much

time as they need to oppose the fulfilment of our plans strongl
and decisively, and to use every possible means to bring abou
their failure. They will completely discourage the Prince c
Orange, and induce him to break off all the negotiations i
progress, some of which, as Your Highness is aware, are alread
very far advanced.'

After blasting this mission at length, he ends: 'But I beg You
Highness to keep secret the fact that I have approached you, an
to burn this letter. I am, in fact, very well in favour with th
Duke of Neuburg, and greatly obliged to him, and I do not wis
to cause any trouble to M. de Bye (Heaven preserve me fror
that!). I am his friend, and I would not for anything provok
his resentment. But the public welfare and Your Highness's ser
vice carry more weight with me than any other motive, and fo
that reason I am content to trust to Your Highness's wisdom an
discretion.'

It was a rather inelegant approach, even when the 'publi
welfare' was in question—or was it simply that Rubens wa
anxious to play a certain part and did not intend to be ouste
by this unexpected rival?

On May 11th the proxy marriage took place betwee
Henrietta Maria of France, the third daughter of the Quee
Mother, and Charles I of England, who had succeeded to th
throne barely a month before. Rubens was present at the cere
mony and only just escaped being seriously hurt. The platforn
on which he was standing collapsed, and he narrowly misse
falling. His friend Valavez was less lucky; he sustained a hea
injury. Although the banquets and receptions organized by
those whom he was at the moment calling 'our enemies i
France' gave him the opportunity to make some useful contacts
Rubens was not satisfied. He submitted to Richelieu a plan fo
the other gallery, but the cardinal was too absorbed in govern
mental affairs even to glance at his notes, and Rubens decided t
depart as soon as his account was settled. He remarked somewha
testily that he would learn the conclusions reached 'in a year'
time', probably at Antwerp.

However, he had very little cause for complaint. He had jus
made the acquaintance of Balthasar Gerbier, a fellow-painte
who was a member of Buckingham's suite. This worldly-wis

man, half French, half Spanish, had lived in France and Holland before entering into the service of England. In the course of their frequent conversations Rubens gave him to understand that at the court of Brussels the former good relations between France and Spain were greatly missed. He obviously hoped that Gerbier would pass this information on to his employer, who had come to France to escort the new Queen back to her royal husband. Gerbier presented his colleague to the minister.

Portrait-painting is an excellent means of studying someone's physiognomy and gaining an insight into his character. Rubens arranged to paint Buckingham's portrait, and thus found himself in the presence of this brilliant dandy, the favourite of two kings and the all-powerful master of a kingdom. Like his right-hand man, Gerbier, Buckingham was thirty-three, a handsome cavalier with steel-blue eyes, a delicate nose and curving mouth. His moustache and small pointed beard were fair, his hair golden. He was an aristocrat, arrogant and subtle, and no audacity was too great for him. His insolence at the court of Madrid had wrecked the plans for the marriage of the Prince of Wales, now his King, with the sister of Philip IV. And it was whispered in Paris that he had fallen passionately in love with the Queen of France herself. The daughter of Philip III was a tall, beautiful woman of twenty-four. Her husband, the King, appeared indifferent to her. It is understandable that Buckingham, who was always daring, should have tried to win her heart. If we can believe Tallemant des Réaux, the enterprising Englishman succeeded in achieving a tête-à-tête with the Queen in a garden at Amiens, and there 'the gallant gentleman threw the Queen on her back and rubbed her thighs with his embroidered breeches; but all in vain, for she called so loudly that the tirewoman, who was turning a deaf ear, was forced to come to her aid'. This setback did not discourage the Duke. One day he appeared in audience before Anne of Austria wearing a coat embroidered with pearls; these were badly sewn on and many fell scattered on the ground, but the extravagant Duke did not even deign to take back the ones that were picked up around his feet.

He had been loaded with honours too young and too easily, and had not the slightest idea of restraint. James I, that unhappy man who had no taste for women, had a tender passion for him which was certainly that of a lover. Thanks to this weak King, the obscure George Villiers became in the space of a few years gentleman of the bedchamber, Viscount Villiers, Earl, Marquess, then Duke of Buckingham, Master of the Horse, Master of Woods and Forests, Governor of the Cinque Ports, President of the King's Bench, Grand Master of Westminster, High Constable of Windsor and Lord High Admiral of England. His mother and brother had had money and titles showered upon them, and all his family had been enriched. Intoxicated by his triumphs, he grew insatiable, and what he coveted above all was glory. Though he sometimes appeared pleasant and friendly, he was on the other hand an impetuous man given to violent rages. He was an implacable hater, but could become so infatuated that he would raise the basest flatterers to dizzy heights, only to fling them back as quickly into the shadows. He despised men and money with equal insolence; and, though for different reasons, his ascendancy over the young King Charles I was, if such a thing were possible, even greater than over that weak monarch James I.

Despite all these useful contacts, Rubens was not happy. He had not been paid, which pleased him not at all. 'Altogether I find I cannot breathe here, and if I am not paid with as much readiness as I myself put into the service of the Queen Mother, it may be that I shall not easily return!' He had, after all, presented a large painting to the Queen Mother's treasurer to help matters on . . . When he got no satisfaction, he decided to go home.

Breda had just surrendered after a memorable siege. It had been a brilliant feat of arms on the part of Spinola. The Infanta was going to visit the conquered town, and Rubens, who was hoping to accompany her, just missed her at both Brussels and Antwerp, 'not without annoyance'. But there was no chance to brood over this disappointment; he tells us that since his return he had been 'overwhelmed by visits and congratulations' from his relatives and friends.

For those of the North, the surrender of Breda was added to an even more serious occurrence: the death of Maurice of Nassau. It is true that the redoubtable *stadhouder* was not always easy to live with, and the States-General had many a tussle with him, for he was of the stuff of which dictators are made. Unrepentant womanizer though he was, he took the side of the rigid Gomarists in their quarrel with the Arminians, simply in order to be in a better position to undermine the civil authority represented by the aged Johan van Oldenbarneveldt; and history has judged him responsible for the execution of the Land's Advocate of Holland, a man who had devoted his whole life to the cause of liberty. Citizens of honour never forgave him that crime, and in particular Vondel, the national poet, harried him ever after with vindictive lampoons. Nevertheless, Prince Maurice was the sword and buckler of the young Republic for some forty years. Apart from battles in the open field, he took thirty-eight towns or citadels after siege; he took by surprise five towns and ten forts, and delivered twelve fortresses surrounded by the enemy. He was a great leader, a brilliant strategist and a reformer of military methods. When some silly woman asked him to tell her the name of the greatest captain of the day, he replied, 'Spinola is the second'. This son of William the Silent and Anna of Saxony trained some brilliant pupils who did him great credit; notable among them were his brother Frederick Henry, and young Turenne, their cousin. However, Spain was hoping that without Prince Maurice the United Provinces would prove more conciliatory and more ready to make peace.

Rubens was soon playing an active part in the negotiations. 'Journeys made in the service of my sovereign lady must be subject to no delays.' He travelled a great deal; we meet him at Dunkirk, with the Infanta and with Spinola who was arming the fleet, and then in Germany. He stayed in Brussels for six months. 'I am very tired of being away from home for so long,' he wrote in November. But he still did not go home.

Although plague was raging in Antwerp, his painting workshop was not idle. But its master was driven by the demon of politics and was busy with the affairs of Spain, which he defended unreservedly. England, France and Holland were also holding his attention, as well as Tilly and Wallenstein and the citizens of La Rochelle. He thundered against Buckingham, who was guilty of an attempt against Cadiz, and sympathized with the young master of this arrogant man 'who rushed in like this and drags his people into the wildest possible venture for no reason at all; for though a war can be started at will, it cannot always be ended at will'. Wise words, and fully justified by the chaotic situation in Europe. Since the revolt of Bohemia, war had been continually spreading thoughout the Empire, and future developments could not yet be foreseen.

Despite these clouds Rubens had not forgotten his private interests. Whatever he may have said, he was deeply grieved to have heard nothing further about the Henry IV gallery. He wrote in vain to the Abbé de Saint-Ambroise; the gentleman in question failed to reply. 'I infer from his silence that the wind has changed, which actually does not worry me very much', he wrote to Valavez; although at the same time he asked him to use his standing at court to find out 'discreetly' the reason for this silence. Rather petulantly, Rubens drew up a balance-sheet for his work in France: 'When I count the journeys I have made and the time I have wasted quite unprofitably in Paris, I feel that my great work in honour of the Queen Mother was a very bad piece of business for me. I cannot count the Duke of Buckingham's generosity on the credit side of this account.'

He omitted to say that his visits to Paris had enabled him to paint the portrait of King Louis XIII in armour, and that of Queen Anne of Austria in State robes. It is true that however flattering it may be to work for royalty, it is also difficult to extract payment from them. This same Louis XIII had commissioned twelve tapestry cartoons depicting the life of Constantine several years before, and Rubens was still waiting to be paid. He was somewhat mollified when he learned that Richelieu wished to buy two paintings from him, but he hastened to ask whether he might not perhaps obtain payment for his cartoons.

Alas, the times were not favourable for those working at peaceful crafts. England was signing a treaty with Holland. The King of France was trying to come to terms with the Huguenots, which meant that France was becoming an enemy more to be feared. Spain was threatened more than ever. And Rubens, forgetting his habitual reserve, exclaimed: 'It would surely be better if these young people, upon whom the fate of the world rests today, could make friends with each other instead of throwing all Christendom into confusion as the whim takes them.'

'These young people' were Charles I, Louis XIII and Philip IV. The eldest of them was only twenty-six.

In February Rubens at last went home. Willy-nilly, preparations were being made for war against the Dutch. Skirmishes were already taking place at sea; and, as always, money was short. Her Highness the Infanta, who, in agreement with her husband, had favoured the setting up of pawn-offices for the relief of the poor people oppressed by the Lombards, found herself obliged in her turn to have recourse to these charitable institutions. Their general superintendent, Wenceslas Cobergher, who was also a painter and architect, proved less recalcitrant than the bankers and advanced money on the security of the Archduchess's jewels.

Rubens was still interested in any curious book, particularly on classical archaeology, that might come his way; but it was easy to see that his real passion was for politics. He may have sent Peiresc and Valavez commentaries on learned works, but the largest and liveliest part of his letters was devoted to European affairs or even to court gossip. Through Valavez, who was about to leave Paris, he soon found another French correspondent. This was Pierre Dupuy, a historian and humanist, who had catalogued the Royal archives and manuscripts, and published the proceedings of the Council of Trent.

Suddenly, in June, Rubens received a cruel blow. Isabella Brant died at barely thirty-four. She had lived so quietly, in her husband's shadow, that one almost forgets that for sixteen years she had been the painter's devoted companion. In fact we know very little about her. She married Rubens at eighteen and gave him a daughter, Clara-Serena, and two sons, Albert and Nicholas, who alone survived. Quietly, she had watched the master's rise to fame. The pictures her husband painted of her are not very revealing. She had large thoughtful eyes and a tranquil expression, and who is to say whether the smile which the painter gave her in the last portrait did not hide a deep melancholy? For despite her rich dress and the sumptuous setting, she appears sad. But—who knows?—perhaps she was already suffering from the illness which was later to kill her.

She was buried in the Abbey of Saint Michael, near Maria Pypelincx, and Rubens adorned her tomb with one of his works, representing the Virgin and Child. A letter to his new friend Pierre Dupuy contained a fitting funeral oration for his wife: 'I have lost an excellent companion, whom in all reason I could—nay should—love, for she had none of the failings of her sex; she was never bad-tempered nor weak, but so good, so gentle, and so virtuous that everyone loved her in life and mourns her now she is dead. Such a loss strikes me to my very soul, and since the only true remedy for all sorrows is the forgetfulness born of time, I must needs put my hopes in that alone. But I shall find it very hard to separate my grief from the memory I shall treasure all my life of the being I have loved and respected above all others.' And he adds that a voyage would probably help him: 'The new experiences offered to the eyes, as the scene changes before them, fill the imagination so that sorrow is for a while forgotten.'

He mourned sincerely, but was already seeking consolation. Life must go on.

X

THE GREAT GAME

1626–1628

A week after the letter announcing his wife's death, Rubens wrote again to Pierre Dupuy. The following week he wrote again. The letters came in regular succession. Was the painter succeeding in controlling his grief? Had forgetfulness really come with such surprising swiftness? Or was Rubens seeking ways of escape? He talked only of politics; and the situation in Europe provided an inexhaustible subject. Charles I had dragged France, the United Provinces and Denmark into a struggle against the Emperor and Philip IV. Though Rubens did not in fact leave Antwerp, his thoughts ranged over the hills and far away. He galloped into Germany after Tilly and Wallenstein. He took an interest in the new canal which was to divert the course of the Rhine to the great dam built by the Dutch. He thundered against the cruelty of the latter, who gave no quarter at sea, and approved the reprisals ordered by the Infanta. He worried about the galleons bringing twenty million in gold from Peru, for which the English fleet was lying in wait. Buckingham occupied much of his attention, but this was no novelty.

The Duke also remembered the Flemish painter, but for different reasons: the year 1625 had not been a good one for the English, and 1626 was even worse. The British army had met nothing but reverses. While Philip IV was making peace with France, England was managing to quarrel with her, and the fault was Buckingham's. He had been anxious to go to France in order to meet the Queen, for his passion for her had not faded. He reckoned without Richelieu, who despite the cardinalate purple had not given up all thought of amorous conquest; he aimed high, but was no match in this field for so engaging a

119

personality as the Duke. There was nothing left to him but to put all possible obstacles in the way of his successful rival. And he rose to the occasion. Louis XIII, duly warned, for the Cardinal had his spies in all quarters, opposed Buckingham's entry into France, saying that it would be 'a source of shame to the King and prejudicial to the peace of this State'. Whereupon the Duke, impetuous as always, swore that he 'would see the Queen in spite of all France's power', and straightway manoeuvred his master into an attitude of hostility. But behind him there was muttering throughout the land. If he could make peace with Spain he would have more scope. Buckingham's aim was to extricate himself from a difficult situation without too much damage to his self-esteem. On the basis of information given by Rubens, Gerbier had the year before told his employer of the Infanta's peaceful inclinations, for Rubens and Gerbier had continued to correspond in spite of the war.

Buckingham suddenly discovered a violent passion for antique marbles. And as Rubens possessed a fine collection, the Duke offered to buy it. Did Rubens, with his amazing business instinct, suspect that this collector's whim had a political bias? Without hesitation he asked 100,000 florins. In order to stimulate the zeal of the intermediary, he promised him a reasonable commission of ten per cent. At such a rate, Buckingham's agent became positively lyrical. The bargain was concluded, and Rubens pocketed a round sum of 90,000 florins. Since the whole collection had cost him 2,000 florins together with a few canvases 'by his own hand', it was a financial master-stroke. The painter accompanied the precious marbles as far as Calais, but did not meet Gerbier as he had hoped. He returned by way of Paris where he stayed three weeks. During his absence, the court, in spite of 'its atmosphere of torpor and placidity', had been tattling at his expense. The rumour was circulating that he had been to England. The Infanta and the Marquis Spinola were convinced of it, and Rubens had all the trouble in the world to get the idea out of their heads.

He did not have long to wait for news from England. In January 1627, Gerbier wrote to Rubens that he had messages for him from his master, and asked for a passport. At the end of February he arrived in Brussels; Buckingham was proposing a truce, with complete freedom of trade, between Spain, England, Denmark and the United Provinces. Rubens passed on this proposal to the Infanta. But Brussels feared that it would be difficult to reach a general settlement, and it was therefore recommended that failing this result, England and Spain should negotiate between themselves. Rubens was asked to make a proposal on these lines, and Gerbier carried the reply back to Buckingham, who acquiesced. His only condition was that the United Provinces should not be excluded from the agreement, because of the alliance between them and England.

The Infanta informed her nephew Philip IV of Buckingham's suggestions. True to its old habits, Madrid was in no hurry to make its opinion known. Rubens grew impatient at these delays, but reassured Buckingham and Gerbier. Then, as his correspondents did not protest, he became anxious, wondering whether his letters had really arrived at their destination. He had not been idle. He had been to Brussels with the Abbé Scaglia, the representative of the Duke of Savoy, who had just arrived in the Netherlands. He had 'received all possible satisfaction' from their interview with the Infanta and Spinola. Thanks to him, Spinola and Scaglia agreed 'very well, receiving perfect satisfaction one from the other, without a sign of mistrust'. Scaglia was going to Holland, where he would probably meet Gerbier. Rubens very much wanted to go too. 'I am of opinion', he wrote, 'that my presence would contribute greatly to the successful conclusion of the matter', and as his employers dared not send him of their own accord, he suggested an excellent arrangement—that Gerbier should summon him to Holland at Buckingham's request. In conjunction with Carleton and the Abbé Scaglia, they would think out the best solution for the differences between Spain and Holland, which were the only ones standing in the way of complete agreement.

'It would be a fine thing to achieve', he remarked. Difficulties could come only from the United Provinces, and those he undertook to smooth out. 'I have friends in high places there, and my old correspondents will not fail in their duty.' After writing this wily but boastful letter he was attacked by scruples and added a postscript: 'I beg you to burn this letter as soon as you have read it, for it could ruin me in my masters' esteem, even though there is really nothing wrong in it; it would at the very least lower my standing with them and make me useless in future negotiations.'

Madrid did not reply, and there was a very good reason for this. In March Olivarez and the Comte de Rochepot, the French Ambassador, had signed a treaty of alliance with the simple object of conquering and dividing up Great Britain! Louis XIII and Philip IV had just ratified this pact, making it difficult to follow up the English proposals, though it would be a bad move to rebut them.

At last Philip IV decided to reply, encouraging the Infanta to go on with the negotiations. She even obtained the authority to conclude a treaty, but with the express recommendation not to do anything about it! Moreover, the King was not satisfied with Rubens' part in the affair—it horrified him that a simple painter should represent the glorious Spanish nation. 'It is a cause of great discredit to this monarchy, as may easily be understood, for its reputation is bound to suffer if a man of so little importance has to be approached by ambassadors bearing such weighty proposals.' The Infanta retorted that Gerbier was a painter too, and Buckingham had sent him to Rubens with a letter written in his own hand. What else could they have done?

In June Gerbier left for the Hague as did also Sir Dudley Carleton. The latter returned to Holland as Ambassador Extraordinary, after a two years' absence which had been profitable in both money and prestige. On the pretext of arranging a sale of pictures and *objets d'art*, Rubens obtained his passport. He went to Breda, and acting on instructions received, proposed to Gerbier a meeting not far away on neutral ground at Zevenbergen. But Gerbier in his surprise suspected a ruse and suggested Delft, Rotterdam, Amsterdam or Utrecht. Still acting on orders, Rubens insisted on Zevenbergen. Gerbier refused categorically. Events were taking a tragi-comic turn.

Finally Rubens agreed to go to Delft, since Brussels consented to it. His presence in Holland did not go unnoticed. The diplomats were anxious—what was the purpose of this visit? For a week Rubens and Gerbier were able to discuss at their leisure the peace of which they dreamed. Their talks had very little practical value. As a negotiator, Rubens was singularly inefficient; he had been given no documents and was not empowered to enter into any contract. Neither the Infanta nor Spinola had the right to negotiate. The wishes of the King of Spain could not be known until the arrival of Don Diego Messia, his representative, who appeared to be in no hurry to come.

More than a month after Rubens had left for home, Gerbier was still waiting. Towards the end of August he lost patience and announced that he was going back to England. As it happened, Don Diego Messia had just left Paris for Brussels. Rubens hastened to inform his colleague; upon which Gerbier returned to the attack, feeling that if he came back empty-handed he would be a laughing-stock. He therefore insisted upon having a certificate in writing that the Infanta was seriously interested in the affair. So far from entering into the views of the two negotiators, Don Diego Messia came armed with an astounding plan, according to which the combined navies of France, Spain and the United Provinces would land in England; there would be a march on London ending in the capture of all Great Britain— and the command of this expedition was to be entrusted to Spinola in person!

All Rubens' dreams were shattered. He gave as his opinion: 'An excess of zeal for the Catholic religion and hate of the common enemy are the main factors of this alliance.' His resentment was great, even though he fought against it: 'In this as in everything we must above all have confidence in the future, and meanwhile keep a tranquil mind.' He was obliged by his orders to write Gerbier a letter full of duplicity. On the one hand he said that Don Diego Messia had 'enlightened the Netherlands governments as to the agreement between the Kings of Spain and France for the defence of their kingdom'; on the other hand he declared that 'Her Highness the Infanta has not changed her opinion', wishing 'nothing in the world so much as peace of mind for the King her nephew and a settlement which would be in the best interests of the people'. And even Spinola 'will for his part render all possible assistance, as duty commands, for the success of so worthy an undertaking'.

Knowing that no agreement was possible, Rubens had to propound the belief that all that Spain desired was peace! He did not, however, give in without a fight. He denounced the duplicity of the French who, notwithstanding their alliance with the Spaniards, continued their aid to the States-General. He pleaded his cause so ably that he won over Don Diego, but the Spanish minister was tied by his instructions and was himself powerless to do anything. Rubens needed to give free rein to his feelings and sent Gerbier a more intimate letter written in Flemish for greater secrecy : 'I implore you to believe that I am doing all I can and that my masters are keenly interested in our affair', but Olivarez 'in whom passion stifles every kind of reason and dominates every argument' was, according to him, to blame for everything : 'The majority of the Grand Council of Spain shares our opinion, but Olivarez has succeeded by his persistence in winning everyone over to his own'. As for Don Diego :

'We have given him a closer insight into the duplicity of the French and pointed out to him the support which the King of France gives of the States General every day, and would like to give to Denmark! We have shown him how the King is laughing at our simplicity, and that the alliance with Spain is merely a bogy to frighten the King of England and force him into an agreement; and in fact is what he will in the end succeed in doing. I have, on the instructions of the Infanta and the Marquis, explained all this repeatedly and in detail to Don Diego. I have spoken to him most freely and candidly. My efforts have not been in vain, but the affair has been concluded and Don Diego cannot modify the instructions he has received from Spain. I will not deceive you, Sir, under a pretence of friendship; on the contrary I will tell you quite frankly that the Infanta and the Marquis are resolved to continue our negotiations, as they are sure that the treaties between France and Spain will come to nothing; they will produce no result and will not even last. And for that reason, moreover, all intelligent men here, both clergy and laymen, are simply laughing at them. But so long as the stupidity of these treaties has not been proved, we cannot hope for any change in the situation, and we shall have some time to wait. Olivarez will surely open his eyes in the end and do better work, but unfortunately by then it will be too late.

'In the meantime we must take care to keep things as stable

as possible; you must try to keep Buckingham favourably inclined towards us. In any case this attitude can do no harm; we are not trying to prevent or delay an act of war, and consequently our position cannot possibly be suspect. For the rest, I have no wish to use vain hopes to keep you away from your master and your dear wife any longer; if I have done so up to now it was with good reason and my intentions were excellent. We will keep in touch and each will keep the other informed of all developments so that we can win the favour of our royal masters and remain in our respective positions. I enclose with this a letter to the Duke, which should make things easier for both of us. I cannot do anything else for the moment; my conscience is clear and I trust completely in the will of God.'

A matter of weeks later, he returned to the attack; he was too stubborn to let go now. He wrote to the Marquis of Spinola with news of Gerbier, who was anxious to come to Brussels for peace talks, since Buckingham was seeking an agreement with Spain at all costs. After vainly trying to raise the siege of La Rochelle, he had suffered a crushing defeat on the Isle of Ré. Two-thirds of the troops enlisted had been lost in that ill-starred expedition led by the Duke in person. It was useless for Gerbier to claim that 'retreat followed by a stronger offensive is a strategem used by all great leaders'; Buckingham had not the means to renew the struggle, and in order to protect himself against the violent personal attacks of which he was the object, he badly needed to make peace with Madrid. English trade, which had made rapid progress thanks to the East India Company, had been greatly harmed by the war with Spain, and the attempt against France had only made matters worse. Finances were in a desperate state, and the country was living by dubious shifts. Gerbier, good servant that he was, gave no inkling of the situation; on the contrary, he declared: 'We are making rapid preparations for a much larger and better equipped expedition than the last.' Spinola, who was on the point of leaving for Spain, replied to Rubens that he would explain the situation to the King as soon as he reached Madrid. He prudently avoided burning his boats; the French were very uncertain allies, and there was nothing imaginary about their help to the Dutch.

In his relations with Gerbier, Rubens showed more sympathy for his English friends than for his Spanish masters, and was obviously anxious to keep on good terms with Buckingham, but he sang a different tune in his letters to Pierre Dupuy. There was no question here of 'the duplicity of the French', but the English on the other hand were judged without indulgence: 'Truly, by the way the English are proceeding, they will soon be able to restore to the ancient flag of St George the device: "Friends of God and enemies of all the world".' When Buckingham took command of the fleet, he wrote: 'I am very surprised that the Duke of Buckingham should have preferred to leave his King rather than give another experienced general the leadership of so unpleasant and dangerous an expedition.' His conclusion is definite: 'It seems to me that his own temerity has put him in such a position that he must either win or die gloriously; for if he survived a defeat, he would be nothing but the plaything of fate and the laughing-stock of his enemies.' When the reverses suffered by the English were announced, he commented: 'They would do well to hurry back and guard their own homes instead of attacking those of others, and the Duke of Buckingham will soon learn from experience that the profession of arms is very different from that of courtier!' Later he rejoices at 'the victory of His Most Christian Majesty over the English, whom he drove out of the Isle of Ré with heavy losses and to their shame'. A few weeks earlier he had written to this same Buckingham, following the failure of his plans: 'I beg Your Excellency, notwithstanding the iniquity of the times, to continue to think kindly of me and to believe that no accident of fortune nor catastrophe in public affairs could ever alienate my affections, but that I shall always serve you most humbly, as I have promised and dedicated myself once for all.'

Rubens' duplicity is flagrant. Was it a natural inclination to deceive? It is hard to say. He was a mere amateur, longing to play a part in politics, and it is conceivable that he would model himself on the professionals. And a diplomat should be able to keep his hand out of sight. Rubens attempted this, with varying success. In his letters to his English correspondents he lacks calm and patience; what is more, he yielded to the temptation to make untimely observations. Such ill-judged remarks betrayed his lack of experience. With Pierre Dupuy he was more at ease. This worthy historiographer and librarian was not, strictly speaking, a friend of the painter, but a useful contact, as he was in touch with all the Court gossip and enjoyed the confidence of Louis XIII. He could speak learnedly on a host of recondite subjects, and for those who, like Rubens, wished to pass for humanists, it was good form to carry on a correspondence with men of this kind. So, even while yearning to interfere in public affairs, Rubens sent Pierre Dupuy tranquil epistles giving the news of the country, the condition of the Cardinal, the plans for a second canal ending at Herenthals, the loss of galleons in a storm, the forthcoming marriage of Spinola and other minor news-items.

Sometimes the tone becomes more elevated. He holds forth on the distress of princes: 'They are not only burdened with debts, having mortgaged all their resources, but have great difficulty in finding fresh expedients to keep themselves going and stretch their credit as best they can.' As for the 'fine speeches that flourish in our Court', they are, he says, 'meant for the people, but not for us'. This is not all: 'To this we must add that the economic system of princes is full of defects, and their affairs are in such chaos that it will be very difficult to straighten them out.' And he concludes: 'For my part I wish the whole world were at peace and that we could live in a golden age rather than in an iron cage.'

He even drops the mask a little, though this happens more rarely: 'If Spanish pride could be made to see reason, we should easily find a way to bring peace to Europe, which shows on all sides an overwhelming desire for tranquillity.' And this representative of Spain, doubtless exasperated by the interminable waiting, exclaims: 'Everyone here is weary, not so much of the hostilities themselves as of the continual difficulties in receiving the necessary funds from Spain, of the grinding poverty in which we constantly find ourselves, and of all the indignities heaped upon us by the malice and ignorance of ministers or their inability to act otherwise.'

Rubens had his work to console him for his setbacks as a diplomatist. The Archduchess had commissioned a set of fifteen cartoons for tapestries intended for the convent of Discalced Carmelites at Madrid. The subject 'The Triumph of the

Eucharist' allowed him to juggle with symbols and allegorical figures to his heart's content. His compositions were full of fire and movement and completely incomprehensible to the common herd.

He had begun his sketches for the Henry IV gallery. They were magnificent: 'The Battle of Ivry', 'The Fall of Paris', 'The Entry of Henry IV into Paris', 'Henry IV receiving the sceptre from the hands of his people', 'Henry IV and Marie de Medici'. Twenty-four were needed. The life of King Henry abounded in heroic episodes, and nothing could have been more suited to the painter's temperament. He finished the portrait of Spinola whose departure grieved him, for he had always got on better with this supple Genoese than with the stiff Spaniards who gravitated around the Infanta. He had his books and also his friends in Antwerp, Balthasar Moretus, Nicholas Rockox, van der Geest and Gevartius.

This last was a remarkable man. After studying at Louvain and living for long periods in Holland and France, he now held the office of Town Clerk of Antwerp. Besides being an important official, he was also a philologist — his edition of Statius had attracted the attention of men of letters — and a Latin poet. During his stay in Paris he made friends with Peiresc, and it was through him that the famous humanist came into contact with Rubens. The portrait of Gevartius is a splendid work, very aristocratic in appearance. Contrary to his usual custom, Rubens used no secondary decoration; the attention is concentrated entirely on the scholar's fine features, and despite his white ruff we are struck by the luminous quality of the flesh, further accentuated by the bright intelligent eyes. Rarely had the master been so inspired by his model, and probably he had not often had a model with so attractive a personality. Probably his very real liking for Gevartius had a great deal to do with it; this was the man whom he called 'the best of my friends and the friend of the Muses' and to whose tutorship he entrusted his son Albert.

His correspondence with Pierre Dupuy continued unabated. The two friends discussed political events and the books they were reading. The siege of La Rochelle caused them great concern. When, on his journey through France, Spinola was

Van Dyck. Self-portrait. (Pinakothek, Munich—Photo Hanfstaengle-Giraudon)

11. Rubens. Self-portrait. (Uffizi Gallery, Florence—Photo Alinari)

received by Louis XIII, it was enough to make Rubens drop his
detached pose and exclaim: 'Truly I cannot help but contemplate the inconstancy of all things human, when I see the Spinola
of the siege of Breda, whom the Kings of France and England
were doing all in their power to defeat, visiting the King of
France in very similar circumstances, being received as a friend
in his camp, and advising the King against his subjects in revolt
and against the King of France who had become his enemy.'

Reassured, he wrote a fortnight later: 'I am glad that the
Marquis has declared himself satisfied on leaving the French
court. He truly deserves to be treated as a gentleman, as I can
testify, who have spent much of every day in his company. He
is the most reasonable and prudent man I have ever known. He
is discreet where his intentions are concerned; he is taciturn, but
rather through fear of saying one word too many than through
lack of logic and eloquence. His bravery is known to everyone,
and I need say nothing about it. At first I feared the Italian, and
even more the Genoese in him, but I have always found him
open, dependable and of good faith.' Rubens was not surprised
that Spinola had not visited the Medici gallery, because the brave
general knew 'no more about painting than any street-porter'.
On the other hand his son-in-law, the Marquis de Leganes, 'can
take his place among the best authorities in the world'.

The Danish *chargé d'affaires* at the Hague, Josias Vosbergen,
came to visit Rubens, who took advantage of the occasion to ask
the Infanta for the authorization to negotiate. He was burning
to enter the lists once more. He accompanied Vosbergen to
Brussels so that the latter might expound his views to the
Infanta. It was still a question of that problematical peace in
which Rubens was absolutely determined to collaborate. The
project did not come to very much. Isabella referred the painter
back to Spinola who was at Madrid. Rubens complied, but as
Josias Vosbergen had no authority, the Spaniards attached no
importance to his statements. But this was no obstacle. Rubens
hastened to pass on the remark to his correspondent. He only
needed to find in Spinola's reply the sentence: 'It is certain that
the King of Spain is very ready to make peace with the states
which are at war with him', to see in it the indication of a new
policy, and informed Buckingham accordingly.

On his side, Gerbier was taking up again his old subject of conversation with Rubens: in spite of Spain's lack of response to her advances, England was still ready to come to terms. Once more Rubens tackled Spinola, pressing him to act. He even took up some of Gerbier's grievances against the Spaniards. He did not say all he thought, but with Pierre Dupuy he was more open; he judged Spinola 'powerless to act as a spur to Spanish indifference and sloth; those inborn vices which the Spanish nation is doing its best to nurture still more'. Finally he insisted that if the negotiations took place they should be entrusted to plenipotentiaries without having to 'refer continually to Spain for orders and instructions'. He would have liked the Infanta to be able to 'treat on equal terms with the King of England'. In view of the prestige he enjoyed in Brussels, it is fairly clear what his tactics were.

This time Madrid took the matter seriously. Philip IV, through the Infanta, demanded to see the correspondence on the subject. This was Rubens' great moment; no one, he said, would be able to understand these letters, written partly in cipher or in Flemish. Private business was mingled in them with public affairs. Someone would have to be chosen to whom they could be entrusted. Or perhaps the King would like Rubens to bring them himself? Philip IV consulted the Junta, which gave a favourable opinion in which the King concurred. 'But', he added in his own hand, 'Rubens must not be pressed; it is for him to decide whether it is in his interests to make the journey.' It was far from being a cordial invitation! No matter—Rubens had achieved his aim, which was what counted. Was he hoping to fly to the help of Spinola who was still being detained in Madrid? Rubens, being an active man himself, was convinced that the Marquis was 'bringing all his talent and all his good will to the task of rescuing the King of Spain and his ministers from the deep lethargy into which they have sunk, so that they may at length open their eyes and put an end to the appalling misery of Europe'. The Infanta and Spinola, he felt, were people who really knew how to govern. But the others! 'All the affairs of Europe are at present in confusion, but they are in the hands of people who are either inefficient or inexperienced.'

One last letter to Pierre Dupuy says: 'Here we are half-way

between peace and war, suffering all the misery and inconvenience of war and having none of the advantages of peace. Antwerp is sinking little by little; she is living on her capital and has not even the ghost of her former trade to support her.' After a long list of other news, he adds: 'I am afraid that our correspondence will have to be interrupted for a few months. I am going to be obliged to make a long journey. But since no plans on earth are certain except at the very moment when they are being carried out, I shall inform you just before my departure; and, so that you may not write to me in vain, I shall tell you if there is any delay or obstacle.'

XI

THE CHESSBOARD OF EUROPE

1628–1630

Rubens hurried through France at lightning speed, allowing himself only one slight detour by way of La Rochelle. The heroic city had been resisting a cruel siege for a year, but the end was near. In the spring Richelieu had built a wall cutting off all communication with the sea. Two attempts by the English to raise the siege had failed. Famine was about to break down the courage of the inhabitants. Writing to his friend Peiresc, Rubens described the siege as 'a sight worthy of the liveliest admiration'. But a few months later, when Pierre Dupuy sent him a heroic inscription in honour of this great feat of arms, he made the harsh remark: 'Let us hope that the author will soon be able to turn his style to good account in the celebration of a finer subject, when the glory of a victory over a foreign foe will overshadow that of successes achieved in a civil war.'

Rubens was now in Madrid. Twenty-five years had passed since his first stay in Spain. So many things had changed. At that time the King was a young man of his own age and the Duke of Lerma his all-powerful minister. Philip III had died in 1621, and his son, Philip IV, was twenty-three years old. He was endowed with every gift that Nature could shower upon a prince; he was both an athlete and a wit. No more brilliant horseman was known, and in tournaments he was first-class. He was an excellent shot; hunting was one of his chief pleasures, and his skill was the admiration of all. He had a lively intelligence and a gift for languages, and was interested in history. The arts attracted him; he loved painting, and not merely as a collector, for he drew and painted himself. His passion was the theatre, and here again he could not confine himself to being a mere spectator. At nine he was already an actor. Nothing pleased him more than to take part in the improvised plays which were sometimes given in the Queen's apartments.

Literature was flourishing in Spain, and every writer was ready to be a dramatist as well. Cervantes was dead, but old Lope de Vega was still tirelessly pouring forth his plays which by now ran into hundreds. The priest whose pseudonym was Tirso de Molina had just written *El Burlador de Sevilla* and created the immortal figure of Don Juan. Alarcon and Calderón were giving promise of future greatness. Living at the court as chaplain was Gongora, widely praised as either the 'Andalusian Pindar' or the 'Spanish Homer' according to choice. This man, who invented a style as brilliant as it was obscure, was the object of a hail of lampoons from those who disagreed with him; prominent among these was Quevedo, that prolific writer of every type of work, whom the King later appointed secretary.

Everyone praised the affability of Philip IV; no Spanish monarch had ever treated his servants with such kindness, and his tenderness towards his sisters was extreme. He was a good Catholic without being bigoted like his father or implacably cruel like his grandfather. Despite his slightly effeminate appearance he had amazing self-control. His large blue eyes looked upon the world with unalterable calm; he had never been seen to lose his temper and he never laughed. He had a very white skin, fair hair, a high forehead, full lips and the prominent Habsburg chin.

At the beginning of his reign he declared his intentions of making all decisions and seeing to all affairs of State autocratically, but he soon tired of this, for he was not a strong-willed man. He continued to play his part as King with dignity, but he left the policy-making to others. He was a *Rey por ceremonia*, to use the Spanish expression. His other weakness, and an even greater one, was women. His amorous adventures were legion, and the number of his natural children increased regularly. Olivarez, who knew his sovereign lord well, was always ready to act as go-between or procurer in order to have a free hand in affairs of state.

The *conde duque* was a strange character. Don Gaspar Guz-man, Count of Olivarez, and later Duke of San Lucar, was originally destined for the Church, but had played his master stroke on the death of the preceding King. The Duke of Lerma had summoned him to Madrid a few years earlier to join the personal suite of the Infante Philip, but he soon realized that he had misjudged his protege, and thenceforth did his best to get rid of him, but in vain. Olivarez was quick to take full advantage of the situation when his young master succeeded to the throne at only sixteen years of age. Even though Philip IV had declared that he would have no favourites, Olivarez quickly and easily obtained the widest possible powers. Fearing the influence of the Queen, Elizabeth of Bourbon, he had his own wife appointed as *Camera mayor,* and this cantankerous, misshapen old woman was given the task of spying on the daughter of Henry IV.

Men of overweening ambition like Olivarez know almost intuitively from what quarter danger threatens; and he accordingly kept a watchful eye on that sweet queen, of whom Calderón could say:

> La mas bella
> La mas pura, mas fragrante
> flor, la flor de lis, la reina
> de las floras

And he attempted with some success to drive a wedge between her and Philip. He gave the King the illusion that he was working day and night, and he did in fact work very hard. He was always surrounded by papers; he thought of everything, and managed to make himself indispensable to the lazy monarch. He lived like an ascetic and was known to be incorruptible. He claimed to lead a harder life than any stable-boy. He was obsequious with the King, who comforted him when he chose to play the overburdened statesman, but haughty and insolent with everyone else. It did not take long for him to become universally detested. He was cruelly handled in an endless succession of pamphlets. People quite openly wished him dead, and there were those who went so far as to wish the King dead if they could thus be rid of the minister they hated.

The various envoys at the court were greatly intrigued by Rubens' arrival. The painter had frequent interviews with Olivarez—what did that mean? It was said that this Fleming was a great friend of Buckingham, and that he had just returned from England; it was supposed that he had come to negotiate a truce with the Dutch or a peace with England. Rubens was summoned before the Junta, which decided that negotiations could profitably be continued. So far, so good; but the news that followed was sensational—Buckingham had been assassinated! What was to happen to the talks? Another of Buckingham's envoys, Endymion Porter, opportunely revealed that the first steps had been taken with the King's assent. Brussels confirmed this. Meanwhile La Rochelle had fallen, and the news became public that a peace between England and France was under consideration; the Venetians were working to this end. It was a blow for Spain, and one which she would have to avert if possible. In London, the Secretary of State, Cottington, and the Grand Treasurer, Weston, were discreetly sounded. Cottington let it be known that he was shortly to arrive in Madrid . . . There was nothing to do but wait.

It would have been impossible for Rubens to remain idle; he had always something with which to busy himself. He painted as others breathe. At the court of Madrid a painter was a privileged person. The King was more interested in the arts than in politics. His collections were marvellous, and his painter in ordinary was a man of twenty-nine in whom Rubens found a brilliantly gifted colleague. His name was Velasquez. The Flemish master took pleasure in conversing with him and lavishing advice upon him.

Don Diego Velasquez de Silva was born in Seville, where he studied with the elder Herrera and Pacheco, whose daughter he married; he was, however, influenced mainly by Ribera. He had been painter to the King since 1623, partly because he had powerful friends, but also because he had achieved success with a large equestrian portrait of Philip IV. He had a studio in the royal palace itself, with a special chair for the King who loved to come and chat with his painter and especially to watch him at work. During his stay in Seville Velasquez had painted religious or domestic scenes, but since he entered the King's service he had confined himself to portraits. His horizons had narrowed; his world was limited to court personalities, Olivarez, and above all the King, whose facial expression never changed. He had nothing productive to learn from his colleagues, none of whom seemed to have understood the genius of that recently dead painter Domenico Theotocopuli, called El Greco, who elongated his figures so as to 'make them look like celestial bodies in the same way as those lights we see from a distance, which appear large however small they may be'.

In rich royal collections, foreign masters predominated. We can imagine the effect which the arrival of Rubens, in all his glory, must have had on Velasquez. For the first time, Don Diego was in the presence of a great living painter. The leader of the Flemish school knew Italy, having lived there eight years. Before him, the Flemish painters—in exactly the same way as the Spanish ones—had shown a certain hardness of form. Rubens showed them how to bring a subject to life by softening the outlines and bathing it in mellow light. He also showed that he had not forgotten the lessons of his beloved Titian; he copied, in his own way, and for his own delight, some paintings by the Venetian wizard. In style, too, the Flemish painter, so different from the Spaniards, had much to impart, combining as he did the influences of the Renaissance and of the Counter-Reformation. He loved splendour, opulent curves and rich ornamentation. He excelled in those splendid nudes which were never to be found in Spain. All these elements he wove into paintings which were bright, turbulent and sensual, and whose verve exerted an irresistible appeal.

It is understandable that Velasquez should have adopted a modest attitude in the presence of this dazzling personage, and it is not impossible that this modesty—to which Pacheco bears witness—was slightly tinged with melancholy. He was, after all, the King's painter, and he had been promised the monopoly of royal portraits. Rubens had only just arrived, and was already painting portraits of the King, the Queen, and other members of the royal family. Everyone was eager to meet him, going into ecstasies over his amazing facility and that overwhelming vitality which led him to fill the backgrounds of his portraits with eagles, half-naked women, crowns and palms in riotous confusion.

The portraits painted by Pantoja de la Cruz, Alonso Sanchez Coello, Bartholomeus Gonzalez, and even by Zurbaran and Velasquez, appeared so very stiff compared with those dynamic paintings through which a fresh and happy breeze seemed to blow. Not that Rubens' portraits had more depth—far from it— but they brought with them an element of novelty pleasing to that court where, thanks to the King, balls, plays and hunting were more important than politics. Velasquez, in his own way, could paint portraits with a psychological insight to which Rubens was never likely to attain, but nevertheless all the success went to the foreigner. When he left Antwerp, Rubens, who never lost his business sense, had brought eight paintings with him on the off-chance; and they had gone to swell the royal collections. Even though gout sometimes kept him tied to his bed, Rubens was as full of energy as ever. Philip often visited him, taking immense pleasure in conversations with his guest from Flanders.

Soon not a trace was left of his prejudices against this commoner who had negotiated in the name of aristocratic Spain. Better still, the King took a liking to the painter, which was hardly surprising, since Rubens had always known how to please the great. But skilful courtier though he may have been, he was none the less clear-thinking. He judged, and his judgments could be harsh: 'For myself, it is only the King that I pity. Nature has endowed him with the finest qualities of mind and body, as I have been able to observe in my daily intercourse with him; and if he had more confidence in himself and less respect for his ministers, he would be capable of overcoming any difficulties that might arise. But today he must suffer the consequences of his own trustfulness and a succession of follies committed by other people; and he is beset by hate which should really be directed elsewhere.'

In April 1629, one positive fact at last came to light: England was willing to send an ambassador to Madrid, on condition that Spain should at the same time send an ambassador to London. Rubens was chosen. It is doubtful whether we should see in this a proof of the King's friendship or the wish of Olivarez to get rid of a possible rival for Philip's favour. It may have been a combination of the two factors. One thing is certain: Rubens was considered capable of carrying out this difficult task. Olivarez pressed him to leave without delay. The King appointed him Secretary of the Privy Council of the Netherlands, probably in order that he should no longer be considered as an amateur diplomat.

Rubens left Madrid with every reason for satisfaction. He was entrusted with an official mission; he had painted during his short stay about forty canvases including a series of portraits of the King and other members of the royal family; he had been free to copy works by his beloved Titian; and he wore on his finger a diamond ring, a parting gift from the King. Once more he sped through France. On May 13th he was in Brussels. The Infanta besought him to continue his journey without delay, as a new complication had arisen: the English King, offended by Spanish shilly-shallying, had just concluded a treaty with France. Rubens paid a flying visit to Antwerp, and accompanied by his brother-in-law Henry Brant, continued on his way. At Dunkirk he boarded an English ship, and on June 5th he was in London.

He was immediately summoned to Greenwich, where he found himself in the presence of the King of England. Charles I was a man of aristocratic bearing, serious and reserved. He was deeply convinced of his royal prerogatives, and his life was an open and continual struggle with Parliament. This situation had grown steadily worse over the last few years. Buckingham's unfortunate policy had a great deal to do with it. The most serious accusations brought against this minister could not alienate the King from his favourite, for he was always constant in friendship. Even though he was a Protestant, he was suspected of sympathy with the Catholics, because he recoiled from the violent measures demanded by the Puritans against the Papists. His wife, Henrietta Maria of France, whom he loved tenderly, was a Catholic, which increased the suspicions. The King was not without good sense, but he showed a lack of prudence and firmness when he blindly supported Buckingham's rash and sometimes inept enterprises. The murder of his favourite had grieved him deeply; however he had learnt one lesson from it—

henceforward he would reign himself, and his ministers would remain his servants.

Rubens explained the Spanish point of view to the King. While rejecting the idea of a preliminary truce, Charles I affirmed his sincere wish to conclude a treaty with Spain; but an indispensable condition was that Spain should agree to make concessions in the Palatinate. That was a bad beginning, since Madrid was not disposed to take a single step in that direction. Rubens learned, moreover, that an offensive alliance with France was being planned; the name of the French ambassador entrusted with the negotiations had already been announced. Rubens obtained the King's promise that nothing would be concluded as long as the talks with Spain were going on. It was something to have gained, but not a great deal, for two men in the forefront of English politics, Richard Weston and Francis Cottington, warned him that the King had gone too far and the Cabinet would dissociate itself from his actions. Rubens was deeply disturbed, and asked the King for written confirmation. He obtained it, but it was couched in terms that were far too vague, and he had the impression that he could get no further. Though the King had welcomed him warmly, as had a few important people like Weston and Cottington, he had against him the pro-French party and the Venetian and Dutch ambassadors.

It seemed to him that his fight was lost before it had even begun; so he asked the Infanta for permission to return home, but without success. He was obliged to stay where he was. He was not in an easy position. When Chateauneuf, the French Ambassador, arrived in London, the French party began with renewed zeal to wreck the efforts of the Spanish delegate. Chateauneuf went so far as to propose a conquest of the Palatinate. There, facing each other like wild beasts at bay, were the representative of His Catholic Majesty and that of His Most Christian Majesty, each striving to win heretical England to his side! It is true that the King of France exterminated the Huguenots in his own country and gave financial support to the Dutch Protestants, while Philip IV, who would not come to an agreement with the States General because of their religion, granted subsidies to Soubise, the leader of the French Huguenots. that was politics. . . . Only the Infanta, who was sincere in her faith and austerely pious, was incapable of understanding these manoeuvres.

The French Ambassador threw all the weight of his allies into the balance — the Pope, the Venetian Republic, the Duke of Mantua and the Duke of Savoy. And behind him stood the most formidable figure of all, a tall thin man, with sharp, unhealthy features—Cardinal Richelieu. He was known to be the real ruler of France. He claimed that he 'watched while the King slept'— and this was scarcely a metaphor, since he spent a large part of his nights in work. He had brought the aristocracy low and conquered the Huguenots. He foiled without difficulty the plots and intrigues of his many enemies. He manipulated with consummate skill the man, at once weak, timid and brave, who reigned as King Louis XIII. His method was simple and he summed it up himself in the maxim: 'It is less imprudent to act like a king than to fail to talk like a subject.' Thus Richelieu served the King his master, but according to his own views. He aspired to muzzle Spain and diminish the power of the Emperor. He took up on his own account the cry of Henry IV: 'Destruction to the house of Austria!' At the beginning of his career he had been taken for a friend of Spain, and Bentivoglio had fallen into the trap. Richelieu had good reason to utter his famous aphorism: 'You must reach your goal as rowers do, with your back to it.' He fought against the Protestants at home, but allowed those abroad to be slaughtered in defence of his policies, thus reaping a double reward. He may have said that his greatest pleasure was to write poetry, but he worked for the greatness of France and his own glory, for he was ambitious and had a very high opinion of himself. He shrank from no means to gain his ends. He loved cats but despised men, and yet he understood men and knew how to use them. For the moment he needed England in order to carry through his plans, and he was ready to pay whatever price was wanted. He sent a second emissary to make fresh proposals, even more advantageous than the first. France, he said, was ready to make war on Spain. They would invade Italy and Burgundy, and the Dutch would attack the Spanish Netherlands. England need only contribute the support of her Navy, and would receive in return all that France was in a position to grant. The prospect was alluring.

Rubens had succeeded in persuading the King to send Cotting-ton to Madrid, but as soon as the news became known the pro-French party sought to prevent him going. Cottington, more-over, was in no hurry to leave, for he was afraid of failure and thought it best to handle the situation with caution. Meanwhile a note summarizing the English demands had been despatched to Spain; the English required that a Spanish plenipotentiary should be sent to England in return for the sending of their own ambassador. Rubens insisted that a solution should be reached as soon as possible. But the usual Spanish dilatoriness had to be reckoned with. At last the nomination of Don Carlos Coloma brought him a little relief; but it was only momentary, for the absence of any reply to the English note, together with the fact that the French were bidding higher and higher, made his situation more and more difficult. These delays, compromis-ing as they did a cause so dear to his heart, infuriated him. He longed to return home. Not that he wished to complain about his stay in England; 'From every point of view', he wrote, 'I am treated well, and with great honour; in fact more respect is paid to me than I really deserve, but I cannot consider staying here longer than I am needed in the King's service. The state of my personal affairs makes it impossible.' This was true.

The Court was an extremely pleasant one. Queen Henrietta Maria was by inclination a patron of dramatists and artists. Sometimes she even took part in pastoral plays at Somerset House with the Court ladies. Despite the violent attacks of the Puritans, many people remained attached to the theatre, and though Shakespeare was dead, Chapman, Fletcher, Ben Jonson, Massinger and Ford were still alive.

In this country, with its inclement weather, Rubens discovered magnificent collections of pictures, and not only in the King's palace and that of the late Duke of Buckingham. His client, the Earl of Arundel, possessed works by Holbein, Raphael, Leonardo da Vinci, Titian, Veronese and a number of German and Flemish Old Masters. His collection of classical marbles was unique. He had introduced into England the use of bricks for building, which was a great step forward for a town like London, built almost entirely of brick, whose population was increasing by leaps and bounds; and not content with that, he had discovered the man who was to free his country from the fetters of Gothic architecture. This was Inigo Jones, the architect of Whitehall and of many other buildings in the Italian idiom. Rubens, who ten years earlier had painted a fine portrait of the Arundel family, now painted another of the Earl by himself, in armour. This warlike portrait called to mind the fact that this powerful patron of the arts was also Earl Marshal of England.

Rubens made the acquaintance of several scholars and amateurs of the arts, including Sir Robert Bruce Cotton and secretary Boswell. He appeared less enthusiastic about Cornelis van Drebbel, the Dutch scholar who invented a microscope and a thermometer, for he gave as his opinion that 'his genius is like those things of which Machiavelli speaks, which appear much larger seen from a distance and in the light of their reputation than they do close at hand'.

On the other hand Rubens did not hesitate to condemn one of England's finest sons, the famous jurist and historian John Selden, who had recently been imprisoned by order of the King. There was nothing surprising in this; Rubens took the King's part in all circumstances. This arrogant, frivolous, headstrong Prince had one quality to endear him to a painter; he loved painting in general and that of his Flemish guest in particular. What artist could show disapproval of the policy of such a monarch?

Rubens received other marks of respect; the University of Cambridge conferred on him the degree of Master of Arts on the occasion of a visit. But all this did not stop him from writing to Gevartius: 'I am longing to come home although I am sorry to return in such painful circumstances.'

Don Carlos Coloma was still keeping the English waiting, and their annoyance, skilfully fanned by the French Ambassador, reached its peak. Weston went so far as to declare negotiations broken off, and wished to recall Cottington. Rubens was very worried, and complained to the Infanta: 'I consider this delay, as things are at present, so deplorable that I curse the hour in which I set foot in this kingdom. Please God that whatever happens I may leave it safely.'

At last Don Carlos Coloma arrived, and Rubens wrote at once to Olivarez: 'I am putting my affairs in order and preparing to return home. .... I really cannot wait any longer without great detriment to my personal affairs; a long absence of eighteen months has put them in jeopardy, and only my presence in Antwerp can set them right.' Might he perhaps have had wind of the successes enjoyed by Van Dyck during his absence?

His former collaborator had returned from Italy, basking in a most flattering reputation, and had been back in Antwerp for two years, producing portraits in rapid succession. His art had a charm and grace unknown to the Flemish painters. His portraits had both distinction and refinement; they were less elaborate than those of Rubens but more penetrating, flattering the model without falsifying and without recourse to superficial artifice. Van Dyck excelled in deep blacks and silvery greys which brought out the creamy smoothness of the skin, and with delicate flattery he gave the middle-class ladies of Antwerp an air of nobility very like that of a Genoese aristocrat. He also painted very high-born ladies like the Duchess of Arenberg and the Duchess of Cray, and a large number of male portraits: ecclesiastics like Bishop Malderus and the Jesuit Schribani; scholars and notables—Woverius, Puteanus, Alexander della Faille; artists—Vorsterman, Paul Pontius, the two Petrus de Jode—father and son—Karel van Mallery, Kasper de Crayer—too many to count. His religious paintings, though still rather insipid and conventional, were none the less highly thought of. His work, like his person, had an irresistible charm. 'Il pittore cavalleresco' was in fact a dashing cavalier with an almost feminine beauty despite his fair moustache and beard. He was as elegant as any aristocrat. It was hardly surprising that he was lionized. Even the austere Infanta, who now wore only a nun's habit, had tried to attach him to her household by offering him an annual pension of 250 florins.

If Rubens suspected all this, it was understandable that he should wish to return home. His work in England was over, and he himself summed it up: 'It was no light task to keep an even keel and to undertake my mission with the feeble resources that remained to me, and at the very moment when the plan for which I chiefly came was coming to nothing.' And he hoped to receive 'if no thanks, at least my pardon'. Madrid had already expressed its satisfaction with him on several occasions. Only once did Olivarez appear displeased. Nevertheless, the painter-diplomat had always acted for the best. Don Carlos Coloma kept him for several more weeks, but at the beginning of March Rubens left London. When he went to the Palace of Whitehall to say farewell, Charles I gave him a sword, a ring, a gold chain and a hatband, and as a crowning favour knighted him. As the Venetian Ambassador wrote, it would have been impossible to honour a minister more.

At the end of March, Rubens embarked at Dover. He stopped at Dunkirk, Brussels, where he gave a report on his mission to the Infanta, then Antwerp.

The Cardinal Infante Don Fernando at the Battle of Nordlingen by P. P. Rubens.
do, Madrid—Photo Mas)

13. Helen Fourment by P. P. Rubens. (Pinakothek, Munich—Photo Hanfstaen Giraudon)

XII

THE TRIUMPHAL YEAR

1630

Rubens was home again in a blaze of new glory. He had played
on the great chess-board of Europe, and his compatriots, reduced
to political dependence, looked with admiration on the man who,
despite his origins, had been able to change the course of destiny
and treat on equal terms with kings and ministers. A mere spectator always responds more easily to prowess as such than he
does to the deeper implications of the game. He knows nothing
of the defeats, the bitterness, the trials and anxieties which are
the price every public figure must pay. He sees only the brilliant,
almost legendary side; the hero whose voice rises above the
howling of the masses, who tramples them like the dust beneath
his feet. Peter Paul knew what all this meant; would be now be
happy? He was back in his magnificent home, with his studio,
his collaborators and his commissions. His friends had received
him with open arms, and the Regent had expressed her satisfaction. Thanks to his efforts, an English ambassador was even now
sailing towards Spain to conclude the treaty which his enemies
had wished to prevent at all costs. He had pitted his wits against
the formidable Richelieu, and the game still hung in the balance.
The English had been grateful for his inflexibility of mind. He
was an envoy of Spain who had won the esteem of his masters
and the sympathy of his adversaries. And yet, deep down, what
did he really think?

He was not a man to confide easily. His politeness was great
and his courtesy exquisite; charming masks, meant to deceive.
His air of detachment and his scientific preoccupations bore
witness to the serenity of his mind. Anything more can only be
guesswork, or perhaps a matter of comparing the opinions he

threw out as he wrote. But none of his correspondents was in a position to juxtapose his letters. His French friends, Peiresc and Dupuy, may have thought in all good faith that he disliked the English, but Gerbier would have been of a quite different opinion; the Infanta was convinced of his loyalist sentiments, in which she was not mistaken; Olivarez did not doubt his devotion to Spain, and, taken all in all, he was not mistaken either. The Dutch, to whom he regularly referred as enemies, had no reason to suspect his feelings towards them. Over and over again he let it be understood that he hated France, and we can hardly discount his outbursts against the policies of Madrid. It is easy to accuse him of double-dealing, and perhaps with truth, though there are two sides to the question. However contradictory they may appear, these opinions were almost always sincere. Then, his detractors may say, he must have been fickle. But even that is not quite true. He was simply himself.

His service to one party was no reason for him to wear blinkers. Of course without certain precautions the whole thing would have been impossible. If he wished to maintain his status he could hardly tell the all-powerful Olivarez what he thought of his policy; nor could he give Gerbier his candid opinion on Buckingham if he wanted to keep his credit with that very influential man. But his correspondent was a spectator, not an actor, and there was no point in mincing words. And so he spoke ill of the English, the French, the Spaniards and the Dutch in turn, because he quite sincerely thought it, and because one of the chief characteristics of the true politician is to believe in his own ideas and methods and hate other people's, even those of his own followers. The will to power has precedence over every other consideration, and if the politician gladly accepts the outward signs of fortune and dignity, it is because they impress the vulgar and the mediocre—which means the vast majority of mankind. It is, in short, another road leading to the same goal—power. As for those who let themselves be seduced by the trappings of glory, they are not true politicians. A true politician never confuses the end with the means.

The really great believe only in themselves, and compel attention quite naturally, always and everywhere they go. But despite this, it is not always easy to move out of one's class. The world has a passion for labelling everyone, and a painter who wishes to make his mark in politics is making too clean a break with tradition. The King of Spain was not the only one to ask: why this painter? There were also all those for whom politics were not a vocation but a profession. They were shocked by this intrusion which upset the established order of things and which they considered contrary to their professional interests. So the painter-diplomat had to use craft to make a niche for himself, then again to win even a minor role, and again to keep it. He had to cope with all the Jacks-in-office, addressing them with feigned humility when their delays irritated him and their ill-will was obvious. A clear-sighted man cannot let himself be defeated by the blindness of others. And every true politician thinks himself clear-sighted. For that reason, despite the prestige surrounding the painter-diplomat on his return from his missions, we can reasonably ask whether he really was pleased with himself.

He appears to have answered that question the day before he left London, when, to everyone's surprise, he called on the Ambassador for the United Provinces. Peace was not yet made between England and Spain, and he was already sounding the representative of the States-General on the possibility of a truce between Spain and Holland. Unbridled ambition, his enemies might have said—or a wish to appear important. But the truth, his truth, was probably simpler. He was not really satisfied with the diplomats whose colleague he had become. He believed only in his own methods. If anything was to be achieved, it was necessary to act. He himself possessed this gift for action; it was an insatiable need, which no attainment or reward could assuage. He was one of those born conquerors whose victories become dust as soon as they are won, and who live only for the future, which is for them the greatest wonder of all.

That is why he ventured to take this surprising step, and in taking it, clearly exceeded his powers. The Dutch diplomat was bewildered, the English were scandalized, and Heaven knew what the Spaniards might say. Rubens did not care. The gallant courtier lifted his mask, forgot foreign princes and thought only of his own country, which was suffering so atrociously. It was for his fatherland that he dreamed of peace . . . dreamed, moreover, in vain.

In June he took the oath as private secretary to the King, and obtained a promise that the post should pass to his eldest son if he died or resigned. He renewed contact with his old friends in France. He took up his brush again, working, among other things, on the sketches for the gallery in honour of Henry IV, whom he called, with justice, the Great, but he complained that after he had received the measurements they had then been decreased. He therefore asked the Abbé de Saint-Ambroise not to cut off the head of the King seated in his triumphal chariot, but to give him grace of half a foot. He still kept closely in touch with politics. When he heard of the sack of Mantua by the Austrians, he wrote: 'I am very grieved at it, for I served the house of Gonzaga for several years in my youth, and my stay in that country was very happy.' Distance and age can modify youthful opinions. The death of Spinola did not surprise him. He knew that in Madrid the Marquis had been the victim of some stubborn intrigues in which the Abbé Scaglia had taken a large part. The brilliant military leader, tired of life, had simply lost the will to go on living, and died after his duties had been handed over to the Marquis of Santa Cruz. Rubens ends: 'According to what is being written on all sides, he has ended this war with his life; it is a mark of the greatness of his destiny and the power of his genius. In him I have lost one of the greatest friends and patrons I had in the world, as a hundred of his letters bear witness.' He might have added that Spain had lost one of her best servants, but what would that have mattered to Olivarez? Rubens carefully refrained from reflections of this kind. He was too involved in the game being played out in Madrid, which, despite all setbacks, finally came to an end; England and Spain signed a treaty. This peace was in some measure his work, whatever certain people might say; and this was a great feat in a Europe tortured by continual wars.

'Labore et Constantia', said Plantin—by work and perseverance much can be achieved. A startling difference in temperaments appeared in the fact that whereas Spinola died in harness at fifty-nine, Rubens, at fifty-three, was considering marrying again. And why not? He was a handsome man with a fine presence, and, moreover, he was rich and famous. Gout, it is true, held him prisoner from time to time, but such small worries seemed not to weigh heavily on him; they served merely to remind him of his human condition, for a man of his stature might well think himself immortal. He may occasionally have extolled the mortification of the flesh, but only as a virtuous precept to round off a letter. A tinge of stoicism was considered a good thing by the high-minded philosophers of the day; but there was no law against preferring sensual pleasure. Whom, then, should he choose?

He could aim high. He had, in fact, been advised to choose a Court lady. But it was not servility that made him a courtier; far from it, it was his love for domination—he was a born leader, and needed to command. He was too recent a recruit to the ranks of diplomacy to be able to play a leading part in public affairs. As he well knew, he was forced to give precedence to better-born people who were not worthy of it. His acquiescence in these deceits was due only to his passion for the game; his longing to play even a minor part came before any other consideration. Marriage was quite a different matter. He had always been the master in his own house, ruling his family as well as his collaborators and pupils. This sovereignty, which no one in Antwerp would have dreamed of disputing, he may perhaps have owed to his genial nature, his intelligence and his charming manners, but he was too clear-thinking not to realize that these were mere accessories, and that really he owed everything to his art. He scarcely spoke of it, but that was because it was enough for him to paint. He painted as others breathed or dreamed. He knew that in the eyes of those enchantment-loving children that all men are at heart, he was a magician; and he intended to remain so.

What did he want with a woman who might perhaps blush to see him take up his brushes? He could play the courtier without losing his self-respect, simply because he possessed a magic way of escape; was he likely to risk it by an ill-judged excursion into matrimony? Indeed not. He wanted no Court ladies. Not that he was afraid to take risks; far from it, as he was soon to prove. He knew that by marrying a girl of sixteen he would provoke laughter and malicious gossip. He did not care, probably realizing that the undertaking was by no means beyond him. That was the essential thing. It mattered little what others said; his own decision was what counted. Sixteen was his son Albert's age. Well—there would be one more child in the great house, a child who at the same time would be his wife. The younger she was, the less of a burden she would be to him, and the more freedom he would have, to lead in his own way the team he aspired to form.

Man is a reasonable animal, and likes to justify his actions. He strives to explain the unexplainable because he loves to put others off the true scent, and even deliberately deceive himself. And, clearly, he does this whenever his secret wish is in conflict with cold reason. When a man of fifty marries a child of sixteen, he can give plenty of reasons to himself and others, but there is only one true one, and that he will not mention: it is because he is a prey to the demon of sensuality, because passion throbs in his blood, and because he is haunted by an almost incestuous desire for a child he has seen growing up and who could have been his daughter.

Her name was Helen Fourment. Her parents were rich burghers with whom he had been friendly for many years; Isabella Brant's sister Clara was the wife of Helen's brother Daniel. The father of the family, also called Daniel, had no less than eleven children of whom Helen was the youngest. Another of his daughters, Susanna, had sat for Rubens many times; she was the widow of Raymond del Monte, and had remarried with Arnold Lunden. Rubens had painted several portraits of this slender woman with great mournful eyes and a petulant mouth. One of them, in which she is wearing a fur hat, is rightly considered one of the best. He had rarely been so finely inspired as in this graceful painting, to which he seems to have brought a special quality of tenderness. That may well have been why scandalmongers claimed that this woman was the painter's mistress.

Helen was very like Susanna, but younger and fair-haired. Her features were less fine, but that was natural at her age. At sixteen the features are still unformed; but she had, if such a thing were possible, a skin even whiter than that of her elder sister. Such freshness, such eternal youth! It was a wonderful privilege to possess, in flesh and blood, the woman of whom he had dreamed, and whom he had painted, all his life. For he had painted Helen, with the gleaming whiteness of her pink-tipped breasts, the milky plumpness of her flesh, and the dazzling transparency of her skin, before she was even born! By a miracle, this voluptuous Flemish girl resembled the woman of his dreams. She was only a child, and possibly not even an intelligent one, but it still did not matter. He had enough brain to judge the vanity of his triumphs. For himself and his kingdom, all he needed was a warm, voluptuous body, young and yielding. He could now grow old, die even, he was in the lead and had nothing to fear; to the end of his days the grace and radiance of youth would light up his life. And by dint of constantly gazing on youth as a living reality, he would at last believe in his own youth, which meant immortality. Peter Paul had known many triumphs, but that of December 6, 1630, was probably the greatest.

The great epic of female beauty, the first verses of which he had shaped long ago, could now reach its glorious climax. He was not a lover jealous of his treasure. It was not enough for him to drink in the loveliness of this body which to him was the most beautiful in the world. He wanted the whole world to share his joy. With ever-renewed delight he traced with his brush the image of his lovely Helen. He loved to dress this beautiful clear-eyed child in the richest adornments he could find, but all this was simply a game. Velvet and silk, brocade and feathers, furs and jewels were all mere artifices, which, as experience had taught him, would lend greater enchantment to the revelation of her body in all its triumphant nakedness. Nothing of her beauty is hidden. He never wearied of admiring her, and she, surprised and delighted, let him. She was for him the Spirit of Youth; she was his Goddess, and as a goddess he offered her to the world. In the artist's imagination she lent her form and her face to every goddess on Olympus, but there was one who took her form more often than the others — Venus, the immortal Goddess of Love. As long as she remained Helen, Rubens was held back by one last scruple, and carefully concealed a little of her charms; but once she became Venus he freed her from all restraint. Venus unveiled was triumphant; and no painter ever glorified the body of a woman—of all women—as he did then.

XIII

THE REVERSE OF THE COIN

1630–1633

On December 6th the bells of St James rang out to celebrate the wedding of Peter Paul Rubens and his young bride. A few days later, King Charles I signed the document conferring on the painter the title of Knight of the Golden Spur. In order to hold this title in Flanders Rubens needed the authorization of the King of Spain, and he hastened to ask for it; he may have been in love, but he did not forget the world. Meanwhile Coloma had left London, and the post of ambassador was thus vacant. Rubens was considered; however the idea of appointing someone who 'practised an art and lived on the product of his work' appeared impossible, and the court at Madrid nominated Juan de Necolalde. As the latter could not take up his duties immediately, the Infanta chose an Englishman as substitute. This arrangement did not please Philip IV, who thought the painter the obvious choice for the interim period: 'Rubens is greatly respected at the English court', he wrote, 'and competent to negotiate on all matters, thanks to the prudence with which he approaches them.' Though the office itself was denied to him, Rubens was thus considered a suitable stop-gap. He objected to this secondary role, though he took care not to say so. On the contrary, he accepted in principle and agreed to a few days' absence. In fact he concentrated all his diplomatic skill on finding excuses for delay.

We might think that since Rubens had been married only a few short months before, he was not anxious to go off on his travels again, or perhaps that he was not interested in political matters—an impression he tried hard to give. Nothing could have been further from the truth. His refusal to leave stemmed from wounded pride. He was still in favour at Brussels, and at the first opportunity his besetting weakness caught up with him again. Events in France gave him a pretext to enter the lists once more. The cold war, carried on for several years between Marie de Medici and her former protégé Cardinal Richelieu, had just entered an active phase. Louis XIII had finally decided in favour of his powerful minister, and the Queen Mother had been packed off to Compiègne. The news caused a sensation.

Rubens was very worried. He did, it is true, congratulate himself, in a letter to Pierre Dupuy, on having broken off his work for the Henry IV gallery as a result of an argument about measurements, 'for I consider all that I have done up to now as so much waste of time'. He contented himself with a vague allusion: 'On the whole, all courts are subject to the hazards of fortune, and the French court more than others. But it is difficult to have a clear view of events seen at a distance, so I will say nothing rather than judge lightly.'

Soon things began to get serious. With the help of her son Gaston d'Orléans and the Duke of Lorraine, Marie de Medici fled from Compiègne to La Capelle which she believed to be on her side. She had reckoned without Richelieu who always knew everything, and she found the doors closed in her face. Flight to a foreign country was all that was left to her. When the Duke of Lorraine sent an equerry to the Infanta to ask for hospitality for the Queen Mother, Rubens was given the task of parleying with him. Without awaiting the result of these negotiations, the Queen Mother arrived in the Netherlands. The Infanta at once delegated the Marquis d'Aytona to welcome her in the name of the King of Spain, and Rubens accompanied the Ambassador. Aytona invited Marie de Medici to come to Mons; she agreed, and her entry into the town took place to the sound of drums, trumpets, musketry and bells.

Madrid was far from looking kindly on this event. Olivarez thought that Marie should be asked to continue her journey as far as Aachen. The Infanta replied that she had been taken by surprise and had not been able to wait for an answer from Madrid. The Spanish government finally gave in, and the Infanta was able to meet the fugitive Queen. It was so touching an encounter that for a moment they forgot protocol and fell into each other's arms.

Rubens' imagination took fire. He wrote from Mons a long letter to Olivarez beginning with attacks on Richelieu: 'The Queen Mother has in fact come to throw herself into the Infanta's arms, fleeing from the violence of Cardinal Richelieu, that man who was her creature, whom she not only dragged out of the mud but to whom she gave the high office which enables him to thunder against her and besmirch her with his ingratitude'. Carried away by his enthusiasm, he exclaimed: 'We have before our eyes a flagrant example of the evil that may be done by a favourite who is moved more by personal ambition than by the welfare of his country and the service of his King, and of the way in which a virtuous prince, badly advised, can allow himself to violate the obligations of nature towards his family and his own mother.'

Realizing that he could kill two birds with one stone, he retreated gracefully: 'On the other hand — as all things are happily balanced by their opposites—the world sees in Your Excellency's case the support and help which a monarchy like ours can receive from an intelligent and prudent minister, whose only aim is the glory of his King.' There follows a piece of well-meant but not entirely practical advice: 'The more Your Excellency repels every advance and every suggestion of collusion with Cardinal Richelieu, the more effectively you will avoid the infamous reputation and popular hatred which generally attach to the favourites of kings, and the more you will justify and confirm on all sides the high opinion everyone has of your sincerity and of the excellence of your methods of government.'

Thereupon he expounds his plan, beginning with a precaution: 'I have never urged war, as Your Excellency can testify, but have always tried to make peace whenever I could.' Having said this, he feels in a better position to make an exception. He urgently presses Olivarez to subsidize Gaston d'Orléans, whose noble supporters he lists with great satisfaction. Once more, it seems, 'Monsieur' is waiting to raise the banner of rebellion, and the opportunity is too good to let slip. Rubens anticipates possible objections: 'It may be that after having made use of our grant, Monsieur will not appear overwhelmingly grateful for it, but we can be sure that a large number of Frenchmen will fall in these civil conflicts, and in this way that cruel nation will be weakened. Whichever of the two parties wins, we shall in any case have one enemy less.'

And as if this Machiavellian approach were not enough, he even has a solution to be used in case of failure: 'Moreover, even if we had to pay fresh subsidies, I consider that the King's money could not be put to better use than keeping civil war going in France, for our own better safety.' Finally there comes a touch of irony, perhaps unintentional: 'I therefore beg Your Excellency to free the proud Spanish nation from the old traditional reproach with which she is generally — and so wrongly — insulted, that she can never take a resolution, nor grasp opportunities as they occur, but that after infinite deliberations she sends *post bellum auxilium*. This cannot be reconciled with Your Excellency's most notable virtue, which is speed.' And probably as a crowning touch to so magnificent an effort, he ends by telling Olivarez, for the first time, that he 'kisses his feet with all his heart'.

Despite all this flattery, Rubens achieved nothing. Olivarez considered that the painter's letter was full of absurdities and Italian verbosity, but he acknowledged his good intentions. No one at Madrid would have dreamed of quarrelling with France in honour of the Queen Mother and the turbulent Gaston d'Orléans. So far from supporting the rebels, Spain offered to mediate between the two parties. Meanwhile the Queen Mother continued her journey. In Brussels she was welcomed by musketry salvos. In the Grand Place, 'magnificently adorned and illuminated, the Town Hall being hung with red cloth fringed with green', she was addressed by the Pensionary of the town. The next day she visited the Jesuit convent 'where she saw entertainments of all kinds—ballet, music, fireworks, fountains, and fights between wild beasts'.

At the beginning of September Marie de Medici and the Infanta went to Antwerp. The town was to be illuminated. The two princesses were present at the Kermesse procession, postponed for their especial benefit, and the Jesuits put on a tragedy for them. They went to see Rubens in his house on the Wapper, and saw also Van Dyck, who took advantage of a brief visit to his native town to paint a superb portrait of the Queen Mother. Last of all they went to 'the fine Plantin printing-house, the fame of which Balthasar Moretus maintains and increases through his own merits'. This house published the account of the celebrations organized throughout the country in honour of Marie de Medici, written, somewhat bombastically, by one of her household, De la Serre, who called himself 'historiographer of France'.

This paid employee was naturally a flatterer of the first water. Antwerp delighted him: 'Speaking of the goodness and charm of its inhabitants, the long experience which I and many others have had of them makes me wish I could leave the public a whole volume about them instead of these few lines. But as time and my limited leisure make this impossible, I will only say, openly and emphatically, that these people are the most charitable to strangers, the most zealous in their religion, and the most obedient to their Prince, of any that I have ever seen.'

He was no less friendly towards 'Monsieur Rubens', but at the same time he sang the praises of Van Dyck in a way that clearly showed the preferences of Marie de Medici and her suite:

'The Queen was curious to see all the rich and beautiful paintings in Monsieur Rubens' house. He is a man whose art, though rare and wonderful, is the least of his qualities; his judgment on matters of state and his political sense are so far above his condition that the works of his wisdom are as admirable as those of his brush. Her Majesty took great pleasure in contemplating the vivid wonder of his paintings, the colours of which seem to have been laid on by some enchanted hand; one never tires of admiring their beauty and perfection.

'But the truth demands that I say openly that Monsieur Van Dyck has borne away the prize against all the greatest painters who have dared, with too bold a hand, to attempt the Queen's likeness; for in truth no art could ever represent Her Majesty enthroned so perfectly as in the new portrait he has painted. It is said that Apelles took the finest features of different faces in order to portray one perfectly beautiful one under the name of Helen; but today the greater talent of this painter shows, in this single portrait of the Queen, all the beauty in the world, taking nothing away from nature, and adding only that touch of genius which makes all adore his art. Her Majesty did him the honour of visiting him, where she saw in his studio the Titian collection containing all the masterpieces of that great master. But I dare to maintain, without flattery, that Monsieur Van Dyck will very soon share with him the glory of his fame, for if that excellent painter was the ornament of his age, this one is the wonder of his.'

For almost two months the two princesses remained in Antwerp. They were present at the sailing of the flotilla which was about to attempt a surprise attack on the island of Over-flakkee in Zeeland—a bold plan, which was intended to give the Spaniards a base at the point where Zeeland joined Holland. The flotilla, commanded by Count John of Nassau—a cousin of the Prince of Orange who had changed sides as a result of a love-affair—and by the Prince of Barbançon, consisted of about forty ships carrying nearly six thousand soldiers. Despite the blessing of the Papal Nuncio, the expedition ended in disaster; the Spanish flotilla was attacked by the fleet of Marinus de Hollare and sunk or dispersed in a few moments leaving four thousand prisoners in the hands of the enemy. Rubens was therefore sent to the Hague before the end of the year to confer with the Prince of Orange beneath a veil of secrecy. This mission, 'although very secret, soon became public and displeased many people who knew what was going on', as the French Ambassador remarked. And his efforts in any case were in vain.

On account of either discouragement or fatigue, Rubens was, in April 1632, showing some slight inclination to give up politics. He had returned to Antwerp, where he was painting and attending to his affairs. His friend Gerbier had become the King of England's *chargé d'affaires* in Brussels, where, it appears, he had considerable difficulties with the entourage of 'Monsieur'. Rubens comforted him: 'I am sorry to hear that the French are causing trouble for Your Excellency with Her Highness and her ministers. However, Your Excellency should not be unduly alarmed; you depend only on your King. But it can certainly make your relations with them very painful!'

He congratulated himself on being safe from similar troubles: 'I retired in time, and never in my life have I regretted a decision so little.' But it does not seem to have been a very firm resolution. It only needed an officer of the Duc de Bouillon to go and see him secretly one month later, and Rubens was back in the field. Bouillon was trying to drag 'Monsieur' into a new venture and was asking the Infanta for guarantees; he wanted her to promise 'in her own name, and in the name of the King of Spain, not only to protect him from the King of France or anyone else who might attack him' but also to ensure 'that Monsieur would be in a position to keep his word', for the Duke did not seem to be very sure of his ally. Before taking the offensive, he wanted to be able to recall his brother the Viscount of Turenne, who was at the French court and ran the risk of being thrown into the Bastille if he did not get away before hostilities began. Rubens was possibly seeking to appear important, as he often did, when he let it be understood that he was the central figure of the affair: 'Although his delegate is going to Brussels to negotiate with the French envoys, the Duke's decision will depend on what I have to tell him on behalf of Your Highness.' The affair came to nothing, as the court at Brussels had more serious worries to deal with.

For eleven years, since the end of the Truce, a state of war had existed between Spain and the United Provinces, causing great suffering to the Spanish Netherlands. Trade was ruined, industry was falling into decay, and confusion was general. Campaign had followed campaign, with varying fortunes, but always to the detriment of the wretched population. Discontentment had reached its height. The Brussels government, notwithstanding all this, continued its narrowly Spanish policy. Everything that might work against this policy was suppressed; for example the account published by Cardinal Bentivoglio of his nunciature in Brussels was confiscated in 1629 because it contained passages that were detrimental to the royal power. And yet the chief instrument of this policy, Cardinal de la Cueva, had left under general censure, as Cardinal Granvelle had left earlier in similar circumstances.

By sea, the Dutch admirals, led by Piet Hein, terrorized the Spanish fleet, and though Piet Hein died in battle, his successors were no less intrepid.

On land, Prince Maurice had been replaced by his half-brother

Frederick Henry, son of William the Silent and Louise de Coligny, a gay, charming Prince and as good a general as his glorious elder brother. Within a few years he had taken Oldenzaal, Grol, Bois-le-Duc, Venloo, Straelen, Sittard and Ruremonde, and he had just laid seige to Maestricht, one of the strongest Spanish fortresses and an important strategic point. That was not all. Spinola's successor at the head of the royal troops, Count Henry de Bergh—of whom Van Dyck painted a masterly portrait—had just gone over to the enemy. Furious at being replaced by the Marquis of Santa Cruz, he invited the Belgians to 'follow the laudable example of their ancestors and free themselves from the heavy and intolerable yoke of Spain'. It must be added for truth's sake that his anger had received suitable monetary encouragements.

The Infanta, alarmed, decided to make fresh efforts for peace. She sent Rubens to Liége to meet a delegation from the United Provinces. It was useless. The Dutch were intoxicated with success, and completely uncompromising. Rubens returned to Brussels to report that his mission had failed.

The situation was critical. Conspiracy was rife among the nobility, and feelings were running high. In an attempt to restore calm, the Infanta convoked the States-General which had not met for thirty-two years. The will of Spain had had only one implacable aim: to annihilate all liberty and suppress all local privileges. The position had grown even worse since Albert's death. Behind and even above the Infanta there had been for years the grim and dominant figure of Cardinal de la Cueva, the Spanish Ambassador. This arrogant, unscrupulous man had had to be recalled; Aytona, who took his place, was more understanding, but he too was Spanish and the natives still had no hand in the running of their own country.

From the very first sitting the States-General demanded direct contact with Holland, and in this they were successful. At the beginning of December a conference opened in the Hague. But the court in Brussels allowed these direct negotiations only as a sop to troubled minds. It was merely a superficial concession. In fact it had no intention of giving up any of its prerogatives, and in any case Madrid would not have allowed it. It was therefore important that a confidential agent should be sent to follow the negotiations and act according to the views of the Court; this ambiguous role fell to Rubens. The Duke of Aerschot must somehow have had wind of the matter, though how remains a mystery. In any case that proud gentleman lost no time in telling the delegates, who were naturally annoyed. A deputation was sent to express their disapproval to the Infanta, who did her best to reassure them, saying that Rubens was not to interfere in the negotiations, but would simply be at their service when they 'needed to see the papers relating to his negotiation of the truce'.

When the delegates returning to the Hague stayed for twenty-four hours in Antwerp, Rubens wrote to the Duke of Aerschot to justify his actions: 'I never had any orders from my superiors but to serve Your Excellency in every way in the conduct of this affair, which is so necessary for the service of the King and the preservation of our country that I should consider anyone unfit to live who, for his private interests, retarded it in the smallest degree.' To this the Duke of Aerschot replied in an insolent letter: 'I might well have refrained from doing you the honour of answering you, considering how grossly you have failed in your duty by not coming to see me in person, instead of having the impertinence to write me this letter, which is only proper between persons of equal station.' If he replied at all it was only because the opportunity to humiliate the painter was too good to miss: 'All I can say is that I shall be greatly obliged if you will learn from henceforth how persons of your station should write to persons of mine.' And to complete his revenge, the Duke distributed copies of the letters exchanged. It caused a sensation in both camps. The delegates were delighted; they felt that Rubens was encroaching on their preserves, and perhaps they feared him, for as Boswell, the English Ambassador at the Hague, said, he had 'more spirit than any of them'.

Aerschot's arrogance may have been odious, but the delegates' protests were fully justified. The Infanta and her advisers, yielding to a movement of national patriotism, had allowed them to make contact with Holland. The delegates had been full of hope, and really believed they could see 'the dawn of peace and tranquillity after the long dark night of cruel war'. They had every reason to feel that Rubens' intervention was a sign that they were not trusted. They had been the playthings of the Spaniards for too long to tolerate the interference of an agent of Spain at the precise moment when they had at last—or so they believed—the opportunity to guide the fortunes of their country themselves. And Rubens was, in fact, acting decisively on the side of Spain against the representatives of his own country. He had asked the Prince of Orange for a passport so that he could follow their proceedings, and probably frustrate them when the opportunity presented itself. The upsurge of ardour which fired these representatives of the clergy and nobility found no answering glow in him. One sign from the Infanta would have been enough for him to throw all his weight behind the policy dictated by Madrid. The vigilance of Aerschot triumphed, and Rubens was forbidden to go to the Hague. The delegates, said the Duke, had nothing to do with painters; and, full of hope, they set to work.

Strongly backed by France, the representatives of the United Provinces laid down conditions which were unacceptable to Spain. The deputies of the States-General were not unduly disturbed; their goodwill was obviously greater than their political sense. They were ready for any kind of concessions if the affair could only be brought to a successful conclusion, and they deluded themselves with the hope that Philip IV would follow them. Not only were they not taken seriously at Madrid, but an appalling deception was practised against them. The King deprived the Infanta of the full powers to act on his behalf which had been granted to her, so that the deputies were uttering empty words, with no mandate behind them. And Brussels was conniving at what Madrid had done, since the Infanta went on giving them instructions as though nothing had changed. Months went by and the talks dragged on. At last, faced with the combined ill-will of the Hague and Madrid, the representatives of the States-General bowed to facts and considered returning home. The state of mind of the Brussels government was clearly shown in an incident of the time: when the humanist scholar Erycius Puteanus dared to publish his *Belli et pacis statera* concluding in favour of peace, a violent attack called *Antiputeanus* was immediately published on official instructions, as a measure against too pacifist a doctrine. On December 1, 1633, the Infanta Isabella died at the age of sixty-seven, and

Rubens lost his great protectress, whose confidential agent he had been for years. The daughter of Philip II was perhaps not very intelligent, but she was always well-meaning. As sovereign, and then as regent, she had realized that only peace could save the unhappy country in her charge. She had protected it from Castilian arrogance as best she could, encouraged in the task by her most faithful advisers, with Spinola first among them. This brilliant soldier, despite the harsh instructions given him by Philip III, was the chief prop of the Court in Brussels. Madrid had only one thought: to crush the independence of the Spanish Netherlands. Because his ideas were too liberal, Spinola had to step down in favour of the Cardinal de la Cueva. The Infanta dared to stand up to the Cardinal and eventually had him recalled; this may have seemed like a victory to her, but in the long run she gained nothing. La Cueva was replaced by Aytona, and even though the latter proved more liberal, nothing was really changed, because he was bound by instructions which remained completely inflexible. Thus, however good the Infanta's intentions may have been, she was never anything more than a tool of Madrid.

She died at a particularly critical moment. The country was at the end of its resources. The clergy were restless and the nobles on the verge of open revolt. And her death, like everything else, made no difference at all. Spain announced her intention of sending another regent, Don Ferdinand, the Cardinal Infante, the King's own brother. The King made some fine promises: 'We will give to our aforesaid countries the peace and contentment which they have hitherto enjoyed: it is our firm resolution to stake our life, together with the kingdoms and estates which God has put in our care, rather than fail to do justice to their cause.' There was, in fact, to be no change. Spain had more to do than to bother about the welfare of her subjects in the Netherlands. She had close ties with the court of Vienna, and had never given up the idea of conquering the United Provinces and breaking their alliance with France, since France was supporting the Swedes against the Emperor and threatening Spanish communications in Lorraine. Finally, since the death of Gustavus Adolphus the Habsburgs—Vienna and Madrid united —had been seized with new ardour. The moment was opportune to bring down the Protestant princes who had lost their glorious ally. It was a fine imbroglio.

Death brings back memories, but more precise than before; it prunes away unnecessary detail and places them in their context. As soon as the agitations of life are over, the dead person seems to become part of an almost permanent pattern. We see him better in relation to ourselves, and ourselves better in relation to him. Rubens had now taken an active part in the political life of this country for ten years. He had been the faithful servant of the Infanta and thus of the policies of Spain. Rubens had often judged the Spaniards harshly, but his wish to play a part had taken precedence in him of every other consideration, which was why he sided with Spain in the affair of the negotiations with Holland. The reason was simple : he was on the side of anyone who was willing to employ him. His compatriots were not willing; the fact that this commoner had negotiated in Holland, Spain, and England, and that his personal success had been remarkable, moved them not at all, so that despite his rise in the world he had not been able to play a decisive part. He had always had to bow before fools or nonentities whom an accident of birth had placed in the front rank. He called himself the humble servant of men who were not worthy to clean his brushes. In his letters he humbly kissed their hands or their feet, according to their importance. But a man who knows his own worth remains in his heart undaunted. Rubens had no illusions about kings and ministers; he knew they were only men, those strange mixtures of virtues and weaknesses. And he was certainly not free from human weaknesses himself. He had clung to his last abortive mission like a drowning man clinging to a straw, hoping to the last to play his part. His enemies claimed that he was driven by ambition or vanity. It was to be expected; people always judge their adversaries in a strangely superficial way. Not one of them seems to have realized that this passion for public affairs, so unswervingly followed, could be a deep irresistible need, and that many minor slips were inevitable, since anything would be preferable to the idea of leaving the field.

But then came wisdom. With any other man we might have said it came with age, and he was in fact nearing sixty. But was that a reason for giving up? He had lost his illusions, but that was all. He could scarcely give up when he had a young wife who was like a child to him, or think himself old when his great house rang with a constantly renewed chorus of babies' cries. In January 1631 there was Clara Joanna, and in July 1633, Frans. His eldest sons were already grown up. He had his friends, his books, his collections. He had his work, which never flagged for a moment. He had carried out a new series of tapestry cartoons, 'The Life of Achilles'. It was one of those commissions which only kings can permit themselves. They were unusual cartoons, too; instead of being painted *in tempera* according to tradition, they were wood panels painted in oils. Rubens, whose own particular stamp marked every branch of art he attempted, certainly intended to give a new lease of life to tapestry. But he was too much a painter, and too spirited to succeed in a craft which demanded a more severe style and a more analytical use of colour.

Rubens completed one large-scale composition which by its brilliance of colouring can be considered one of his most successful works. It was a great retable for the altar of the Brotherhood of Saint Ildefonso, a foundation of Archduke Albert, in the church of St James-on-Coudenberg in Brussels. On the central panel the Virgin is giving the Saint his priestly robes, the Archdukes appear with their patron saints on the volets, and, on the reverse of the volets, the Holy Family is shown under an apple tree. The painter had rarely been more finely inspired than in this set of five works, in a bold florid style yet free from the often chaotic turbulence which he loved so much. His vision had become more pleasing and his touch more ethereal.

In the same spirit he returned to one of his favourite themes: 'The Adoration of the Magi'. With the Divine Child as the centre, he loved to indulge his fantasy in the various exotic guises he lent to these legendary characters who came from the East bearing gifts, their only guide a star. Sometimes the scene took on a more intimate air, but more often it was the pretext for a magnificent setting, for the painter was attracted principally by the spectacular aspect of the episode. His verve was greatest when he could make play with gleaming silks, exotic physical types, princely gifts, and animals. For that reason the painting he did for the high altar of the Abbey of St Michael in Antwerp remains one of his greatest successes. However often he returned to the same theme, altering the emphasis and varying the effects, he never surpassed that masterpiece.

He painted himself with Helen in the garden of the house on the Wapper; and later that familiar setting became the background for scenes even more poetic. He evoked happy couples, and charming groups of men and women, richly dressed, who seemed to move in a world from which all cares were banished. It was the art of a happy man, and one who was generous with his happiness. It had been hard to stifle his passion for politics, and a born conqueror does not easily give up the struggle. But then came peace, and the discovery that there are joys less artificial than the thankless game of politics. He was a happy man, and though he had everything he could wish, he had no need to fear satiety, for he knew what he must do; he had one perfect way of escape—his enchanted brush.

XIV

THE AGE OF WISDOM

1634–1636

Despite the poverty of the times, Rubens' workshop was never idle. The great ones of the earth still showered their favours upon him, except that they found it hard to pay him. He was always busy with work of all kinds, from great paintings commissioned by princes to the illustrations which his friend Moretus entrusted to him. His assistants gravitated around him, and though their names might change, they all remained subject to the same discipline. The master made rapid sketches which they reproduced on a larger scale, according to the dimensions required, on the canvas or wooden panel. Like the leader of a campaign, Rubens supervised the work, corrected a detail or completed a figure. In large compositions he retouched especially the lower part, which was nearest the level of the eyes; the rest was left to his assistant. How else would he have found time to do all that was asked of him? He could not remain indifferent to such things as newly published books, new aspects of physics or the latest discoveries in Roman archaeology.

After the departure of Vorsterman who joined Van Dyck, Rubens engaged Paul Pontius, a pupil of Vorsterman who, though less powerful than his master, was able to reproduce all the subtleties of colour with considerable charm. For Rubens, this was the essential. He cared little that engraving was deviating perilously from tradition and that the craft was losing its purity in the quest for somewhat facile effects. He wanted faithful reproductions of his paintings; the implication that copperplate engraving had to be subjected to his needs and its independence curtailed did not worry him. At last he found suitable interpreters, the Bolswert brothers who came from

Holland. The elder, Boetius, was characterized by heavy hatching and strongly incised outlines. His effects of relief and light and shade were carried out firmly and accurately, and though his technique had a certain rigidity, Rubens worked to give it more flexibility, with some success. Schelderic, known as Schelte, excelled in subtle effects of gradation, and effortlessly combined grace with strength; his strength was more sensitive and softer than that of Boetius. His transcriptions of Rubens' landscapes in particular, placed him amongst the foremost interpreters of this branch of art. The two of them formed a brilliant team, ideally adapted to the master's views.

Besides these two virtuosi of the burin, Rubens employed a wood engraver, Christopher Jegher, a German who had become a citizen of Antwerp. Woodcuts, essentially more popular, were sold in fairs and markets. Rubens was not a man to despise any means by which his fame and prestige could be maintained. He was not satisfied with the minute but rather stilted work of the native wood-engravers, and intended to put his personal stamp on this craft as he had on so many others. Guided by Rubens, Christopher Jegher cast aside all the accepted ideas and produced woodcuts with a breadth of design unknown before him.

Once they had been printed, engravings whether copper or wood were simply merchandise which had to be sold. Within the country there were numerous outlets, but abroad a licence was indispensable. There were times when pirates had to be dealt with; Rubens had an engraver who copied his work summoned before the Parlement in Paris. His son Albert was already able to help him in this affair. In order to have his licence renewed in France he called upon his friend Peiresc to assist him, since owing to the tense situation between France and Spain it was necessary to be well protected in order to succeed.

The political horizon remained dark. To explain their failure, after talks lasting a year, the delegates had sent the Duke of Aerschot to Madrid. It was not a good idea, for the nobles had been conspiring together since 1631, wishing to 'follow the laudable example of their ancestors and free themselves from the heavy and intolerable yoke of Spain'. The Infanta had already had wind of the affair, and on her orders François Carondelet, the ambitious dean of Cambrai, had been forced into a monastery for having gathered together a few discontented nobles such as the princes of Barbançon and Epinoy, the Duke of Bournonville and Count Egmont. Charles of Arenburg, who had become a zealous Capuchin, had influenced the decision of his brother the Duke of Aerschot, the most important figure among the Belgian nobility. The conspirators had so far done nothing, and the defection of Count Henry de Bergh, who had been bribed to go over to Holland, remained an isolated incident. They were moved by vanity rather than by any desire for action, and they expected France to do everything, while France was waiting to see them in action before giving them any support.

Gerbier, who was still the King of England's representative in Brussels, put an end to their shilly-shallying by selling all the details of the plot for 20,000 crowns. Immediately, on the King's instructions, the Marquis d'Aytona had the leaders of the movement thrown into prison, while the Duke of Aerschot was arrested in Madrid. Philip IV announced the news to the States-General assembled in Brussels, ordering them at the same time to return to their provinces; they obeyed without a murmur. Such was the pitiful end of this dream of independence. And war began anew. A defensive alliance had just been signed between the United Provinces and France, and the *stadhouder* Frederick Henry was proposing that they should divide up the Spanish Netherlands.

Finally the long-awaited Regent, Don Ferdinand, arrived in Flanders. He was a young man of twenty-five, who had been Archbishop of Toledo at ten, and later became a cardinal; he was the father of three children. He had just entered upon a military career by taking an important part in the victory of Nordlingen won by the Imperial forces over the Lutheran army commanded by Bernard of Saxe-Weimar and the Swedish general Horn. This brilliant feat of arms after a long succession of reverses gave Spain a new lustre. The Cardinal Infante was glorified as a hero of Catholicism. He brought fresh troops from Germany, and at once hope was renewed—but a hope without much foundation, for the confusion remained inextricable.

Rubens could write: 'For the last three years I have, thank God, given up with a quiet mind everything not concerned with my profession.' It is true that he was inclined to boast in asserting:

'My journeys to Spain and England were very successful', and it was with great pride that he proclaimed: 'The negotiations concerning the flight of the Queen Mother and the Duke of Orleans—which resulted in the permission granted to them to find asylum here—were confided to me, and to me alone. I could provide a historian with precise and truthful information very different from what is generally believed.' And he adds somewhat complacently: 'It is true that I was in the complete confidence of Her Highness the Infanta (whom God hold in His glory) and of the King's first ministers, and had been able to win the esteem of my foreign colleagues. It was then that I resolved to break free, to cut the golden knot of ambition and regain my liberty, as I felt that one should be able to retire on the way up and not on the way down, and abandon fortune while she is still kind, not wait until she turns her back.'

He had to beg the Infanta to excuse him from further missions, and that favour he 'obtained only with great difficulty'. Though he lived 'peacefully, by God's grace' with his wife and children, he asked his friend Peiresc to put on his letters: 'Secretary to His Catholic Majesty in his privy council' and not 'Gentleman in ordinary of the household'. He said this 'not for vanity, but to ensure the security of his letters'. It was childish enough not to deceive anyone. He was not a man to give up honours easily, and if he bade farewell to his missions it was because he had to; his wise decision was a complete fabrication. But what did it matter? At a time when things were going from bad to worse, he could congratulate himself on the course he was taking, even if it was rather the result of events than of his own free will. He added: 'I want nothing more but to enjoy my retirement'; but we should not attach too strict a meaning to these words.

At the beginning of 1635, Antwerp was preparing to celebrate the triumphal entry of the Cardinal Infante, and the magistracy entrusted the decoration of the town to Rubens. 'I have no time to write or even to live' he confided to Peiresc. His inventive genius took fire, and he poured out designs and sketches. He created projects of unparalleled magnificence: porticos and triumphal arches, theatres and decorated chariots. The best painters in Antwerp worked under him: Jacob Jordaens, Cornelius de Vos, Erasmus Quellin, Theodore Rombouts,

Cornelius Schut, Theodore van Thulden and the two van Balen brothers. Quite twenty of them put their talents at his service. Six sculptors were of their number, carving both stone and wood. Among them were Quellin, van Mildert and van den Eynde. Gevartius provided the text of the inscriptions, calling Olympus to his aid so as not to fall below his friend's standard, and his texts, imitated from the classics, could vie with Rubens' allegories in splendour and obscurity. Scholars struggled to solve these enigmas, and the ignorant masses simply gaped at them, and asked no more.

Hundreds of craftsmen were pressed into service—carpenters, painters, gilders, smiths, drapers, artificers, tapestry-weavers, tin-smiths and glaziers, not to mention the labourers, contractors, watchmen, clerks, porters, bellringers, shopkeepers, trumpeters, messengers and others who, in various minor roles, contributed to the success of this magnificent ceremony. Eleven triumphal arches were erected in different parts of the city. The one on the Meir was the most beautiful; its twelve porticos, each supported by four columns, were adorned with twelve white stone statues representing the emperors of the house of Austria, and twelve other statues of mythological deities. The whole was shaped like half a hexagon and surmounted by an obelisk. Theatres were built in other places. The decorated chariots of the 'Ommegang' were exhibited as curiosities to admiring crowds. Everywhere there was a profusion of garlands, maypoles, festoons and flags.

At night the city was illuminated and a marvellous firework display ended the feast. Antwerp had always been lavish, but now it surpassed itself. Never had a ruler been welcomed with such a riot of colour. And nothing else seemed to matter. The expenses, estimated at 50,000 florins, rose to 70,000. In order to pay the debts, the magistracy sought to bring in new taxes which were refused, and the painters and other creditors went to law for their money. But to the good citizens of Antwerp these were but trifles—a monotonous repetition of an old familiar theme. The essential thing was that something great and beautiful had been achieved, that the city had been transformed by a genius nurtured on experiences from Italy combined with the pride of a citizen of Antwerp. That Rubens had received 5,000 florins for his pains was a mere detail. He had been able to set the scene as he wished—that was his good fortune and that of his collaborators, and also of his fellow-citizens who had become, through his sovereign will, the actors in his drama. Art was no longer kept for temples and palaces, but took possession of the streets and became an integral part of a town overflowing with holiday spirit. Every citizen played his part in it, for this art, magnificent and gigantic in scale, needed colourful crowds in all their finery to give life to the splendid setting; and nothing could better have suited the people of Antwerp, who called themselves 'Sinjoren', meaning 'lords'.

But the great stage-manager of this triumphal reception could not be there himself. Gout had laid him low and forced him to bed, and the Cardinal Infante had paid him the inestimable compliment of visiting him in person.

Like all the princes of his line, Don Ferdinand was an enthusiastic lover of painting, and who but Rubens could satisfy his needs? The master had moreover a charming personality, and though his body might be immobilized, his mind remained alert. And as for the living model of so many master-works, the Cardinal Infante had no hesitation; he wrote to his brother the King that she was the most beautiful woman in Antwerp.

Nothing except gout could keep Rubens inactive. He was engaged in litigation against an engraver in Paris who was copying his prints, thus doing him 'considerable harm', and he asked Peiresc to intervene, since his adversary was claiming that he, Rubens, was 'extorting enormous sums from France'. Rubens did not agree. 'All that is untrue', he wrote, 'and I am ready to state under oath that I have never, either directly or indirectly, sent to France any other prints of my engravings than those intended for the Bibliothèque Royal, given as presents to a few friends, or sent in small quantities, at your request, to M. Tavernier. The latter has never asked me for any more, and I should not mind seeing my prints banned from France, since the rest of Europe would be ready to pay me homage, which is more precious in my eyes than a little money.' Clearly it was a proud retort, though not remarkable for its logic; if Rubens was really so disinterested, why the lawsuit and what 'considerable harm' had he to fear? At any rate he was quite prepared to 'come to an agreement' with his opponent. He then offers himself the following testimonial: 'I am a peaceable man, and I hate lawsuits and every other sort of quarrel like the plague; and I think the chief wish of a gentleman should be to live in peace *publice et privatim et prodesse multis, nocere nemini.*' And he adds, somewhat haughtily: 'I am sorry that kings and princes do not share my point of view.'

Meanwhile he had delivered the paintings commissioned when he was in England for the palace of Whitehall in London. They were ceilings intended for the banqueting hall, glorifying the reign of James I in splendid allegorical style. The formula was that used for Marie de Medici, but the manner had changed, become more turbulent. Every composition was crammed with detail and swarming with movement. For this work Rubens was paid the considerable sum of £3,000 sterling. He was great enough to magnify the dullest of lives—and in any case lives treated by his brush could scarcely remain dull. Everything he touched he transfigured with such eloquence that the subject was forgotten. And doubtless the magician was finally falling under his own spell.

Public affairs were going from bad to worse. The final break between France and Spain had come, 'which makes me very unhappy', said Rubens, 'for I am a man of peaceable character and tastes, and have set my face against wars, lawsuits, incidents and quarrels *publice et privatim*'. And he went on with his lawsuit in Paris.

In May 1635, Helen gave him a third child, Isabella Helena. Shortly afterwards he bought the Castle of Steen at Elewyt. It was a vast domain with woods and fields through which a river flowed. Since 1627 Rubens had possessed an estate at Eeckeren, north of Antwerp, which he used as his country house. This was the 'Hof van Orsele', a house built on an islet in the middle of a lake, which lacked elegance, as it dated from the fifteenth century and looked like a fortress. The Castle of Steen at Elewyt was quite different. It was a vast country seat well provided with turrets, a drawbridge and a mock keep—just enough to remind the world that the lord of the manor was well able to rival his ancestors. The new nobility did not shrink from a little ostentation, and the 'Lord of Steen' was among them. As with his house on the Wapper, he could amuse himself by transforming, and above all by beautifying, his princely retreat. He could also use it as a model and as a setting; the manor house, transfigured, could be the background for all the shifting brilliance of an imaginary tournament.

In addition Rubens, as father of a family, had acquired this estate as an investment; what, otherwise, was he to do with his money? In Antwerp, he lived in a palace overflowing with riches. He was one of the chief collectors in the city of pictures, marbles, agates, ivory carvings, books and drawings. He possessed houses, lands, and securities in quantity. Despite the poverty of the time, money flowed into his coffers. Princes still sought after his canvases, and, sooner or later, paid for them. Rubens' judgment of them is offhand: 'I have long been acquainted with the dilatoriness of princes as far as money is concerned, and I know that they find it easier to do ill than good.' To him, as it happened, they did only good.

In order to annoy the French, who had just concluded an offensive and defensive alliance with the United Provinces, the Cardinal Infante had taken by surprise the city of Trèves which had been placed under French protection. The Elector was taken to Brussels under guard. Urged on by Richelieu, Louis XIII decided to avenge this insult. A herald was sent to Brussels and another to Madrid, to declare war on Spain. At once a French army, led by Marshals de Châtillon and de Brézé, invaded Luxemburg, beat Prince Thomas of Savoy at Avins near Rochefort, and joined up with the *Stadhouder's* troops. The two allied armies then penetrated into Brabant and captured and sacked Tirlemont. But resistance was soon organized. Supported by fifteen thousand Imperial guards brought by Piccolomini, the Cardinal Infante undertook a victorious counter-offensive. 'To such an effect', wrote Rubens to Peiresc, 'that instead of having sixty thousand enemies in the heart of Brabant, as we had a few weeks ago, we are today masters of the whole country.' And he added some rather unflattering comments on the 'two mighty armies' which 'through indecision, bad strategy, slowness, confusion, imprudence and indiscipline' had been 'forced in the end to flee shamefully'.

For a moment his old passion appeared to be reawakened. Although it was hardly kind to France to write this to a French

friend, Rubens spoke the truth. The war had shifted on to the
territory of the United Provinces, a thing which had not happened for years, and the result was complete panic. To some
good souls the moment seemed propitious to speak once more of
peace. The Bishop of Ghent, Antoine Triest, who was devoting
himself to this noble cause, approached Rubens, who also
thought this an opportune moment to begin talks. Always eager
to push himself forward, he was ready to go and visit Prince
Frederick Henry. So as not to arouse suspicion, he arranged to
go accompanied by his sons on the pretext of inspecting paintings and other curiosities. The plan was soon unmasked, and all
Spain's enemies worked to prevent the journey. 'That man
Rubens is full of tricks', said the Venetian Ambassador. 'He is a
very clever negotiator, and has been employed by the Spaniards
on other very serious occasions.' They were also afraid that he
might be planning to go to England. The French Ambassador
did everything in his power to prevent Rubens being granted a
passport, and he finally had his way. Rubens, who had gone to
Brussels, returned empty-handed, but, as always, managed to
save face. Replying several months late to a letter from Peiresc,
he claimed that he had been 'kept in Brussels by private business,
and not at all by official missions as you imagine'. Had his
correspondent had wind of something, or, knowing his man, had
he simply guessed? Rubens explained: 'I admit that they
sounded me right at the beginning to find out whether I would
accept this mission, but they did not seem inclined to give me
free rein, and made difficulties over my passport; I at once contrived to waste as much time as I could, and found all sorts of
loopholes. Since, on the other hand, there was no shortage of
people anxious to obtain a mission of this sort, I managed to
preserve my peace of mind, and, thank God, I can stay at home
in tranquillity.'

And he is doubtless sincere when he states in the same letter
that he has 'conceived a horror of Courts'. But it must be said
that he conceived a horror of them because he did not succeed in
playing the part he wanted there. Otherwise, despite his fifty-
nine years, he would willingly have entered the field again. He
was, of course, in great favour at court. In April 1636 the
Cardinal Infante had appointed him painter to his household,

the same title as he had once received from the Archdukes. It was one more empty bauble—as though this passionate politician had to be reminded that he was a painter. And what a painter! The Cardinal Infante, wiser than the Infanta Isabella, honoured the painter and neglected the diplomat. The evolution of Spanish politics had probably something to do with this, for the last faint tendencies to particularism had been wiped out in the Belgian provinces. So much the worse for the provinces—we may say— and so much the better for Rubens. He was secretary, knight, envoy—and these honours were mere bagatelles. His business was painting.

XV

FULFILMENT

1636–1638

He was close on sixty. There was not a collector in the world who did not know his name and seek out his works. For twenty years, with the help of a team of assistants, he had been struggling with the ever-rising flood of commissions. His richest and his most knowledgeable clients imperiously insisted on works 'by his own hand' as though he could cope single-handed with their demands. His capacity for work was indeed enormous but not unlimited. So he had to resort to evasions to soothe those kept waiting, telling them where necessary that the work they had commissioned needed all his attention, and that it would be really marvellous if only they left him time to finish it at his leisure. Gaining time meant being free to attend to other, perhaps more absorbing work, being able to choose and to fulfil himself completely.

He had passed the stage of strategy and conquest. He still accepted commissions, probably less for the gain involved than to maintain his status as master. Personal glory makes great demands; the younger it has been acquired, the harder it is to keep it intact. Posthumous glory is another matter; it is touched by no sense of conflict. The living man has to defend his glory like a fortress gained in battle; its loss would mean a decline in his own eyes. And there is only one way to defend it: work. He must prove by his work that he can always surpass his rivals.

Van Dyck had left for foreign parts, had returned, left again, and once more returned; he had been in England since 1635, but no one knew whether he would stay there. Each of his appearances in Antwerp was like a test of greatness in comparison with his former employer, and each time Van Dyck's prestige

14. Rubens' house in Antwerp (1684). Engraving by Harrewijn. (Brussels, Bibliothèque Royale, Prints Department)

15. Plan of
Antwerp
(1565) by
Virgilius
Boloniensis.
Detail.
(Plantin-
Moretus
Museum,
Antwerp—
Photo

appeared to increase. And yet, did not his retreat prove that he did not feel himself great enough to eclipse the reigning master? With Van Dyck gone, there remained Jordaens, the son-in-law of Adam Van Noort, whose pupil he was, long after Rubens. This native of Antwerp had come under the influence of Caravaggio without having visited Italy. He was an unusually powerful painter whose personality showed itself in a vision like a sculptor's, great concentration in his composition, and colouring perhaps even more brilliant and vibrant than that of Rubens. It was honourable for the leader of a school to have such rivals, and glorious to triumph over them.

It was flattering to be represented in the collection of one of the greatest kings, but it was no less useful to be well represented in the 'constcamer' of one of Antwerp's leading citizens. About the middle of the preceding century the fashion had taken root for possessing a 'constcamer', that is to say a room devoted entirely to works of art, and since then the enthusiasm of collectors had increased enormously. Their houses were filled with paintings from the ground floor to the attic, not excepting the kitchen, the lumber-room and the servants' bedrooms. In the principal rooms they hung side by side right up to the ceiling, hiding the sumptuous embossed leather with which these places were adorned, making the walls seem to disappear and creating such a fairy-tale atmosphere that several painters had been tempted by so fantastic a subject. Cornelius de Vos painted Rubens' *constcamer*, and Willem Van Haecht enshrined the visit of the Archdukes in 1615 to the justly famous collection of Cornelis van der Geest.

Every person of note in Antwerp prided himself on a collection of works of art; among others the painter's friends Jan Brant, Nicholas Rockox and Daniel Fourment. All these collectors were impelled by real passion. Works which pleased them were unblushingly copied, so that every *constcamer* had as many copies as originals. Their taste was very eclectic. Despite the wave of enthusiasm for Rubens, they still clung to the cult of the elder Bruegel, his sons, and the Grimmer family. They loved Quentin Metsys, Joos van Cleef (known as Mad Cleef), Frans Floris, Cocxie, the Mostaert brothers and van Conincxloo. They left large-scale subjects to churches and palaces, preferring portraits, genre painting, landscapes, flowers, still-life or charming allegories. They were particularly fond of the graceful landscapes of Joos de Momper, and also of Adriaan Brouwer, whose bohemian subjects flattered their own propensity for drinking-bouts and minor orgies. They also loved the Italians, whose drawings they collected in default of paintings: Raphael, Michelangelo, Veronese, Titian, and Bassano. Antique marbles or their copies, engravings and tapestries completed their wealth.

It is understandable that Rubens should have wished to maintain his sovereignty in each of these homes where painting was so devotedly worshipped. He admitted his preference for large-scale compositions, and yet painted a large number of small panels; this was surely in order to be hung in *constcamers* where the wall space was often very small. He was one of those old fighters who never gave up; the forces seething within him were too strong. Even now he was always short of time. He had said goodbye to politics and to Court life, he lived part of the year in the country, and still never had any time. The more he hurried, the more he took from life. That was what mattered, especially at sixty. When younger it is easy to think ourselves immortal, but at sixty we dwell on life because our thoughts are turning towards death. Art, love, knowledge, riches, family or friends are reflections of life, of our own life, the only one which really counts, because we alone live it, because we stand alone and watch other lives going on around us. Of course there is God. Basically there is only one alternative; to believe only in oneself or to trust completely in God—the way of heaven or the way of earth. But there are also those who steer a middle course, who pretend to trust in God but believe only in themselves. When not incapacitated by gout, Rubens went to Mass every day, but his mind did not dwell on God. He acted always as a man, a lone individual among individuals. 'God helps those who help themselves.' He was steeped in stoicism, and a stoic is a Christian without faith. Richelieu, having exterminated the French Protestants, supported Protestant Holland and Germany against Catholic Spain; was he then a Christian? Or the Cardinal Infante, who led armies on the field of battle? Poverello, or Fra Angelico, yes . . .

Times had changed. The Council of Trent had established a

new doctrine for the Roman church. The Jesuits were teaching a
less rigid code of morals. Being good psychologists, they took
intention into account, and made religion a pleasanter thing, ably
assisted by architects, painters and sculptors burning with enthusiasm for the new style. Rubens felt that a good Catholic had no
need to worry; if he did his duty without misplaced zeal nothing
more would be asked of him. He was not in the least given to
metaphysical heartsearchings. He lived his life intensely and
trusted in God for the rest, according to the time-honoured maxim.

He worked for many clients, but above all he worked for himself and for his own pleasure. His technique was changing imperceptibly. Even though he had always mixed his colours very
thinly, he now managed to refine them even more. His brushes
barely touched the canvas or panel; they moved caressingly, and
his dreams took shape, fluid, like gossamer. His assistants, however skilful, could no longer keep up with him, and they had to
give up collaborating with him. His colours seemed to have
become intangible, immaterial. It may have been the result of
his long periods in the country. He was discovering nature,
which was no longer a background, hitherto left to skilful
collaborators, but had come into the forefront of his paintings
and become a character.

He had never, to tell the truth, been entirely uninterested in
nature. From time to time he would paint a landscape as though
to show that there was no branch of art with which he was not
concerned. At first he painted rustic scenes like 'The Return of
the Prodigal Son', a balanced, harmonious work entirely by his
own hand. In the same vein, he painted 'Winter': the stable,
the cattle, agricultural implements and a scrap of landscape. But
little by little the landscapes had increased in scope. 'The Farm
at Laeken' is a fine example of a well-ordered composition further helped by forms accurately and powerfully modelled. There
came other landscapes, with herds, or a cart stuck in the mud,
and trees now beginning to move in the wind. And at last there
were storms; wind, lightning, and rainbows. Fierce blasts blew
through the leaves, giving dramatic movement to the scene;
these were the landscapes with 'Atalanta's Race', 'The Shipwreck of Aeneas' and 'Philemon and Baucis'.

The lessons of Van Conincxloo, Josse de Momper and Jan

Bruegel were over; they were all too calm and too meticulous. Their finicky preoccupation with detail destroyed the element of lyricism. What mattered to Rubens was movement, wind-tossed landscapes with clouds, lightning-flashes, sun, rifts in clouds and contrasts of light and shade. Too great precision in drawing was useless to him. When a gale is blowing it is not possible to distinguish the outline of a leaf; the leaves are now only a shuddering mass. When a storm rages, one solitary colour gives the sense of tragedy which drowns every other tone. Even if the atmosphere is sombre or dark, the painting must not become dull. Colour has its sacred rights; it must remain warm even if the atmosphere seems to exclude that possibility completely. Rubens was craftsman enough to have recourse to a red preparation—as in the 'Shipwreck of Aeneas'—which, itself transparent, gives a new brilliance to sombre grey tones. Thus, by the magic of colour and by the dynamic movement of the lines, Rubens succeeded in giving landscape painting a completely new aspect, at once heroic and lyrical. Then, satisfied that he had marked it with his own particular stamp, he could calm his ardour and paint more tranquil landscapes.

Once he had let loose all the forces of nature as he must have seen them in the windswept plains of the Polders, he was free to feast his eyes on the gentler beauties of the Brabant countryside which he had learnt to know well since becoming lord of the manor of Steen. There, nature was all moderation and quiet charm, and the eye could rest on an almost flat horizon, endlessly changing with the weather and the time of day. He delighted in this shifting play of light, and his enthusiasm led him to abandon his transfiguration of landscapes in the heroic style. He painted 'Nightfall' and 'Morning'. In 'Moonlight' he evoked a starry night, and in 'Landscape with Bird-catcher' the morning mist. He dared to paint the sun itself. The lover of full rounded shapes became the subtle wooer of an elusive atmosphere. All these sights were new to him, and he came to them without affectation or pretentiousness.

He looked at the world around him, no longer with the eager eyes that once saw everything on a heroic scale, but simply, in quiet enjoyment. He came down from Olympus, and left the Bible alone, at least when he could escape the demands of his

insatiable clientele. Then he abandoned himself to the simple joy
of painting, creating pictures which expressed his delight in his
family and his surroundings: his wife, his children, his garden,
his country seat. A setting he loved was the Italian garden of
his house on the Wapper, with its pavilion and its portico; he
could put in it his wife and his little children, and add himself in
all his finery. He could fill it with young men and women in
amorous conversation and call his painting 'The Garden of Love'.
It was a magnificent subject—and what optimism at his age,
despite the hard times and the crippling gout! The Garden of
Love was his garden, and his Helen was there, moving happily
among these happy couples. She lent herself with docility to all
his whims, this Helen of his, and he decked her with the richest
adornments or left her naked as he chose. He was no anxious
lover guarding his beloved's beauty with jealous care. Her milk-
white flesh was there for all to see. He showed her dressed in a
black pelisse, but joyfully left her arms, her legs, and her breasts
uncovered. This painting he called the 'Pelsken' — the little
pelisse—and kept it for himself and for her.

He never tired of contemplating and painting this fair-skinned
Flemish girl, perhaps a little heavy for some, but for him so
exactly corresponding with his dreams; opulent curves and
dazzling whiteness—everything, in fact, which he loved. Was
she anything more than a lovely child? We do not know; and he
scarcely seems to have cared. Her expression is sweet and
unaffected. Whether she is stiff in heavy silks and velvets, naked
or nearly so, she appears unruffled. Only once does she seem
more thoughtful, when he painted her seated, head bowed, with
her two children. Was this a finished picture or a brilliant
sketch? He had never achieved so fine a result with so little
apparent effort. Its fluid, almost immaterial colouring suggests
rather than describes. It is the poetry of happiness—a mother
and her children in perfect contentment. It springs from the
happiness of a man who has all he wants from life—and he was
over sixty years old!

Age was telling on him—not on his hand, which was more
lively than ever, but on his body. He seems to have realized this
when making a hasty sketch of himself. Of course a magician
like him could make great play with an ample cloak and a wide-

brimmed hat. But there was still the face, and a mirror does not lie. His eyes were deep-set, his cheeks hollow, and under his moustache his mouth was falling in. However much his pencil may have skimmed over the paper without emphasizing any feature, he could not work miracles. Besides, this drawing was only a stage in his work. If he was going to cheat, he had first to know what the weak points were, and cheat he did. His magic brush undertook the hard task of putting new life into that tired face. As always, he strove to achieve a likeness whilst idealizing at the same time. The black hat and cloak made it easier to bring out the patches of lighter colour in the face and the hand lying on a sword-hilt. The dark hair—could it have been a wig?— remains in the shadow of the hat. The moustache and short beard are brown; the moustache, more impressively curled than in the drawing, conveniently covers the mouth. The face, with the traditional play of faint shadows, comes out brilliantly. There remain the eyes; the eyelids are a little heavy and the eyes dimmed. Some have chosen to see melancholy, even sadness in them; could it have been because he was not prepared to carry his rejuvenescence any further?

He had painted himself fifteen years earlier at the request of the Prince of Wales, the future Charles I, who, it is said, had to overcome his modesty. Here too he wore a large black cloak and a wide-brimmed black hat. He had no need for tricks, and he evaded nothing; eyes, mouth, hair were faithfully drawn, for then he was in his prime. He traced with a firm hand the first lines to show on his face, knowing that far from detracting from his looks they enhanced them. This time he slid over what he was afraid to emphasize. But even coquetry has its limits. In his drawing he admitted that he was over sixty, but he wiped away at least ten years from the canvas. And that was probably enough for him; he was on his guard against exaggeration which would have made him look ridiculous. His efforts to appear younger were a kind of homage to the life he loved, to his young wife, his children, himself, the whole world; they proclaimed an unfailing optimism. And the slight blurring of his gaze was a tribute which had to be paid to the truth, the only way to gain acceptance for that boldly flattering image.

In his relations with the outside world, nothing had changed.

Rubens was still the Lord of the Manor of Steen, the secretary of His Catholic Majesty in his privy council, the Knight of the Holy Ghost and the painter of the Cardinal Infante, a man, in fact, who mixed only with the great. In Antwerp itself his friends were magistrates of the commune, highly placed civil servants and rich patrons of the arts; They were men like Rockox, Brant, Gevartius, Moretus and Van der Geest, studious, scholarly types, generally devout and not without a tinge of Ostentation, the founders of chapels and hospices which they took pleasure in adorning magnificently. This was only one side of the picture. Drunkenness and gluttony were still greatly to the fore, and junketing was in favour in all circles. The authorities did their best to fight back with decrees and edicts—although it might have been supposed that the great burdens and losses borne by the community as a result of the recent war would have naturally induced everyone to observe a certain moderation —but it was in vain. One was even brought out 'against the great irregularity, gluttony and drunkenness in marriage feasts'; henceforward the number of guests was limited to forty, and marriages were not allowed to 'last more than one day and up to the afternoon of the next day'. On rare occasions some virtuous citizen upheld the authorities; thus Puteanus published his *Comus* in order to denounce this scourge. It won him more abuse than praise, particularly from the townspeople of Antwerp. Even scholars and humanists like Beyerlinck and Woverius — two great friends of Rubens — entered the lists against the over-zealous professor. Despite the edicts, Richard Verstegen managed to describe twenty-five different kinds of drunkards. Guilliam Ogier had just composed *De Gulsigheydt* ('Gluttony'), the first piece in a cycle on the subject of the Seven Deadly Sins, a theme which Adriaan Brouwer had already treated in painting.

After living for a time in Holland, where he was a pupil of Frans Hals, this Flemish painter had settled in Antwerp some years earlier. He excelled in characteristic scenes which he interpreted with quite exceptional freedom of style and understanding of human nature. It may have been due to the influence of bourgeois and calvinistic Holland; there is not a trace of the Counter-Reformation in his work. His subjects, always contemporary and realistic, his colouring, usually monochrome, and the very small size of his pictures set him apart from his brilliant colleagues who painted heroic subjects for the churches. Bitterly, and yet at the same time lyrically, he depicted man—man who smokes and drinks, and sometimes fights, because he is an obscure, unhappy creature — and the message implicit in his works is enigmatic yet full of brotherly warmth. His pupil, the former baker Josse van Craesbeeck, worked in the same manner. And Jordaens himself, that bold champion of heroic painting, with all his glowing tributes to the glory of the Christian religion or of mythology, was also edging towards a more familiar style. He was painting more and more family festivals in which three generations are gathered round a table, drinking, eating, shouting and singing. And his inspiration had never before achieved such warm colour-harmonies, based on browns and carmine reds.

However much one tries to escape from nature, she is bound to triumph in the end. Up till now Rubens had allowed the common people no part in either his life or his work. But he had learnt from other painters, and from writers and humanists too. These men of the North, though they passionately loved Latin poetry, returned to their mother-tongue when treating certain subjects, because they could not separate themselves from the masses who clung to them as the clay soil clung to their boots. Such is the fate of man. Some rise so high that they have lost all contact for ever; but they are wrong. A man who has left the people always returns to them by however secret and circuitous a route. Had Rubens really needed to be taught this? Now that he had reached the heights of fame and fortune and was on the threshold of old age, it must have been easier to sweep aside all obstructions and do as he liked without regard for anyone or anything.

In one marvellous painting he uttered a hymn to joy—the unbridled joy of a Flemish *kermesse*. The fact was that despite his wealth and honours, he was a plebeian at heart, and the Duke of Aerschot was right to say he was not of his world. And praise be to the gods for that! That picture would never have been painted had he belonged to that world of stiff aristocrats, enamoured of illusory privileges. The blood of the people of Flanders flowed through his veins — that quiet, patient folk whose gaiety bursts out as suddenly as a fanfare. It was joy for joy's sake, unreasoning, untouched by the suffering and sorrows of the times. Joy sang in his bright colours and in the mad swirl of his drawing.

There were, of course, the village festivals of the elder Bruegel. But they were not gay; Whoever saw a smiling face in the works of this famous painter? He may have been called the 'Droll', but, as Carel van Mander tells us, it was because of his fantastic scenes in the manner of Bosch. Bruegel's peasants sometimes dance, at a wedding or some other festive occasion, but they dance decorously, and their faces remain anxious. They are at best only just beginning to enjoy themselves. Rubens, as always, goes straight to the point and shows the celebrations at their height. Intoxicated with pleasure, couples dance as though possessed. There is eating and drinking, music and dancing, harbingers of joy, that all-pervading joy which gives life to a whole people. Hands move boldly, their gestures leaving no room for doubt. Prudes and puritans may be shocked, but only because they do not understand the meaning of joy, that mad ecstasy that carries all before it, down to the smallest detail, in one glorious whirl of exaltation.

The day that he painted that hymn to joy, for his delight and ours, he dropped his mask at last; he was now simply a man like any other, drunk on life, eager to taste every kind of pleasure, greedy and insatiable. He loved life, despite his sixty years and more, and his Catholic exterior hid a pagan heart. He returned to the theme in his 'Peasant Dance', although, wild as it is, it has not the breadth of the 'Kermesse'. It is a joyous group, but not a crowd. And though the movement is livelier, the gaiety has a different accent. A couple are kissing; a man leans towards the girl beside him, but the dance is already carrying him away. In the 'Kermesse', on the other hand, joy is universal, from childhood to old age. Some children suck the breast, others drink from the wine-jars, the grown-ups dance; hands slide over breasts, buttocks, and bellies, and there are kisses, full on the lips. The old men drain the pots to the dregs. Voluptuous curves form the finest hymn of joy there has ever been, set in the peace of the Brabant countryside.

Rubens continued of course to paint religious subjects, since they were commissioned. But he took his time. The painter

Geldorp asked, on behalf of the banker Evrard Jabach, for a retable for the church of St Peter in Cologne, and he replied calmly: 'As for the time I shall need, I must have a year and a half, so that I may do as your friend asks without hurrying and without inconvenience to myself.' He demanded a year and a half without even knowing what he had to paint! Since it had to be an episode in the life of St Peter, he suggested 'his crucifixion with feet upwards, because I believe I could do something quite out of the ordinary with that, keeping nevertheless within the limits of my talent'. That was what religious subjects meant to him—but it was a question of business, and he had his own philosophy. He concluded: 'In any case the final choice must be made according to the tastes of the man who is paying for the picture.'

Ten months later he declared that the painting was 'already well under way'—which we may have leave to doubt—and he adds: 'However, I should very much like not to be hustled into finishing it; I would be glad if you would leave it to my discretion so that I can finish it at my convenience and enjoy doing so.' He was, he said, 'overwhelmed with work'. He certainly had a hand in everything. He painted 'The Martyrdom of St Lievin', for the Jesuits of Ghent, with the speed of a man possessed. 'The Road to Calvary', in spite of the subject, is a festive scene. 'The Martyrdom of St Ursula' and 'The Massacre of the Innocents' are heroic scenes where vitality outweighs every other preoccupation. His design has become purely lyrical and his touch feather-light. His earlier canvases, so greatly praised for their verve, seem stiff in comparison with these new works, ethereal in their lightness, and painted purely for pleasure.

When work is one's chief source of spiritual exaltation, it is hard to give anything up at all. The most Rubens would do was to cease supplying drawings to his friend Moretus; he left the task of illustration to his collaborator Erasmus Quellin. For the rest, his output continued abundantly and regularly, and a large number of assistants ensured that production went on. New names appeared, replacing the old ones or side by side with them: Willem Panneels, the faithful guardian of his house during his journeys abroad, Abraham van Diepenbeeck, Jan van den Hoeck, and many others.

But the names matter little. They were satellites drawn into his orbit. Very often those who left him lost the glory which they mistakenly thought their own, for most of them shone only with his reflected light. To him all that mattered was results. He ran a business, and had to satisfy his many customers. His prestige and his reputation were at stake as a purveyor of religious pictures of every type and various sizes to be delivered anywhere in the world—distance no object.

He would even ask any client who could so much as hold a brush to retouch works that had been damaged in transit. He asked this service of Justus Sustermans, his colleague and the younger by twenty years. This man, a native of Antwerp, whose portrait Van Dyck painted during his stay in Florence, was the official portrait-painter of the Medici family, and in a way their artistic representative. He had painted, with facile elegance, a large number of persons of note : Pope Urban VIII, the Emperor Ferdinand II, Prince Christian of Denmark, Galileo. Rubens could, without losing face, ask him to retouch a little : 'I am afraid that having been packed up for so long may have done some slight harm to the colours of this picture, which was freshly painted, and most especially to the flesh-tints and white, which could turn yellow. I hope that as you are yourself a great painter you can easily remedy this by exposing the work to the sun from time to time. If, moreover, your intervention proves necessary, I gladly authorize you to retouch my painting wherever accident or my carelessness obliges you to do so.'

There had been yet another addition to his family, a child born in February 1637 and called, like himself, Peter Paul. For the sake of all this burgeoning life around him, and also because it was his destiny, he worked hard and supervised the work of others. He painted a great series for the hunting lodge of Torre de la Parada in the neighbourhood of Madrid, belonging to the King of Spain. It was an important commission and altogether worthy of a painter of Titanic stature—a hundred and twelve compositions! The themes of this huge undertaking came from Ovid's Metamorphoses and the 'Labours of Hercules'; there were 'Apollo and Marsyas', 'Apollo and the Python', 'Arachne and Minerva', 'Ariadne and Bacchus', 'Atlas holding up the world', 'The Triumph of Bacchus', 'Cephalus and Procris', 'Cupid riding a dolphin', 'Deianira', 'Deucalion and Pyrrha', 'Europa', 'Fortuna', 'The Harpies', 'Hercules leaning on a Club', 'The Apotheosis of Hercules', 'Hercules and Cerberus', 'Hippodamia', 'The Death of Hyacinth', 'The Fall of Icarus', 'Jason with the Golden Fleece', 'Juno suckling Hercules', 'Jupiter and Lycaon', 'Jupiter and Semele', 'Mercury and Argus', 'Nereid and Triton', 'The Fall of Phaeton', 'Polyphemus', 'Prometheus', 'Pluto and Proserpine', 'The Fall of the Titans', 'The Birth of Venus', 'Vertumnus and Pomona', 'Orpheus and Eurydice', 'Venus and Adonis', 'Diana and Callisto', 'Perseus and Andromeda', and many other subjects of the same type, varied in theme but with one thing in common: the opportunity they gave for glorifying the nude, in every imaginable attitude. Some may be calm, but most are lively, rising sometimes to the point of turbulence. No one seems to have taken exception—when an artist is in fashion, even his faults are admired.

The method never varied: the master made sketches and his workshop carried out the work according to the dimensions required. He had at hand Erasmus Quellin, Jan Cossiers, Cornelis Schut, Luke van Uden. Cornelis de Vos, Jan Van Eyck, Peeter Symons, J. B. Gouwi, J. B. Borrekens. They were skilful men, trained in his style, biddable workers with no fire of their own. There was no one at the time to notice this; it takes many years before men can separate outward appearances from the deeper meaning. It was therefore enough that Rubens should supervise the work and touch it up a little here and there. When a subject pleased him he kept it for himself, and it was like a different language. But there was nothing he could do; he had no time and his clients were always in a hurry. He rolled up scarce-dry canvases and sent them on their way before getting on with others. And there were always others to come.

In his solitude at Steen, he forgot important commissions and painted for his own pleasure. And though there may have been painters to equal him, there were none to surpass him. He painted with absolute mastery, with no hesitation or second thoughts, and a lightness of touch which could not be equalled. Other painters—and painters of no small skill—fought fierce battles wth their materials. He dominated them to such an extent that every stroke of his brush was the final one, and he achieved the miracle of canvases of a clear bell-like brilliance, which were scarcely touched with colour. He was moving further and further away from crucifixions and other scenes of martyrdom. He no longer strove after difficult attitudes in which to amaze the world with his skill. The die was cast. Since his imagination needed themes, he found them once more in mythology. It gave him a pretext for painting luscious nudes; whether the subject was 'The Three Graces', 'The Judgement of Paris' or 'The Rape of the Sabine Women', the nude was always triumphant.

Sometimes the themes changed, but the result was always exactly the same; the bronze serpent, the massacre of the innocents, or Bathsheba, was always a hymn to the glory of the flesh. When, exceptionally, he painted his Helen as Saint Cecilia—probably a theme imposed on him—he exposed her breasts more generously than the subject required, but he had to cover her body, and he surrounded her with chubby *putti*. He very soon undressed her again and made her into a luscious Andromeda; and the tearful glance of the captive is exactly the same as the inspired expression of the saint.

He cared little for the thoughts of these heroines with their changing names. He never tired of glorifying Woman in her most permanent and universal possession — her body. It was through her body—the artist's inspiration, the source of pleasure and the generating force of the human race—that she held sway over him, as over all men worthy of the name. And it was not enough for him to embrace a woman and so calm a desire which was no sooner satisfied than it blossomed again as though by a miracle; he needed to fondle her in his dreams, and so he gave her new life in a thousand forms by the enchantment of his art. No painter had ever painted flesh whiter and at the same time more vibrant with life, and no artist had ever glorified flesh so eloquently.

We realize that Rubens painted it with such ardour because it set his senses afire. He loved this flesh with a passion that became stronger as age weighed heavier upon him. Now his self-betrayal had gone far enough. A few years before he would have toyed with folds of drapery or floating veils to mask a part of the flesh, but now these trammels irritated him. His goddesses were becoming more and more naked; and he preferred them so, since he refused to make any changes to a 'Judgement of Paris' commissioned by the King of Spain, which the Cardinal Infante would have rather seen more veiled. He no longer believed that 'the taste of the man who is paying' was all-important, and he would not yield even to a King. That canvas, commissioned or not, had been painted for his own pleasure. In it his Helen triumphed as Venus, as she embodied so many other heroines of his dreams.

He had been painting unveiled women for thirty years—why should people have suddenly judged them too naked? The Cardinale Infante was no prude. Why should he appear shocked? He may perhaps have sensed all too clearly the evolution of Rubens' style. The first naked women, the 'Venus Frigida', 'The Toilet of Venus' and 'Susanna and the Elders' were remarkable for their rounded forms and the luminous quality of the flesh. Their masterly execution could be admired without qualms. But these nudes had changed imperceptibly. Their shapes, painted with a lighter hand, had become less precise, had less of the motionless gleam of white marble. One might almost say that they had begun to palpitate.

In 'Angelica and the Hermit' we begin to understand how nakedness can be carried too far. We can look undisturbed at this picture because of its small size. The pale flesh with its rosy shadows, the meltingly soft pose prolonged by the red draperies, the white veil and the grey background all produce an impression of insidious sensuality. But, we repeat, its size is a saving grace, preventing us as it does from entirely forgetting that this is a painting. If the figures were to become life-size, the effect would change. This is not all; the forms too were being transformed, as we realize when we look at the 'Three Graces' and 'The Judgment of Paris'.

The pattern of the human body has undergone quite a new interpretation. The lines have lost their harmonious, academic perfection, and are broken at every moment by the natural unevenness of flesh. The line from back to thigh, passing over the rump, is no longer a perfect, sweeping curve, but a sinuous movement outlined by the plump back and hips and the heavy buttocks. The same applies to the arms, legs and belly. The women are perhaps too fat, but their flesh pulsates with life. And we may well ask whether they have not been rendered in just that way in order to express that wickedly enchanting pulsation. For, in the last analysis, that is the reason for this sudden revulsion—these images are too sensual. They are too direct; they play on the senses, and call up too vivid a picture of Woman — not idealized or transfigured by dreams, but the eternal Eve whose flesh is a weapon, more terrible the more cunningly it is shown to us.

The voluptuous Titian painted woman whose sensuality was in a way spiritual; it is hard to tell whether those languorous bodies are waiting for love or have already known it. With Peter Paul there can be no doubt; these bodies have shivered at the touch of a man; they have known the satiation of love. They proclaim it so indiscreetly that we can understand the reaction of those who were upset by these eloquent images and demanded that they should be veiled. Rubens at the end of his career cared nothing for these paltry anxieties. And in order that no one should mistake his intentions, he painted the 'Shepherd and Shepherdess', in which he freely offers his Helen to a shepherd who is very like a satyr. The attack is fierce and the defence yielding. And Helen's face seems to smile in anticipation of the pleasures promised to her flesh. Peter Paul had painted the very image of desire — that desire which still burned within him despite his age; for if his mind was Olympian, so also were his senses.

XVI

. . . AND A FINE END

1638–1640

Apart from a few independent spirits like Erasmus and Rabelais, who wrote to denounce the stupidity of war, no one had ever raised his voice against this ancient method of arranging or disarranging the order of things. Artists—painters, sculptors and engravers — had often glorified battles and military heroism. None had ever dreamed of decrying war. Bruegel perhaps, in his *Dulle Griet*, but was he thinking of war only? He seems to have had a much wider purpose. It was apparently all the stupidity and cruelty of men that he set out to condemn in that brilliant pageant of devils.

Perhaps because the times were hard, or as a consequence of the war which had been ravaging a large part of Europe for so many years, there was one exception, an artist who had died not long before. His name was Jacques Callot, and he was not unknown in the Netherlands. At the time of the siege of Breda, Spinola gave him the task of mapping the area. Van Dyck had painted his portrait, which was engraved by Vorsterman. He came from Lorraine, and had seen his unhappy country invaded by the Swedes, the Austrians and the French; and he produced two series of engravings called the 'Miseries of War', an implacable indictment of the cruelty of men. These little pictures, incisively drawn, become great by the breadth of their style. There is no more glorification of military heroism. Callot shows us the other side of the picture, that is to say the sorry truth—massacres, torture, pillage, fire and rape, the real face of war. Callot's strength lies in his utter simplicity. He had no need to pile on the agony; he had only to think of his native land ravaged by undisciplined mercenaries.

And then the engraver was imitated by a painter. When Justus Sustermans commissioned a painting on behalf of his masters, Rubens suggested the subject of 'The Evils of War'. This was not one of his usual subjects; and yet need we be surprised at his choice after all he had seen and heard around him? However his testimony was not as direct as that of his colleague from Nancy. He described the evils of war without abandoning his normal style.

In March 1638, after despatching the canvas, he sent a description of his work to the Medicis:

'The protagonist is Mars, leaving the temple of Janus (Your Lordship knows that Roman law is laid down that this temple should be closed in time of peace); he steps forward armed, his sword dripping blood, towards the people whom he is threatening with great misery. Venus his lover, accompanied by Cupids and cherubs, strives to hold him back with her kisses and caresses, while the fury Alecto draws him forward, torch in hand. Beside them are War's inseparable companion, Famine and Pestilence. On the ground lies a woman with a broken lute; this is Harmony who cannot live with discord and war; and we also see a mother with a little child in her arms, showing that fruitfulness, maternity and charity are crushed by war which corrupts and destroys everything. Your Lordship will also observe an architect lying prostrate with his instruments; for what peace builds for the beauty and elegance of great towns, the violence of arms ruins and overthrows. Then, if my memory serves me well, I think Your Lordship will also see on the ground beneath the feet of Mars a book of drawings; I have tried to show by this that war scorns letters and the arts. There is also perhaps a broken quiver, arrows and darts, with the cord which tied them; the quiver is in fact the emblem of concord, as the caduceus and the olive are symbols of peace—these too are thrown into a corner. Finally, the woman with face veiled, sad and dressed in mourning, without jewels or any adornment, is unhappy Europe, who for so many years has suffered from continual depredations and outrages of all kinds, innumerable miseries and all the inexpressible sufferings of every one of us. She holds the globe supported by an angel or cherub, and surmounted by a cross, the symbol of Christianity.'

It is somewhat complicated, but the work is very beautiful. It is painted with splendid fire, and impresses by the unity of its composition, despite the fact that all the figures are deliberately drawn in one single movement towards the right. We may perhaps wonder, however, how many people understood the artist's symbolism. It is a work in the heroic style, idealizing the subject to the full. Was this Rubens' intention?

He painted 'The Evils of War', and he was still to paint 'The End of War', a less perfect composition perhaps, inspired by the same generous ideas; and we must be grateful for his intention, since war had followed him from childhood and he had always been obsessed by it. He had seen every country in Europe locked in conflict, and his own native land had always been the scene of battles, sieges and attacks. The greatest leaders, from Spinola to Piccolomini, had not succeeded in establishing the one thing which would have made up for all their devastation—peace.

Neither proud Spain nor stubborn Holland would give in. The year before, the Prince of Orange, Frederick Henry, had retaken Breda, and thus Spinola's victory, which Velasquez had just immortalized in a masterpiece, was brought to nothing. In June 1638 the indefatigable *stadhouder* tried to seize Antwerp by force, but his second-in-command, Count William of Nassau, was beaten at Calloo by the Cardinal Infante, and lost his only son in the battle. The Dutch army, panic-stricken, abandoned its artillery, flags and supplies. It was a complete collapse. From Antwerp, Rubens must have seen the smoke of the battle. As though this one single episode could put an end to the campaign, Antwerp celebrated this Spanish victory magnificently. The *Ommegang* came out for the occasion, and to the traditional floats in the procession there was added a brand-new triumphal chariot celebrating the victory of Calloo. It had been designed by Rubens. In the evening the city was illuminated and bonfires blazed everywhere. Joy was universal—a joy as bright as the bonfires and as soon extinguished. The war went on.

When summer came, Rubens retired to Steen, where he could forget the folly of men. He painted and attended to his affairs.

As always, he was racked by gout. He was often confined to bed, but went back to work as soon as his illness gave him a little respite. His hand and his brain knew neither fatigue nor weakness; he remained the same hard worker he had been all his life. To him, making the fullest possible use of his time meant living more intensely. From Steen he wrote to his dear friend Lucas Fayd'herbe that he was 'urgently in need of a panel'. It must be sent to him 'without delay', or Fayd'herbe must bring it himself; that was how Rubens understood his retirement at Steen. This young sculptor from Malines had been in his service since 1636, looking after the house on the Wapper as Panneels had done before him. The master advised him : 'As for you, come as soon as you can, so that the house can be locked up, for as long as you are there you cannot prevent others from getting in. I hope you have put my gold chain in a safe place according to my instructions, so that, with God's help, we shall find it when we return.' At the same time he made arrangements for the gardener to send him pears and figs at the right moment, and asked for some bottles of 'Ay wine', 'for those we brought with us are empty'. His gout did not prevent him from liking champagne.

The year 1639 passed like the one before, with the war still as background. The Spanish forces had been dogged by ill-luck. Of the sixty-seven vessels, carrying thirteen thousand men, which had set out for the Netherlands, only nine had escaped from a new and terrible leader, the Dutch admiral Tromp.

Despite his attacks of gout, which were becoming increasingly frequent, Rubens never stopped working and taking an interest in new projects. When King Charles I of England expressed a wish to have Queen Henrietta's apartments at Greenwich decorated by Jordaens, Gerbier at once entered the field. This wily individual went to great lengths, arguing and intriguing, to get the commission transferred to his illustrious friend, and when he realized that London was not to be persuaded, he tried, like the good businessman he was, to secure at least half of the commission. Since nine ceilings and thirteen panels were required, he suggested that the ceilings should be given to Rubens, on the pretext that Jordaens had no knowledge of such work. As Gerbier's zeal was never disinterested, we can guess who was pulling the strings. In any case it was in vain.

The following spring Rubens received some models from Francois Duquesnoy, the sculptor from Brussels who since 1618 had been living in Rome, where he had carved out a successful career for himself. Pope Urban VIII had commissioned a gigantic St. Andrew from him to stand against one of the fourteen pillars supporting the dome of the basilica of St Peter, and Duquesnoy had carried out work in contemporary taste, as grandiloquent and theatrical as anyone could wish. It was an opportunity for Rubens to congratulate his colleague: 'As both a personal friend and a fellow-countryman, I am delighted at your success and feel I have a share in your glory. If I were not held prisoner here by old age and gout, I would come in person to admire and contemplate works so perfect and already so famous. I hope that at least I shall see you again among us in our beloved Flanders, which will one day be proud of your works. And I should be happy if this day could come before I am dead, so that I might gaze on the masterpieces which took shape under your hands.'

This letter is dated April 17th. A few days earlier he had given a glowing testimonial to Lucas Fayd'herbe who was leaving him: 'He has profited to the full from everything which our arts of painting and sculpture have in common, thanks to my instruction, his application and his fine intelligence.' The master makes special mention of a work by his pupil, the figure of Our Lady in the church of the Beguines at Malines 'which he carried out so excellently in my house, and which I doubt if any other sculptor in the country could have done better'.

Sadly, his condition was worsening. Towards the end of the same month he was almost paralyzed. At the beginning of May his condition improved. On the occasion of the marriage of Lucas Fayd'herbe, he sent his pupil a charming letter of congratulation: 'I have learnt with great pleasure that on the first of this month you planted the may-tree in the garden of your dear wife. I hope that it will grow well, and will one day bear fruit.' He had asked the young sculptor for a little child in ivory, 'it is not urgent, and you have on hand the making of a child of far greater importance'. It was the same passionate love of life as always. And besides, he was setting a good example himself. He had scarcely recovered from his sufferings when he drank once more of the cup of physical pleasure. He knew he might die, but while he still lived he intended to make full use of this precious gift. To Fayd'herbe he uttered not a word of his condition. On the contrary, he invited him to his home: 'We will always be very pleased for you to visit us.'

Towards the end of May he became rapidly worse. On the 27th he made his will. After laying down how his goods were to be divided according to justice and equity, he demanded that his heirs should remain in harmonious agreement and refrain from any legal chicanery. On May 30, 1640, at about noon, an attack of gout affected his heart, and all was over.

On the same day the body was taken to the church of St James, and laid in the Fourment family vault. On June 2nd the funeral service was held, together with the traditional banquets. In February 1641, eight and a half months after her husband's death, Helen Fourment was delivered of a daughter, Constantia Albertina, the final proof of the painter's vitality. Then began the settling up of the estate, when lawyers, valuers and tradesmen reigned supreme. Pens scratched and documents piled up; it was five years before all the business was finished.

First of all an inventory had to be made of 'pictures, works of art, antiques, letters of credit, documents and deeds'. And the work began of dividing up all the family treasures of 'the late Monsieur Pietro Paulo Rubens, knight, gentleman of the household of her late Serene Highness of noble memory, Lord of Steen, etc.' The plate and jewels were shared between the heirs, his sons Albert and Nicholas, the children of his first marriage, and Helen Fourment and her five children, Clara Joanna, Frans, Isabella Helena, Peter Paul and Constantia Albertina. The medals and agates went to the two eldest sons. Albert, who had succeeded his father as secretary of the privy council, received in addition the library. The family portraits were given to their respective models; thus the 'Pelsken' fell to the widow. The rest were dispersed. The ivories, the plaster-work, the shells and even the globes were sold. The dead man's wardrobe was also sold. Then there were the paintings, the master's own as well as those belonging to his collection. The inventory mentions more than three hundred items. The Venetian school came first with Titian, Tintoretto, Veronese, Palma and Muzziano. There were a great many portraits which formed the contribution of the Northern painters: Jan van Eyck, Hugo van der Goes, Durer, Holbein, Quentin Metsys, Willem Key, Lucas van Leyden, van Hemmessen, Moro, van Schorel and Floris. One exception was the elder Bruegel, represented by thirteen works, mostly landscapes. Also on the list are Perugino, Henry met de Bles, Joos van Cleef, Cocxie, Paul Bril, Ribera and Elsheimer. Among his collaborators and his Antwerp contemporaries are Van Dyck, Frans Snyders, Paul and Simon de Vos, Seghers, Wildens, Ykens, Sebastian Vrancx and Van Es. The Dutch painters form a rather unexpected group: Palamedes, Poelenburg, Heda, Porcellis and de Vlieger; these minor masters are offset by one single Frans Hals.

But, most surprisingly, there are seventeen works by Adriaan Brouwer. How can we explain the master's love for this genre and landscape painter whose nature appears so far removed from his own? Brouwer was Flemish, but went to work with Hals before returning to Antwerp, where he died when scarcely past thirty. He seems to have charmed Rubens by the utterly simple lyricism of his little pictures. Rubens had perhaps freed himself from the trammels of matter, but he never attained to that simplicity which reduces the subject practically to nothing. However much he whipped his trees and leaves into a heroic swirl of movement, his landscapes were always composed. Brouwer simply abandoned himself to his dreams. He painted not so much a landscape as a state of mind, and he was the first to do this. Rubens was perceptive enough to realize it unerringly. Another surprise in this inventory is the large number of copies left by the master. There were more than thirty after Titian, of which twenty-one were portraits. Raphael, Leonardo, Tintoretto, the elder Bruegel, Anthony Mor and Elsheimer were also judged worth copying. It is an indisputable proof of the great painter's humility. He studied the work of his colleagues with brush in hand.

One sale realized 52,000 florins, another more than 8,000. Four paintings bought on behalf of the King of Spain brought in 42,000 florins. The same King also bought for 27,100 florins another batch of canvases including three by Titian, two by Tintoretto, three by Veronese, one by Paul Bril, four by Elsheimer, one by Muzziano, five copies after Titian and thirteen paintings by Rubens. It is worth noting that the King paid from

1,200 to 1,800 florins for copies done by Rubens after Titian, but gave only 400 for a self-portrait by Titian! About fifty pictures went for very varied prices. 'A man from Cologne' paid 1,200 florins for a 'St Peter', and the Prince of Orange offered 300 florins for 'Silvia', but on the other hand 'Atalanta's Race' fetched only 36 florins. A few works were bought by the family. Helen Fourment acquired, among others, a 'Conversation a la Mode' for 120 florins, while Albert gave 1,250 florins for a large landscape showing the Castle of Steen. Finally, Arnold Lunden bought two portraits of his wife, the sprightly Susanna Fourment, whose likeness figures no less than seven times in the inventory.

After the paintings came the houses, and first of all the princely palace on the Wapper. Its value was so great that no buyer could be found, and Helen Fourment lived in it until her second marriage in 1645 to Jan Baptist van Broeckhoven, lord of Bergeyck and former magistrate of the city of Antwerp. Next to the house on the Wapper were eight cottages with small gardens. One of these, the last occupant of which had been David Ryckaert, was used as a library and as a storehouse for 'a few bad pictures and copies'. The others were let. The country estates included, at Eeeckeren, north of Antwerp, the 'Hof van Urssele' with its farm, its avenue of trees and its large garden; at Zwyndrecht and at Burght, in Flanders, two small farms with land; land also at Cappelle-au-Bois in Brabant, and a farmhouse and land at Doel on the Scheldt. Finally the greatest possession of all, the manor of Steen with its castle, its fields, meadows and woods. This magnificent estate was worth a fortune on its own, estimated at 100,000 florins. He left half to his children, and Helen Fourment received the other half.

There would be no point in listing the mortgage deeds; there were too many of them. The mind boggles at this impressive fortune accumulated through one man's work. Even the paintings, from which all this wealth sprang, were put to many uses by the heirs. Don Francisco de Rochas, who negotiated the buying of pictures on behalf of the King of Spain, was 'honoured' with a 'Saint Augustine' for 'having facilitated the aforesaid sale'. The painter Gaspard de Crayer, who acted as intermediary, received 'A nymph with a basket of fruit', and the treasurer Van

Ophem a 'Saint Cecilia' for the 'good payment'. 'Satyrs with a basket of fruit' went to Peter the groom who had bought a horse for the deceased. The tax-collector received a canvas 'for having obtained better payment of the monies due to the deceased'. Physicians, an innkeeper, and even the mason in charge of the work at the Castle of Steen, received pictures in compensation.

In order to keep certain promises, copies were made, and we note that master Jordaens, professional painter, was given the task of finishing two pictures by the master, an 'Andromeda' and a 'Hercules'. No better choice could have been made. As Gerbier wrote: 'Rubens died three days ago, so that Jordaens is now the first painter here.' He was moreover a modest man, as the accounts show. He was paid 240 florins for his trouble, and the two canvases finished by him, to which two others were added, were sold to the King of Spain for 4,200 florins, that is, an average of 1,050 florins each. It was business as usual.

The dead man had had some drawings kept back, some by his own hand and some by other masters which he had lovingly collected. As a last act of homage to his art, he left them either to one of his sons 'who wished to take up the art of painting', or failing that, to one of his daughters 'married to a painter of reputation'. But his sons were *jonckers*—gentlemen who did not work with their hands—and none of his daughters thought of marrying a painter. The interested parties were so convinced of the uselessness of this clause of the will that they disregarded the provision that the drawings should be kept until the youngest of the children had reached the age of eighteen. And the drawings went too.

In 1642 a chapel was built in the church of St James, behind the choir, and according to the wishes of the deceased it was adorned simply with a painting by his hand showing 'The Virgin with the Christ-child in her arms', and a statue of Mary carved in marble. Some consider this painting Rubens' last and most perfect masterpiece. Can we agree, as some people have insisted, that the painter had wished to assemble all his loved ones around the Madonna—his two wives, his youngest child, his father? Some have even seen Peter Paul himself in the brilliant St George. But his Magdalene is dark, and Helen Fourment was fair. Could he have been thinking once more of the dark-haired Isabella Brant? And if this is a direct evocation, why the picture of a father he scarcely knew, and why is his mother, the valiant Maria Pypelincx, not there? It is possible, even probable, that Rubens gave this canvas, chosen to adorn his tomb, a very precise meaning, but how can we penetrate it? He himself wrote of his subjects: 'They can hardly be guessed at, and to recognize them the author's own commentary is necessary.' And he made admissions like: 'I can no longer find the arguments of my pictures as I wrote them, and my memory is perhaps not as reliable as I would wish.' He was wise to go no further. The canvas may keep its secret; it is still one of the most brilliant achievements of the great painter. Men, women, children—what do their names matter? It is a glowing picture of life, painted tenderly and lightly by a master-painter who was also a completely happy man.

Rubens was now far beyond all human eventualities. The man was gone, but his work, scattered to the four corners of the earth, gave to his name a lustre that has never been equalled. There is not a collection worth the name that does not proudly boast at least one or two of his paintings. Even today many of his pupils' exercises shelter behind his glorious name, but what does that matter? His glory is of the kind that defies the critics. The simple souls who visit museums, treading as though on hallowed ground, gape in wonderment at heroic pieces from his studio. As for the art-lovers who prefer to contemplate his extraordinary sketches, recognizing his genius more easily in them, or to dream over the few masterpieces untouched by mercenary hands—thanks to him they can experience the embodiment of joy in painting, which, in the last analysis, is simply a sublimation of the joy of life. And that is a supreme quality of Peter Paul's art, the road by which, despite the glitter and bombast which could lead it astray, it reaches the greatest possible heights of human achievement. His work was a hymn to joy. Living as he did in troubled times, having known exile and brushed very close to poverty, dreaming of peace and seeing only war, he still kept his faith in life, and joy radiated from his almost in spite of himself. It was man's final, glorious reply to the self-created miseries of the unhappy human race.

CONCLUSION

All art presupposes a choice. It is, in fact, an essential part of creation—the choice determines the work, and is its strength or its weakness. In certain forms of expression such as the novel, the author is his own master. This is not the case with the author of a biography. He is, it is true, free to choose among the mass of documents whatever seems to him eloquent, significant or revealing, and that is one of the important aspects of his work. He may not gloss over any facts or testimonies, unless he rejects them; and in that case he must justify himself.

This is a justification.

The introductory pages gave sufficient indication of the spirit in which this book was conceived; so there is no need to go over the same ground again. For reasons of conscience two testimonies have been in one case passed over, and in the other reduced to a question mark.

The first, often quoted, has contributed greatly to the legend of Rubens the superman. It is the account of Otto Sperling, physician to the King of Denmark, of a visit he made to the painter in 1621, which he related as follows: 'We paid a visit to the celebrated and excellent painter Rubens, whom we found at work, and while continuing to paint he listened to readings from Tacitus and dictated a letter. We were silent for fear of disturbing him, but he conversed with us without interrupting his work, and without stopping the reading; he also went on dictating the letter as though to give us proof of his amazing gifts.' Even Max Rooses, who counts among the master's great panegyrists, judges with considerable good sense that the Danish doctor's account is an impossible fairy-tale.

The second concerns Rubens as a page. The story is well known. On leaving school and before beginning his apprenticeship as a painter, Peter Paul is said to have been a page in the household of the Countess of Lalaing. This detail, which is found in all biographies of Rubens, comes from Roger de Piles who

printed it in his *Conversations sur la connoissance de la peinture*
(Paris 1677) on the basis, as he says, of 'memoirs which his
(Rubens') friends and relatives kindly sent me'. His documenta-
tion thus seems to have been authentic and irrefutable. But on
analysis this biographical material shows several errors or gaps.
It need not disturb us that Cologne was given as his birthplace;
this tradition was created by Maria Pypelincx, and there is no
proof that her children ever knew anything about the Siegen
affair. The testimony of Peter Paul himself does not mention it:
'I am very fond of Cologne, where I was brought up until the
age of ten' (Letter to Geldorp, written July 25, 1637). Was he
being careful, or did he really not know? The secret has been
well kept.

But there is not a word about Rubens' first master, Tobias
Verhaecht, and little Clara Serena has been forgotten. Other less
important details have also been found to be inaccurate. Should
that not be enough to attract the attention of biographers?
There is no sign of it. In the absence of any new proof which
might force them to change their minds, they went on blissfully
repeating all the nonsense piously written down by de Piles.
Here is a description of his way of life:

'He got up at four every morning, and made it a rule to begin
his day by hearing Mass, unless he were prevented by gout, with
which he was greatly troubled; after this he began work. He
always had with him a reader, who was a paid servant of his,
reading aloud from some good book, usually Plutarch, Livy or
Seneca.

'As he derived very great pleasure from his work, he lived in
such a way as to be able to work easily, without harming his
health, and for that reason he ate very little at dinner, for fear
that the fumes of his meat might hinder his application, or, if he
succeeded in applying himself, it might hinder his digestion. He
worked like this until five in the evening, when he mounted his
horse to take the air outside the town or on the ramparts, or did
something else to refresh his mind.

'When he returned from his outing he usually found some of
his friends in his house, who had come to sup with him, adding
thus to the pleasures of his table.'

And here is a picture of the superior man:

'Although he was very attached to his art, he nevertheless used his time in such a way as always to give some part of it to the study of such liberal arts as history and the Latin poets of whom he had a perfect knowledge, and whose language, as well as Italian, was very familiar to him, as we can judge by his manuscript notes on painting, in which he quotes some passages from Virgil and other poets that were relevant to his subject. We must not therefore be surprised that his thoughts flowed so generously, nor that there was such richness in his invention and such erudition and clarity in his allegorical paintings, and that he developed his subjects so well, introducing only those things which were proper and peculiar to them; so that, being perfectly conversant with the action he intended to represent, he could enter into it more thoroughly and give it more life, while still keeping it completely in character.'

And finally, the good colleague who 'gave his opinion (to painters) with fatherly kindness, sometimes taking the trouble to touch up their paintings. He never found fault with any work, and could see beauty in every style.'

There is an obvious tendency to hyperbole. It is quite possible that Rubens employed a reader (which would to some extent explain Sperling's effusions). Nowadays some painters work with the radio on. One might call it background reading, similar to background music. It is equally possible that Rubens rose early, and that he was frugal. But this account is pitched in too high a key. It is hard to imagine Rubens getting up at four in the morning in winter and starting work after attending Mass. He could have ridden out on horseback after five o'clock only in summer. He was not as sparing of his time as we are expected to believe; he always had plenty of time for public affairs, and it was not his fault that he did not devote even more time to them. And although he had some knowledge of a wide range of subjects, we know nothing of the real extent of his education. We could go on . . . but it is sufficient to say that this author has a tendency towards heroic exaggeration.

Since Rubens left the school of master Verdonck at a very

young age, we may wonder when he could have been a page, considering that he had, not two, but three painting masters, Verhaecht, van Noort and Vaenius. And then, why a page? Was it really a suitable career for the son of a widow who had to try to prepare her sons for life? Psychologically, a period as a page looks very well in Rubens' life. If young Peter Paul simply walked into the career of a painter, the effect would not be the same. The idea is magnificent; a young man surrounded by frivolity—we actually know nothing about his surroundings, but imagination can do much—who turns away in disgust and devotes himself to art. We do know, on the other hand, that Rubens was fond of outward shows. Signor Pietro Pauolo, as he liked to call himself, could, by having been a page, have proved that if he worked with his hands it was to fulfil an irresistible vocation, but that he had always belonged to high society.

Does this mean that the page episode was an invention? The hypothesis is not untenable. Maria Pypelincx had done her best to wipe out the memory of her husband's misadventure. If her son Peter Paul had not become a famous painter, and if her husband had not had an affair with the wife of the great William the Silent himself, historians would not have sought after the truth so ardently. Everyone will agree that the story of the page is much more innocent. We are reminded of those commoners who, having become public figures, add coats of arms to their family portraits. Was it vanity? Possibly, but let us not jump to conclusions. Rubens' biographers were evidently worried by the discrepancy between his uneventful life and the heroic character of his work. Hence the tendency—encouraged by the shortage of documentary evidence—to see greatness in the artist's slightest acts.

We scarcely need to mention, for example, his first visit to Spain, which the most exalted of witnesses promoted to the status of a diplomatic mission. All that Rubens actually did was to accompany the presents sent by his master. And then there are the persistent allusions to an illustrious birth. These allusions reappear in recent accounts, despite proofs to the contrary, as though the great man's admirers were reluctant to abandon a hypothesis which gave such scope for romantic development. Peter Paul, son of John Rubens and Anna of Saxony, brought up

as her own child by Maria Pypelincx, a wronged but magnani-
mous wife helping the guilty pair to hide their crime! Peter Paul
would thus have been half-brother to Maurice of Nassau, which
would have explained many things! The subject is worthy of a
Greek tragedy, and for those who love emotional situations it is
disappointing to find that it is quite untrue. In their passionate
longing to increase his prestige, his fanatical admirers have tried
to show us Rubens the man as no way inferior to Rubens the
artist. Obsessed by the fear that the man might appear lacking
in depth, they imagined they were saving the situation by turning him into a 'perfect gentle knight', a fount of knowledge and
a paragon of the virtues. It is true that once we have stripped off
the tinsel, the picture of the essential Rubens with which we are
left is not very clear. This in no way proves that he was superficial. Can a man who keeps his own counsel be so considered?
(A really superficial person is one who judges in just that way).
Rubens was essentially a secretive man, which does not neces-
sarily imply depth. Secretiveness is a characteristic of a man who
withdraws deliberately, as an exercise of will, or who hides his
true self through natural reserve. Some are both strong-willed
and reserved, and Rubens was most certainly one of these.

In what remains of his correspondence, he speaks once only
of Isabella Brant; we remember how. Twice he mentions Helen
Fourment, the first time to tell Peiresc—four years late—that he
has remarried, and the second time to tell Lucas Fayd'herbe that
he and his wife would like him to visit them at the Castle of
Steen. He speaks only once of his mother, to explain his departure from Rome, and his letters contain one single affectionate
sentence, on the subject of his elder son: 'I love that child like a
second self.' That is all—and these were his nearest and dearest.
It is true that many letters have been lost, but the ones that have
been preserved are written to such a variety of correspondents
and spread out over such a long period of time that we can
deduce from them that he did not usually wear his heart on his
sleeve. If things went wrong he always sought to save his face;
in modern boxing terms we would say he could take a lot of
punishment. The philosophical serenity shown in his letters
would not prove very much—the humanists made a feature of
stoicism—if it were not corroborated by the optimism of his art.

Those paintings, full of the joy of life, of youth, health and enthusiasm, are perhaps the only valid witnesses since they are devoid of all affectation.

This man, who transformed Calvary and the sufferings of the martyrs into pictures notable for their heroic, florid and decorative qualities, never moves us by interpretations of human anguish. Fromentin might retort—what about the 'Communion of St Francis of Assisi?' We can reply that if this painting had not been unusual among the master's work, its subsequent history would not have been so exceptional. Suffering man is not beautiful, and human agony can only be visually expressed by ugliness. This is no obstacle to great art; we have only to think of Grünewald. But it was not to the taste of Rubens, who was brought up on the Renaissance and classical antiquity, and cared only for the ideal of beauty. Is this why his portraits are more decorative than expressive? Human beings are generally ugly or insignificant. To give them more expression, the artist must emphasize their features, which means making them uglier still. They can never be beautified without detracting from their character. Van Dyck succeeded in this to some extent, but he does not bear comparison with painters like Velasquez or Rembrandt who looked beneath the surface, without worrying about ideal beauty. Rubens got out of the difficulty by the use of a decorative background, and thus reconciled the demands of his clients with the more imperious ones of his own taste.

Rembrandt, great solitary that he was, remained all his life face to face with human anguish, and all his life, step by step, was reflected in the many pictures he left of himself. Rubens escaped from man and his attendant miseries by creating a world of his own. All his women—the observation is not new—have a family likeness to each other, and his men too can be reduced to a few well-built and muscular general types. It is quite likely that Rubens was not interested in individuals. Is that a sign of superficiality? It is possible to escape by climbing to the heights as well as by plunging into the abyss; by becoming a rebel like Rembrandt or an egocentric, dominant character like Rubens. If we need proofs, they are here:

It is easier to judge an artist at the peak of his career, which, for many great painters, means during his last years. When, three years before his death, Rubens was asked to paint an episode from the life of St Peter, he suggested the crucifixion 'with feet upwards' because he hoped to derive 'something out of the ordinary' from that attitude. But he kept asking for extensions of time, as he wanted to 'enjoy finishing' this picture which, according to him, interested him more than any other (when he died he still had not finished it). During this time he painted, for his own pleasure, works which were light, sensual, and sometimes frankly licentious.

To say that he got up every morning at four and heard Mass before starting work is a rather negligible red herring. Rubens' religion was the joy of life, and he performed his Christian duties without being disturbed or unduly moved by them. What he saw in a crucifixion was simply an attitude to be reproduced. Basically his only law was to be true to himself, and his only religion was the burning faith which all truly great men have in their own destiny.

He has been called a religious painter, which he is if we confine ourselves to externals, but not if we take the word in its deepest sense. He was often a Catholic painter, giving strict obedience to the rules laid down by the Council of Trent, which insisted on works lofty in style, capable of inspiring noble sentiments in those who saw them, and refuting, by means of eye-catching images, certain affirmations of the Protestants. All these scenes from the lives of the saints are so many almost physical bonds between the Church and the faithful. They were the manifesto of a Church which was trying to be more fraternal than that of the Protestants; an assurance to the faithful that they personally could come into the presence of God and become part of the great hierarchy of Heaven; and a protection against that terror of the void which grips so many human beings.

When he did this, Rubens was merely a servant doing his job honestly, but it is scarcely necessary to repeat that thousands of painters have accomplished similar tasks without anyone being moved by the didactic side of their work. Those who still attract us are superior beings whose voice is still heard despite all artifice and constraint. Rubens is not loved for his religious subjects, and is often loved in spite of them. And if the undeniable enthusiasm which he poured into many of his subjects is a proof of his religious sentiments, we must also admit that he was basically a pagan, considering the even greater ardour he expended in the service of the gods of Olympus. Truth to tell, this great painter of living, moving bodies found most inspiration and most true poetry in the naked female body, because he loved women.

He was less refined and aristocratic than Titian—in short, he was Flemish—but he shared his admiration of womankind. He glorified women unceasingly in paintings of ever-increasing sensuality, despite the wave of religious feeling which was sweeping over his country. Helen Fourment may not have been very intelligent, but does that prove that she was not a suitable wife for him, or that she caused him suffering? This is, nevertheless, a constantly recurring hypothesis of his more fanatical admirers; he was so intelligent and so cultured, and then there was such a difference in their ages—she must therefore have cuckolded him. They do not put it quite so crudely, but in the eyes of these judges the Vienna portrait is a crushing indictment of Helen. But what do these accusers make of the generosity with which the master constantly exhibited the charms of his lovely wife? Is this like a jealous husband? Or do they think Rubens was a complaisant husband—the 'magnificent cuckold'? The idea is absurd, and obviously there must be another explanation. Those people who erected for Rubens a pedestal of virtues and moral qualities have passed over the only plausible hypothesis—that Rubens loved women in a completely physical way. That was why he married a child of sixteen who was certainly a delectable morsel; he could have the pleasures of the lover first, and then those of the artist. And that was enough for him. There are men in plenty who ask nothing more of women, whatever they may say; and it is precisely the dominant types who have this characteristic.

Was this not Rubens' right? But the obstinate may dismiss this as mere gratuitous supposition, and the prudish may even call it sacrilege. They are forgetting his works, which are more eloquent than any commentary. All the experts agree that the master's later works are the most beautiful. And the paramount emotion in these works is gladness, like the ever-repeated song of a happy man. It is the most perfect possible vindication of Helen Fourment.

As a painter Rubens could tolerate only satellites around him, as numerous examples show. He sometimes spoke of Van Dyck when the latter belonged to his studio, but later, not a word. In the course of his travels he met one of the greatest painters in the world, Velasquez; and he seems to have forgotten him completely. It is true that he greatly admired Titian, but Titian was dead, as were most of the painters represented in his collection. As for the living ones, they were, apart from a few of his collaborators, all second-rate. The one exception is Adriaan Brouwer, and we may trust that this was for love of his art. In Rubens' time this artist, brilliant though he was, had not won the reputation he deserved (and he has not won it yet).

The same thing applied to the engravers. Rubens accepted only vassals. If one of them showed a slight inclination towards independence, like Vorsterman, he fell out with him.

In politics Rubens fulminated now against one party, now against the other, and if the cards he played were always Spanish ones, it was because they were the only ones in his hand. It would be too much to see complete adherence in this—certain letters are in this respect significant—but Rubens is without doubt a politician, and true politicians are in agreement only with themselves. Every real politician is a dominant character. Hence the abjurations so deeply disturbing to virtuous minds; but what seems a betrayal in a politician is really an act of faith in himself. When a politician feels himself threatened, when he is afraid of losing his power to dominate, he will change his doctrine or his party, and will sometimes betray his followers to save himself. In his attempt at self-justification he will finally convince himself of the validity of his arguments, thus becoming his own dupe. Doctrines, parties and convictions are only pretexts justifying—and often hiding even from himself—the inner needs of his being, for whether politicians are faithful or unfaithful to certain political dogmas generally depends merely on circumstances. But no one will admit this, the politician least of all. He proclaims the supremacy of an Idea, and will not own that this Idea is only the form—a very unstable one—taken by a deep-rooted obsession that leaves its victim no rest.

Rubens was a man like that. All his efforts were directed towards the better expression of the will to power which lay within him. Money, fame, titles, diplomacy were only means towards the fulfilment of his need to rule. It is absurd to bring in moral considerations and judge the man by the normal standards of good and evil. If he chose to be virtuous, it was because virtue suited his purpose. If he remained loyal to the Infanta, it was because she was always ready to employ him. He was almost always on the side of peace because he thought he could contribute to it, and perhaps he himself believed that he loved peace for its own sake. But when that base man Gaston d'Orléans came with his intrigues to Brussels, he was suddenly on the side of war; he was in touch with Marie de Medici and obviously hoped to play his part in the adventure. It is no use to talk about logic. Logic is a method of reasoning, but it is not life. And life, to him, was everything—his own life, which he had to live.

And that was the point—to live his life. But there are small appetites and large ones, and Rubens was a glutton. Far from being that paragon of middle-class virtues which his short-sighted admirers often made of him, he was essentially a leader and a conqueror. All his life he exploited to the full every opportunity that came his way. It is from this angle that we must consider his relations with his fellows; they were tools to be used as he needed, to satisfy his passion for self-assertion. He was an egoist, naturally; so are all great men. And like all who stand on the highest peaks, he stood alone.

CHRONOLOGICAL TABLE

1577 — Rubens born at Siegen (June 28th).

1587 — Death of his father, John Rubens.

1598 — Rubens became master of the Guild of Saint Luke.

1600 — Departure for Italy (May 9th).
Engaged at Mantua by Duke Vincenzo Gonzaga.

1601 — Journey from Mantua to Rome.

1603 — Journey to Spain.
Gifts handed over to the King of Spain (May 13th).

1604 — Return to Mantua, then to Rome.

1608 — Death of his mother, Maria Pypelincx (October 19th).
Departure from Rome (October 28th).
Rubens reached Antwerp (December 11th).

1609 — Rubens appointed painter to the Archdukes Albert and
Isabella (September 23rd).
Marriage to Isabella Brant (October 3rd).

1610 — Rubens bought a piece of land on the Wapper, at
Antwerp.

1611 — His daughter Clara Serena born at Antwerp.
Death of the painter's brother Philip Rubens.

1613 — Rubens became Dean of the Romanists.

1614 — Birth of his son Albert.

1616 — Work completed on Rubens' house on the Wapper.

1618 — Birth of his son Nicholas (March 13th).
Van Dyck became master of the Guild of Saint Luke.

1622 — Journey to Paris (January 11th). Contract with Marie
de Medici for the gallery in the Luxembourg Palace.
Return to Antwerp (March 3rd).

1623 — Journey to Paris (May 3rd). Marie de Medici and
Richelieu visited the Luxembourg gallery.
Return to Antwerp (July 14th).

1624 — Rubens raised to noble rank by the King of Spain.
Visited by Prince Ladislas Sigismond of Poland.

1625 — Rubens arrived in Paris (February 4th).
Return to Antwerp (February 12th).
Journeys to Brussels and Dunkirk.
Visited by Buckingham.

1626 — Death of the painter's first wife Isabella Brant (June 20th).
Numerous visits to Laeken and Brussels.
Visits to Calais and Paris.

1627 — Journey with Gerbier.

1628 — Journey to Spain (August 28th).

1629 — In Madrid until April 29th. On the 27th, Rubens was appointed secretary of the Privy Council.
Journey to London.
Audiences with Charles I at Greenwich.

1630 — Knighted by the King of England (March 3rd).
Departure from London (March 8th).
Return to Antwerp (April 6th).
Marriage to Helen Fourment (December 6th).

1631 — Marie de Medici arrived in Antwerp.
Journey to Holland.

1635 — Rubens bought the castle of Steen at Elewyt.

1636 — Prolonged stay at the castle of Steen.

1637 — The Cardinal Infante visited Rubens in Antwerp.

1640 — Rubens made his will (May 27th).
Death of Rubens (May 30th).

INDEX

GEORGE ALLEN & UNWIN LTD
London: 40 Museum Street, W.C.1

Auckland: P.O. Box 36013, Northcote Central, N.4
Barbados: P.O. Box 222, Bridgetown
Beirut: Deeb Building, Jeanne d'Arc Street
Bombay: 15 Graham Road, Ballard Estate, Bombay 1
Buenos Aires: Escritorio 454-459, Florida 165
Calcutta: 17 Chittaranjan Avenue, Calcutta 13
Cape Town: 68 Shortmarket Street
Hong Kong: 105 Wing On Mansion, 26 Hancow Road, Kowloon
Ibadan: P.O. Box 62
Karachi: Karachi Chambers, McLeod Road
Madras: Mohan Mansions, 38c Mount Road, Madras 6
Mexico: Villalongin 32-10, Piso, Mexico 5, D.F.
Nairobi: P.O. Box 30583
New Delhi: 13-14 Asaf Ali Road, New Delhi 1
Ontario: 81 Curlew Drive, Don Mills
Philippines: P.O. Box 4322, Manila
Rio de Janeiro: Caixa Postal 2537-Zc-00
Singapore: 36c Prinsep Street, Singapore 7
Sydney, N.S.W.: Bradbury House, 55 York Street
Tokyo: P.O. Box 26, Kamata

DAILY LIFE IN FLORENCE
UNDER THE MEDICI

J. LUCAS-DUBRETON

The very name of Florence, especially associated with the Medicis, brings to mind at once all the splendours of the Italian Renaissance. For in this period of the city's history there lived and worked some of the greatest artists of all time: Botticelli, Donatello, Ghiberti, Brunelleschi, Filippo Lippi, Cellini and Ghirlandajo, to name but a few, and the writers, including Boccaccio, were not less illustrious.

What was it like, then, to live in Florence at such a time? How did the people live, in private and in public? How was the city governed and defended? How did the artists live, the poets, craftsmen, princes, peasants, artisans, merchants and churchmen? What was the lot of women; what did Florentines eat and drink; what were their morals; what were their homes like; how did they conduct their ceremonies, their weddings and their funerals; how did they amuse themselves; how did they endure under siege and in the midst of plague? All these and many other questions are answered in this stirring and fascinating study, full of anecdote and history.

DAILY LIFE IN EIGHTEENTH CENTURY
ITALY

MAURICE VAUSSARD

Unlike France, or Britain, or Spain, Italy in the eighteenth century was still only a geographical expression, consisting of oligarchical republics like Venice and Genoa, a kingdom like Naples, a papal state and several independent states varying widely in their governments and traditions. Although customs and habits of thought showed certain common features, nevertheless there were considerable divergences in legislation and economic development especially, and these complicate any attempt to give an overall picture of daily life throughout the peninsula. Yet it was during this century that developed those forces which were, in the ensuing century, to effect the independence and unity of the country. That is why this study of Italian life in the eighteenth century is so important.

It is also an exceptionally lively and picturesque era, and Maurice Vaussard has produced an engagingly realistic account of the conditions of life in town and country, from north to south, and in all levels of society.

GEORGE ALLEN & UNWIN LTD